The Translator in the Text

Northwestern University Press
Studies in Russian Literature and Theory

General Editors
Caryl Emerson
Gary Saul Morson

Consulting Editors
Carol Avins
Robert Belknap
Robert Louis Jackson
Elliott Mossman
Alfred Rieber
William Mills Todd III
Alexander Zholkovsky

The Translator in the Text

ON READING RUSSIAN LITERATURE IN ENGLISH

Rachel May

NORTHWESTERN UNIVERSITY PRESS / EVANSTON, ILLINOIS

Northwestern University Press
Evanston, Illinois 60208-4210

Copyright © 1994 Northwestern University Press
All rights reserved. Published 1994
Printed in the United States of America

Library of Congress Cataloging-in-Publication Data
May, Rachel.
    The translator in the text : on reading Russian literature in
English / Rachel May.
        p.   cm. — (Studies in Russia literature and theory)
    Includes bibliographical references.
    ISBN 0-8101-1157-8 (alk. paper). — ISBN 0-8101-1158-6 (pbk.)
    1, Russian literature—Translations into English—History and
criticism. 2. Translating and interpreting. I. Title.
II. Series.
PG2985.M36   1994
891.709—dc20   94-22792
                                                           CIP

The paper used in this publication meets the minimum requirements of the American National Standard for Information Sciences—Permanence of Paper for Printed Library Materials, ANSI Z39.48-1984.

To the memory of

Edward J. Brown

and

Frank H. Allen III

Contents

ix   LIST OF TRANSLATION EXAMPLES

xi   ACKNOWLEDGMENTS

xii   NOTE ON TRANSLITERATION

1   INTRODUCTION
Discourse and the Translated Novel 2
Translation across Boundaries: Some Trends in Translation Studies 6

11   CHAPTER ONE. TRANSLATION CULTURE
Translation and the Receiving Culture 11
Nineteenth-Century "Informational" Translation 13
Turgenev as Victorian Writer 22
Dostoevsky and Tolstoy 27
The "Russian Craze" 30
Constance Garnett 37
The Soviet Period 42
Recent Trends 49

57   CHAPTER TWO. NARRATOR AND TRANSLATOR
The Personal Narrator 57
Outer Forces: The Politics of Style 59
Inner Forces: Toward a Grammar of Translation 65
    Deixis 66
    Interjections and parentheticals 68
    Pragmatic connectors 72
    Tense shifts 76
    Colloquial register 77
The Personal Narrator and the Translator 83

89 CHAPTER THREE. NARRATED MONOLOGUE: TRANSLATING A SHIFTING VIEWPOINT
Introduction 89

Narrated Monologue in Russian Literature 91

Interjections and Unambiguous Shifts in Perspective 91

Tense Shifts and Narrated Monologue 96

Impersonal Constructions 99

Narrated Monologue—An Extended Example 102

Narrated Monologue as Cultural Category 105

Translating the "Penetrated Word" 109

Postscript: Things Left Unsaid 116

119 CHAPTER FOUR. TRANSLATING THE WRITTEN TEXT: REANALYZING FORM AND STRUCTURE

Form and Meaning 119

Sentence as Focus: Aleksandr Solzhenitsyn and Anatolii Kim 121

Punctuation as Visual Art: Abram Tertz 130

Translation and Punctuation 132

141 CONCLUSION: TEACHING LITERATURE IN TRANSLATION

145 APPENDIX ONE

Fact vs. Fiction: Two Translations of Bulgakov's *Master i Margarita*

155 APPENDIX TWO

Observing the Grotesque: Two Classics of Formalist Criticism and English Translations

167 NOTES

187 REFERENCES

203 INDEX

List of Translation Examples

1.1 Turgenev's Style 26

1.2 Constance Garnett's Dostoevsky 33

1.3 Constance Garnett and the Critics 39

1.4 Magarshack and Garnett 44

1.5 The New *Ivan Denisovich* 48

1.6 A Change in Translation Style 51

1.7 Ivan and Smerdyakov 54

2.1 Gogol's Narrator 58

2.2 Precursors and Epigones of Socialist Realism 63

2.3 Deictics 67

2.4 Yurii Trifonov's Sympathetic Narrator 69

2.5 Particles and Parentheticals in *The Brothers Karamazov* 70

2.6 Parentheticals 71

2.7 Zoshchenko and Pragmatic Connectors 72

2.8 The Bricklaying Lesson 74

2.9 Initial *I* 76

2.10 Present-Tense Narration 77

2.11 Colloquial Language 79

2.12 Solzhenitsyn's "Intonation" 80

2.13 Vasilii Shukshin 85

3.1 Characters' Interjections 92

3.2 Shifts in Perspective 95

3.3 Tense Shifts 97

3.4 Tenseless Expressions 98

3.5 Rasputin's Impersonal Narration 101

3.6 Tendriakov's "The Mayfly" 103

3.7   Repetitions in *The Double*   111

3.8   The Penetrated Word   113

3.9   *Notes from Underground*   117

4.1   Topic and Focus I   124

4.2   Topic and Focus II   126

4.3   Anatolii Kim and the World in a Sentence   128

4.4   Tertz and Painting with Punctuation   133

4.5   Prose Rhythms: Solzhenitsyn's *One Day*   134

4.6   Faulkner in Russian   135

4.7   Yurii Trifonov   137

4.8   Writing about Sentences   138

Acknowledgments

As always, this book reflects the ideas and inspirations of a great many people. Let me take this space to thank some of them. My colleagues and teachers at Stanford University, where this project first took shape, listened patiently and attentively to my inchoate, maybe incoherent early forays. In particular, Jehanne Gheith, Natasha Sankovitch, and Thomas Hodge always seemed to be available to hear and respond to rough ideas; Lazar Fleishman reviewed many of my alternative translations; Mary Louise Pratt and Johanna Nichols gave much insightful advice; Catalina Ilea was, as always, helpful above and beyond the call of duty. For one year this project was assisted by a fellowship at the Stanford Humanities Institute, to which I am forever grateful. The other Fellows and the administrators brought intellectual verve, viewpoints from a multitude of disciplines, and true "fellowship" to the formative stages of my thinking on these ideas. I am also grateful to my colleagues and students at the State University of New York for listening to and reading through various drafts of my ideas. Christina Y. Bethin, Therese Malhame, Ira Livingston, and Cynthia Porter gave me many valued suggestions.

This research was assisted by two grants (one for dissertation research, one for postdoctoral research) from the Joint Committee on Soviet Studies of the Social Science Research Council and the American Council of Learned Societies with funds provided by the Department of State under the Russian and Soviet Studies Research and Training Act of 1983 (Title VIII).

Thank you, finally, to Thomas Brockelman. Above all, just for being there, but also for being willing to learn more than you ever wanted to know about this subject and always responding with thoughtfulness and good humor.

The two men who were most instrumental in helping me get this project off the ground are, sadly, no longer with us to receive my thanks. This book is barely a ripple on the ocean of inspiration they brought into the world in their lifetimes, and it is sorely lacking in the humor and exuberance that were their hallmarks. Nevertheless, I hope it is not presumptuous to dedicate it to their memories.

Note on Transliteration

To give the reader some sense of the development of English-language discourse on Russian literature, I have not standardized the spelling of Russian names in quotations. Thus Tourguenieff, Tourgeniev, and Turgenev should all be understood to refer to the same historical figure. In my own transliterations I have used the Library of Congress system except for well-known names (Dostoevsky, Tertz, Yurii), or names that are consistently spelled a certain way in cited translations (Golyadkin, Nastya). This inevitably produces some odd consistencies (Smerdyakov but Tendriakov), for which I apologize to the sensitive reader.

Introduction

> The word in language is half someone else's.
> –M. M. Bakhtin, "Discourse and the Novel,"
> trans. Caryl Emerson and Michael Holquist

WHO OWNS THE WORDS of a prose fiction text? The author, surely, wrote them, but within the text characters and narrators speak them and the implied author takes responsibility for them. Outside the text, the reader interprets the words, the editor and publisher have a say in their arrangement, and the culture at large lays some claim to them (as, for example, "modern Russian fiction"). We think of the inner and outer influences on the words of a novel as distinct and study them separately (historical criticism, reader-oriented criticism, narratology, formalism, etc.). But there is one event in the life of a novel that affects all these levels at once: its translation.

Although translators generally receive little recognition and less legal claim to the words they produce,[1] the process of translation shifts all the relations of ownership within and around a text. Externally, this is obvious: the whole point of a translation is to change the work's readership and surrounding culture. What is more, its words no longer originate with the author. These shifts also profoundly affect the world within the text. Language imperatives, translation norms, and new cultural expectations alter the relative force of the various voices in the text, sometimes beyond recognition. The narrator may address the reader differently, or not at all. The characters may or may not interact with the narrator as before. And the author and reader in the text must shift in relation to every other entity there—collapsed together or separated further by the translator's presence.[2] In the end, what a translation *does* is to reconstruct the work at all levels, from bottom to top and from top to bottom. Imagine trying to rebuild an onion: translation repacks all the strata of a text, sometimes arranging them loosely, sometimes fitting them well, sometimes striving to reproduce one stratum exactly at the expense of all the others, but inevitably affecting each layer by changes in the others. To the extent that translation studies have focused on isolated effects (language differences, cultural divergences, questions of authorship or authority), they have neglected the essentially multilayered quality of the translation process. What follows is an exploration of the dynamics of rebuilding a whole onion, by observing the reverberations English translations cause at various levels in Russian novels.

In keeping with its project of crossing and exploring boundary lines within and around texts, this book addresses several traditionally separate audiences. By considering together questions of production, reception, and interpretation of translated texts, I hope to include translators, readers, and teachers among my audience. For those who read Russian literature (and, perhaps, other literatures) in translation, this book suggests more informed and active ways of approaching the texts. It offers teachers of those familiar survey courses called "Russian Literature in Translation" a way to explain that this is not the same as teaching "Russian Literature," and a way to do so not as an admission of defeat but as an assertion of the subtle interplay between the two cultures and languages. There are things translations do not tell us about Russian literature, but there are also things we can learn about our own culture by reading them. And for those interested in translation, or in the interplay between language and literature, this book offers a more global way of looking at translations—as language, as narrative, as cultural icons—than many recent theoretical works.

DISCOURSE AND THE TRANSLATED NOVEL

I hesitate to call this a Bakhtinian reading of Russian literature in translation, as I self-consciously incorporate many other approaches. However, Mikhail Bakhtin's insistence upon seeing novelistic discourse as polyvalent, upon rejecting the absolute distinction between inner and outer, and upon seeing boundaries as fluid and essentially transgressible, all inform the pages that follow, and they offer a good starting point.

In "Discourse and the Novel" ("Slovo v romane," 1934–35), Bakhtin dismisses the field of stylistics for concentrating solely upon features internal to the text, the "linguistics of the utterance" and the "stylistics of 'private craftsmanship,'" while ignoring the broader context, the "social life of discourse outside the artist's study" (1981, 264, 259). He calls for an understanding of the "centripetal" as well as "centrifugal" forces acting upon the text (272), shaping it from without as well as from within. Above all, Bakhtin describes the novel as the meeting place of one's own language and that of "another," where each word incorporates past and present, familiar and alien, tradition and change. In the end, he says, the stylistics of the novel should aim not to describe the words or even their use, but to represent "the [artistic] image of a language" (336).

Among the centrifugal forces Bakhtin discusses are the mechanisms for representing the various consciousnesses within the novel, ranging from authorial interventions to narrative voice to character speech. That the boundaries between them are permeable is, for Bakhtin, the essence of novelistic discourse, of heteroglossia. He lingers upon the three ostensible ways of transcribing speech: direct, indirect, and "quasi-direct," which, he says, altogether "permit languages to be used in ways that are indirect, conditional, distanced. They all signify a relativizing of linguistic consciousness in the perception of language borders—borders created by history and society, and even the most fundamental borders (i.e., those between languages as such)—and permit expression of a feeling for the materiality of language that defines such a relativized consciousness" (323–24). Thus the novel becomes a chain of quotations of varying degrees of authority and distance, and the way voices cross borders becomes the defining characteristic of its style.

The true interplay of voices, for Bakhtin, is only possible if the centripetal forces acting upon the novel are also working to blur boundaries. With characteristic bluster (and an ironic *creation* of bounded categories to explain his system of unbounded discourse), he divides the history of the novel among early, essentially monologic works (the First Stylistic Line) and later, dialogic works (the Second Line). The first group depends upon a "discourse divorced from its material" and an expository approach to language, defining its "literariness" and "respectability" (379, 381): "The categories of popularity and approachability are pertinent here—accommodations that are made to the apperceptive background so that utterances may be easily dealt with against that background without its being dialogized, without calling forth any sharp dialogic cacophony between context and what is said, in other words, the smoothing and ironing-out of style" (381). In contrast to this view of contextualized language from above, the Second Line starts from heteroglossia, builds its novels from below, out of the interplay of languages and voices, and replaces the "category of literariness" with "a trial and self-critique of novelistic discourse" (414). Thus the world outside the novel becomes the world within the novel, and its message is essentially about language.

The link between the inner and outer forces acting on the novel is, of course, the author, or the "framing authorial context":

The framing context, like the sculptor's chisel, hews out the rough outlines of someone else's speech, and carves the image of a language out of the raw empirical data of speech life; it concentrates and fuses the internal impulse of the represented language with the exterior objects it names. The words of the author that represent and frame another's speech create a perspective for it; they separate light from shadow, create the situation and conditions necessary for it to sound; finally, they penetrate into the interior of the other's speech, carrying into it their own accents and their own expressions, creating for it a dialogizing background. (358)

They are, in other words, not simply creating the work but interacting with it. They bring the world within the novel to life, but they also must work with its own "light" and "shadows," its own speech.

How does the translator fit into this system? One answer might be that he or she does not fit at all; if the novel is about language, then it must be read in the original. But translations do exist, they are called novels, they stand in for originals throughout our culture. The vast majority of Russian novels read in the United States are read in translation, and it would be folly to expect otherwise. Translators have become a part of the novel as well, and the system must expand to include them. But traditional ways of producing translations and discussing them make little accommodation for the multiple, and multidirectional, forces Bakhtin identifies. As we will see, translators incline, by and large, to replace the inner dialogism of a text with discrete voices, and the heteroglossia "from below" with greater literariness "from above." Both of these acts represent a significant shift in the understanding of the framing context: instead of "creating a dialogizing background" for "another's speech," translations reinterpret the author's role as more stable, more authoritative, and, finally, more exterior to the text.

The most obvious shift in translation is that of the framing context. The change of languages entails a change in the possibilities for reference outside the work. Translators sometimes supplement their texts with notes, prefaces, and other apparatus. These are frequently necessary to allow readers to understand cultural references or peculiarities of the original, but they also change the text's relationship to its readers. Explanatory apparatus creates the sense of a global perspective, of an eye or mind viewing the work and its surrounding culture from without. In other words, it shifts the implied author's frame of reference into a more external frame. At the linguistic level, translation also changes the range of ambiguities allowed within the work: each language allows some information to be implied while requiring that other facts be stipulated. (English, for example, does not specify gender in common nouns but almost always indicates personal subjects and possessives; Russian codifies gender but has a wealth of impersonal or person-ambiguous constructions.) In the case of the shift from English to Russian, there are, moreover, linguistic differences in the transcription of speech (especially indirect and quasi-direct speech) which alter the borders among voices in the text and, therefore, the interplay of consciousnesses that is so essential to Bakhtin's reasoning.

Even more significantly, translation changes the author's own relation to the novel. Whereas Bakhtin describes the author as interacting with the play of voices in the text, sculpting from the raw material of "someone else's speech," for the translator the entire work is someone else's speech into which all its once-alien voices are subsumed. All too often this means that the translator redefines the work from above, asserting boundaries between voices and replacing a fluid narrating voice with one more authoritative. It would seem that the translator, having less "authorship" over the text, asserts *more* authority rather than playing with the boundaries of that authority. Words that were "half someone else's" for the author are, for the translator, *all* someone else's; in the process of taking control of them, the translator commonly reevaluates them as *all* his or her own.

The translator is abetted in this by centripetal forces acting upon translations that differ from those affecting original literature. As Lawrence Venuti writes in his introduction to *Rethinking Translation*,

> A translated text is judged successful—by most editors, publishers, reviewers, readers, by translators themselves—when it reads fluently, when it gives the appearance that it is not translated, that it is the original, transparently reflecting the foreign author's personality or intention or the essential meaning of the foreign text. . . . [Such strategies] take a characteristic form: they pursue linear syntax, univocal meaning or controlled ambiguity, current usage, linguistic consistency, conversational rhythms; they eschew . . . any textual effect, any play of the signifier, which calls attention to the materiality of language, to words as words, their opacity, their resistance to empathic response and interpretive mastery. (1992, 4)

Thus the centripetal forces the surrounding culture exerts upon translations correspond to the expository approach to style that Bakhtin decries. The very process of translation is, after all, an "accommodation to the apperceptive background," because it brings the work closer to a new set of readers. Unlike the original novel, the translation seeks above all "popularity and approachability." The most common praise in a review of a translation, if it mentions the translation at all, is that it is "readable" or "fluent."

In the end, these centripetal forces find corresponding centrifugal tendencies in translated novels. In those cases (especially in recent translations that owe a conceptual debt to Bakhtin and narratology) where editors and publishers have allowed translators to exercise more freedom, more true authority, voices within the translated novels have found more free play as well. More commonly, the imposition of authority from without does away with internal ambiguities. Venuti's lament about the loss of "attention to the materiality of language" mirrors Bakhtin's comment about the gains from relativizing speech within a work, that it permits "expression of a feeling for the materiality of language that defines such a relativized consciousness."

The first chapter of the present book observes some of the external forces shaping translations of Russian literature, the "translation culture" that has evolved over the last century and a half. What gets translated and by whom, which translations survive, who reads them and how—all turn out to be intertwined questions. Furthermore, the factors determining the existence and reception of translations have implications for the language and style, the voices internal to the texts. Subsequent chapters look at forces moving in the other direction, the centrifugal forces that have largely been neglected by translation scholarship. In particular, chapters 2 and 3 consider various methods of internal citation, indirect and quasi-direct speech, and intrusions by other, unnamed voices. Some of these effects are achieved through devices linguistically specific to Russian and are therefore difficult to translate. However, many effects that are readily available in English are routinely discarded by translators. Chapter 4 explores some of the visual effects of the text, particularly punctuation, as another important site of interplay between author, narrator, and reader. Translators tend to explain their often cavalier treatment of punctuation by the search for what "sounds right" to them. However, psycholinguistic research shows punctuation to be a fundamentally visual effect that does not lend itself to such "aural" criteria. Instead, punctuation appears to be a locus of translational control, the place where translators assert the most authority.

Translators of works by different authors, in different periods, turn out to make remarkably similar alterations to internal communicative structures. They reanalyze interjections, shifts of perspective, or odd punctuation to assert a clearer, more objective, more authoritative literary stance. This allows me to posit a sort of translator-consciousness that intervenes in the "relativized consciousness" that Bakhtin identifies as central to the novel. The translator, it seems, acts not only upon the text but within it, engaging in rivalries with the various voices in the text, as well as with the author, publisher, and reader outside the text.

TRANSLATION ACROSS BOUNDARIES: SOME TRENDS IN TRANSLATION STUDIES

If pressed to define literary translation, most would include in their definition some notion of an imperfect approximation to an unattainable ideal. This tacit understanding underlies, in particular, most practical criticism of actual translations in reviews and translators' prefaces. (Consider Vladimir Nabokov's famous characterization of his version of *Eugene Onegin* as "Dove droppings on your monument.")[3]

With the development of translation studies as a scholarly field, this inherently defeatist view has given way, gradually, to less barren approaches that choose to see translation either as holding its own place in the "polysystem" of literature, or as a window onto a richer, multilingual conception of meaning. The former approach has flourished in the past decade as "descriptive translation studies." First identified as such in Theo Hermans's 1985 volume, *The Manipulation of Literature*, this offshoot of translation studies has chosen to view translations apart from original texts, as a class in themselves, and to adopt toward them a "descriptive, target-oriented, functional and systemic" approach. A forerunner of these ideas appears in V. N. Komissarov's 1980 work, *Lingvistika perevoda* (*The Linguistics of Translation*), where he suggests that the primary question a translation critic should ask is not how closely the translation resembles the original but how well it fulfills the goals set by the translator (110). But descriptive translation studies say less about the translator or the process of translation than about the culture surrounding it. As Hermans puts it in his programmatic introduction,

> The new approach tries to account in functional terms for the textual strategies that determine the way a given translation looks, and, more broadly, for the way translations function in the receptor (or target) literature. In the first case the focus is primarily on translational norms and on the various constraints and assumptions, of whatever hue, that may have influenced the method of translating and the ensuing product. In the second case explanations are sought for the impact the translation has on its new environment, i.e. for the acceptance or rejection of a given translation . . . by the target system. (1985, 13)

Examples of the descriptive approach include Hermans's own survey of translators' prefaces and introductions as a key to understanding the role of translations in Renaissance Europe, or André Lefevere's study of the process of canonization of translations in Germany (Bassnett and Lefevere 1990).

A hybrid of descriptive translation studies and the more normative approach is seen in two recent studies of English and Russian translations: Robert Reid's 1986 exploration of multiple translations of Mikhail Lermontov's *A Hero of Our Time*; and Lydia Polubichenko's study of various Russian versions of *Alice in Wonderland*. Reid (1986, 59) looks for clues about changing attitudes toward Russian literature, as well as for critical insights into Lermontov's work itself, in his diachronic study of ten translations. Most interesting from the standpoint of translation studies, he posits a "corporate text" that consists of all the translations plus the original, which "can be used to test the legitimacy of critical hypotheses about theme and structure formed on the basis of single text readings." Successive translations, according to Reid, provide ever more information about the "normative translation." That is, they move the corporate text ever closer to some "true" meaning (or, more accurately, some maximally agreed-upon meaning) of the text. Polubichenko (1984, 201) observes the treatment of selected paragraphs from Lewis Carroll's novel for their "philological topology," or the way they treat sentence structure and syntactic rhythms in the text. By looking at several Russian versions she is able to make generalizations about how such structures are understood by readers, although she also indulges in some vague speculation about the author's intentions, as seen in "the original supraphrasal unity."

In spite of their essentially normative qualities, these essays hint at the other major trend in translation studies, one that sees translation and original as parts of a larger whole. Walter Benjamin's 1923 essay, "The Task of the Translator," serves as the seminal work for this branch of translation studies.

Instead of viewing translation as a war against inadequacy, a striving to surmount difference or impose norms, Benjamin celebrates translation as the expression of the essential "kinship" among languages. Shifting focus away from the question of equivalence, he speaks of original and translation as fitting together in a greater whole. Translation thus brings the original closer to its fulfillment, not farther from its uniqueness. He rejects any idea of conveying "informational content" in translation. The goal is instead the expression of "the unfathomable, the mysterious, the 'poetic'" (70), a means of pointing the way to "pure language."

To the extent that "The Task of the Translator" offers a prescription, it is in favor of strict syntactic literalism in translation, which, Benjamin says, should be "a direct threat to comprehensibility" (78). Nevertheless, more practical-minded theorists have found in this essay much grist for their discussions of actual or possible translations. They have shifted the celebration of "difference in translation" (to borrow the title of Joseph Graham's important 1985 anthology) from one of a disembodied pure language to one that highlights the richness of physical and temporal contexts. One result is to alter the prescription for translators. Philip Lewis, a translator of work by Jacques Derrida and a contributor to Graham's volume, replaces Walter Benjamin's concept of "strict syntactic literalism" with that of "abusive translation," or "the strong, forceful translation that values experimentation, tampers with usage, seeks to match the polyvalencies or plurivocities or expressive stresses of the original by producing its own" (1985, 41). Thus, the goal is not incomprehensibility, but defamiliarization. If a work is worth translating, then it should not just slip unobtrusively into the target language. It should be allowed to stretch and challenge that language with the same vitality that its original possesses—possibly even a greater vitality, born of new linguistic and metaphorical contrasts. Venuti's 1992 collection offers some examples of abusive translation. Most notable among the advocates of abuse is Suzanne Jill Levine, who writes here and in her own book, *The Subversive Scribe,* about her uproarious version of Guillermo Cabrera Infante's *La Habana para un infante difunto,* which she "subversively" calls *Infante's Inferno.* Her understanding of the Cuban text is simultaneously subtle, playful, and personal, and her celebration of the polyglot punning of the translation process is a model of writing about the translator's art.

Other contributors to Venuti's and Graham's collections consider translation not as importation of a work into an alien culture but as an integral component of multilingual societies. These are the situations in which language is obviously politicized, in which boundaries are unclear and travel across them is frequent and multidirectional. As Sherry Simon writes about the Canadian experience, "Translation, it turns out, not only negotiates between languages, but comes to inhabit the space of language itself. The many languages of the literary text speak of the fragmentation of language communities and the increasing complexity and heterogeneity of cultural space" (1992, 174). In such postcolonial essays as Simon's, as in Tejaswini Niranjana's more extended look at English translations of Indian literature in *Siting Translation* (1992), translation appears as a colonial phenomenon, an assertion of territory and historicity, symptomatic of the various power struggles that inform writing and reading in a broader sense.[4]

One feature of "abusive translation" that distinguishes it from more traditional approaches is its willingness to shift the focus, at least partially, from the author to the translator. The defeatist preoccupation with a work's "translatability" now gives way to a question about how daring or original a translator might be. This shift is one of the several connotations of Douglas Robinson's title *The Translator's Turn* (1991). Robinson's text hinges on a contentious argument about subjectivity, positing a "somatic" foundation for our relationship to language and interpretation. "We learn shared meanings [i.e., language] by learning the proper (ideologically controlled) feelings that drive them; and we share them with other people through the empathic power that bodies have over other bodies, emotional states over other emotional states" (10). From there, Robinson formulates a "somatics" of translation theory, always striving to recognize the translator's real engagement with the text and with language.

My own approach in the chapters that follow gleans from all of these methodologies, looking at actual translations together with their originals for clues to the cultural, linguistic, and emotional forces that shape them. I have chosen as the bellwether for my analysis of actual translations their treatment of narrative voice, because I believe that the translator-narrator relationship holds a key to both centrifugal and centripetal forces acting upon the texts. Chapter 1 considers the cultural, territorial, and historical constraints on style and language which guide the way speakers of English might receive Russian narrative voice. Here, the descriptive approach to translation studies is most in evidence. Chapter 4 offers more of a celebration of "difference," attempting to understand what punctuation might mean in the light of what translators do with it. The same approach is evident in chapter 3, which discusses fundamental differences in reported speech as indicative of different concepts of narrative autonomy. Finally, the notion of translator as emotional actor and creator in the text informs both chapters 2 and 3, which explore the language and culture of literary voices. At no point do I discard the original (in contrast to most "descriptive" scholars), and unlike many followers of Walter Benjamin I try to stay close to actual readings of texts. Above all, I attempt to keep the translator always close to heart. For I believe that the essence of translation lies in its simultaneous action upon all the various owners of the words, internal and external, specific and abstract, with the translator redefining the nature of that ownership at every level.

Chapter One

Translation Culture

> [The] awakening of the Anglo-Saxon people to Russian lit-
> erature—something which happened to all intents and pur-
> poses between 1885 and 1920—should rank as a turning
> point no less momentous than the discovery of Italian liter-
> ature by the generations of the English Renaissance. The
> teacher of Russian literature to English-speaking youth
> today is a beachcomber along sands still wet from the incur-
> sion of that tidal wave.
> —Donald Davie, "Mr Tolstoy, I Presume?"

TRANSLATION AND THE RECEIVING CULTURE

If a college course bore the title "Russian Art in America," or "Russian Sculp-
ture in Marble," students would assume the prepositional phrase to carry
important thematic information: What has been the fate of Russian art *when
brought to America*? What distinguishes *marble* sculptures from other Russian works? However, a title such as "Russian Literature in Translation" carries meaning in a different way. Here, the "in translation" phrase is but a convenient signal that the course is open to all students, regardless of their
knowledge of Russian. Beyond that, it is simply meant as a course in Russian
literature. But the prepositional phrase adds a substantial layer, even many
layers, of meaning to the title. Like "in America," the phrase "in translation"
signals a geographical and cultural displacement; like "in marble," it highlights the medium, the texture, and the particularity of the presentation of
the work. As the original was the product not simply of an author but of a cultural context, so the translation is often inextricable from its surrounding culture, which includes its language and readership but also prevailing attitudes
toward translation itself. The history of English-language translation of Russian literature, which maps the centripetal forces shaping our reception of
Russian novels over time, is itself one of those centripetal forces. Even more
than original works, translations are inseparable from their cultural history.
The translator is first and foremost a reader of the text, bringing to the text a

set of cultural assumptions—about the text itself, about the role of the translator, about readers and language and literature. Even if the translator is bilingual, consults daily with the author, or otherwise attempts to be implicitly faithful to the text, there are inevitable pressures exerted by the receiving language on the one hand and by the editor and other cultural mediaries on the other (see Venuti 1986, 179–81).

The completed translation then comes under further pressures from its receiving culture. Ironically, it is because we tend to assume that translations are imperfect that we behave as if they were not. The longstanding assumption that translations are necessarily flawed substitutes for original works has led editors, readers, and teachers of literature to avoid the subject of how translations act upon their source texts. Instead, we read (and sometimes even publish)[1] translations as if they were the original texts. The obvious result is a devaluation of the labor, not to mention the artistry, of the translator. Another result is the canonization of particular translations. If readers choose to see their version of the text as unmediated, they will also think of it as the "true" or at least the familiar, and therefore preferred, version. This phenomenon has proven particularly strong in the case of Russian literature in translation, partly because of the continually shifting political and cultural ties between Russia and the English-speaking world, partly because of the importance of Russian authors in world literature, and largely because the vast majority of English-speaking readers of Russian works read them in translation. Whatever the reasons, canonization of translations has profound effects on both their production and their reception.

Among English-speaking readers, foreign literatures rise and fall precipitously with the tides of fashion. A few influential writers or critics "discover" an exotic import and soon no one is reading anything but Spanish picaresques, French naturalist novels, Latin American magical realism. While the political climate may create the right conditions for the wave to develop, the main impetus causing it to swell is usually aesthetic, and it results in imitations or a whole new school of literature in English. Imports of Russian literature, however, seem subject to a more resolutely political tide table, dependent on swings in national relations, public opinion, and propaganda. During periods of russophobia in the 1820s and 1830s, and again during the Crimean War and the cold war, Russian literature has been either ignored or treated as a tool for demonstrating the evils of Russian society, and translations have served less-than-literary purposes. At these times, "factual" material in the texts has taken precedence over language, form, and style. When public opinion, or at least the opinion of Western intellectuals, has swept the other way, as from the late nineteenth century through the early 1920s, translations have demonstrated more interest in the literary qualities of the original works. In fact they have often shown excessive zeal in this regard, adjusting lexical and syntactic peculiarities in order to make Russian novels conform to Western literary expectations.

The great swings in mood and fashion surrounding Russian literature have attracted the attention of many scholars. M. P. Alekseev (1944, 1989), Gilbert Phelps (1956, 1958, 1960), Donald Davie (1965), and Harold Orel (1954, 1977) treat the general topic. All concentrate on the pre-Soviet period and are concerned primarily with the impact of Russian literature on English writers and their production. (Orel's work has the most bearing on my discussion here, but it tends to be sketchy and chronologically confused, so I have reordered and expanded upon much of his information.) F. W. J. Hemmings (1950) offers insights into French reception of Russian literature around the turn of the century. Others look at the translation and reception of specific writers: among them are Carl Proffer (1964) and Alekseev (1989) on Nikolai Gogol; Royal A. Gettmann (1941), Cyril Bryner (1958), Augusta Tove (1966), and Alekseev (1989) on Ivan Turgenev; Tove (1963) on Anton Chekhov; Robert Reid (1986) on Mikhail Lermontov; and Helen Muchnic (1938–39) on Fyodor Dostoevsky. There also are a few works devoted to translators, including Alekseev (1964) on William Ralston, and Tove (1958), Carolyn Heilbrun (1961), Roberta Rubenstein (1974), Charles A. Moser (1988), and Richard Garnett (1991) on Constance Garnett. The individual stories these scholars tell combine to illuminate the historical culture of English translations from Russian, in particular of the mutual impact of translators and reading public.

NINETEENTH-CENTURY "INFORMATIONAL"
TRANSLATION

In the late eighteenth and early nineteenth centuries there were a few important popularizers of Russian literature in England. The Reverend William Tooke translated Russian poetry in the eighteenth century, wrote on Russian history, and became a corresponding member of the Academy of Sciences in St. Petersburg (Cross 1969, 106–7). Sir John Bowring's *Specimens of the Russian Poets* (consisting mostly of translations by way of German) went through three printings between 1821 and 1822. Russophobia swept England in the 1820s, and the trickle of translations and travel memoirs dried up. When relations warmed in the 1840s translators began to bring out Russian novels, but they focused on those that were derivative of English works, by such undistinguished writers as Mikhail Zagoskin and Ivan Lazhechnikov. These were "imitations of Scott's romances, . . . melodramatic in structure, romantic in tone, and much concerned with lightning, white-churned water, rocks, and mist" (Orel 1977, 2; see also G. Phelps 1956). An 1838 article in *Foreign Quarterly Review* disparaged Russian writers as slavish imitators of their French and German counterparts.[2] When more original works were introduced, they were generally rejected on aesthetic grounds. As Gettmann notes, the "genuine" interest in Russian literature at this time was "not genuine enough to accept Gogol" (1941, 12). One critic dismissed his "Old World Landowners" in 1841 as *sans* everything and anything, except thorough inanity and feebleness."[3]

Events surrounding the outbreak of the Crimean War gave rise to renewed anti-Russian sentiment, but also renewed curiosity: Russia became for the English "deeply and painfully interesting."[4] One commentator later recalled his perception of Russia in 1855 as of "a huge unshapely mass, with a glossy polish on the outer surface, but fierce forces within, kept in control by a tremendous pressure of power, or superstition, or stolid faith, but really untamed and full of savage vigor."[5] This mysterious land became the subject for innumerable articles in all the major British periodicals.

Instead of silencing translators, the new russophobic wave made propagandists of them. Supported by publishers who scrupled little about sources or fidelity to originals, they turned to better novels but produced worse translations, or more often pirated adaptations. Throughout this period the translations that did appear were designed to serve political rather than aesthetic ends, providing "information" about Russian life that bolstered the prevailing stereotypes.[6] Alexander Herzen, in his French and German commentaries on Russian social movements, often remarked on the influence of Russian literature on the course of these movements, which led Western readers to look to Russian belles lettres for historical and social insights. The work that received the most attention was Turgenev's *Sportsman's Sketches* (*Zapiski okhotnika*, 1852). Propagandized by Herzen as an important document of the abolition movement, its artistic merits often were lost to readers' view. Alekseev writes, "While a few German writers with access to Viedert's superb translation of *Sportsman's Sketches* began to raise profound questions about the social significance of realistic art before pronouncing it a masterpiece, French journalists took Ernest Charrière's distorting, inaccurate translation, with all its ridiculous errors, raised its banner and tried to use it as wartime propaganda" (1989, 221). The political significance of the work has continued to be exaggerated in the West, where many are still convinced that Turgenev's sketches were largely responsible for the emancipation of Russia's serfs (Alekseev 1989, 249).

The "informational" bias of early English translators of Russian novels appears in the very titles they chose. Lermontov's *A Hero of Our Time*, Gogol's *Dead Souls*, and Turgenev's *Sportsman's Sketches* came out as, respectively, *Sketches of Russian Life in the Caucasus* ("by a Russe, many years resident amongst the various tribes," 1853); *Home Life in Russia* (by "A Russian Noble," 1854); and *Russian Life in the Interior* (1855). As a rule, these translations disregarded the artistic qualities of the works, such as form and style, in favor of the content, which, in turn, they often distorted with stereotypes of Russian villainy and backwardness. Turgenev, who was himself a translator and fluent in English, was appalled by the mistreatment of his *Sketches*, which was actually an Englishing of the inadequate French version by Charrière (Alekseev 1989, 226–27).

Ironically, though Turgenev would later be hailed in the English-speaking world as a model for realist writing, his work was not considered especially informative about Russian life, outside of its political dimension (Gettmann 1941, 16). Gogol and Lermontov were, it appears, more highly valued as "vital" sources. The introduction to (Lermontov's) *Sketches of Russian Life in the Caucasus*, which is also attributed to the anonymous "author," is mostly an encapsulated history of Russian letters, especially printing. complete with statistics. (There are also knowledgeable thumbnail sketches of Russian writers, including Lermontov, but no mention that he might have had something to do with the work at hand.) The writer of this introduction states, "I think I have said sufficient to prove that Russia is in every way entitled to more curiosity, if not interest, than is usually accorded to her" (6), suggesting that the purpose of this volume is less literary than informational (see also Reid 1986, 77–78). The translator-adaptor has wrought extensive changes on the text, adding flourishes of plot and description and changing names. This version simply omits, without explanation, one of the most stylistically polished segments of the novel, "Taman'," perhaps because it is too psychological and elliptical, too poor in "facts," to serve the edition's purposes.[7] Lermontov's novel received more faithful treatment in subsequent translations, beginning the following year, although Reid details their continuing, if more subtle, deviations from the original, particularly in structure. It was common, for example, to change the order and names of the chapters or eliminate certain ones altogether, and one version adds a sequel (Reid 1986, 77–80; G. Phelps 1958, 431).

The most famous of the pirated novels is the distortion of *Dead Souls* (*Home Life in Russia*, 1854).[8] Its propagandistic mission becomes clear from the publisher's preface (i–ii), which claims that the volume's purpose is to "throw light upon the domestic life of our ancient allies and present foes" and to give "an insight into the internal circumstances and relations of Russian society which only a Russian could afford us." The text, according to the preface, is documentary rather than fiction, and "the main facts are well known in Russia." What is more, the publishers claim, the work is not a translation at all, but was given to them in English, marred by "such verbal errors as might be expected, when we bear in mind that the author has written in a language which is not his own." The editors confess to having corrected the English grammar. They do not mention the other deviations from the Russian original (how could they, if they do not acknowledge its very existence). These include a thoroughgoing restructuring of the text and the introduction of a condescending narrator who takes every opportunity to remind English readers of their superiority to the Russians. As early as the third chapter the narrator offers to fill in his readers on the details of Chichikov's life and his motives for coming to "Smolensk" (in Gogol's version, the mysterious City of NN). He introduces Chichikov's biography much earlier than Gogol does, summing up his plan in terms that are representative of the tone of the work:

> In itself, the nefarious scheme devised by our hero, affords an extraordinary instance of the cunning inherent in the Russian character, for its whole success was based on the knowledge he possessed of the utter baseness of the national character. None of the actors in this strange drama will appear to exhibit the slightest compunction about defrauding the government, as long as they can gain any slight advantage to themselves, and even the certainty of condign punishment in the very possible event of detection, cannot cause them to refrain from their innate propensity. The fact is an humiliating one, but in our character as the historian of an actual event, we have not dared to omit a single trait which may seem to elucidate our story. We only wish it was in our power to draw a pleasanter portrait of our countrymen, and we fervently trust that the time may yet arrive when such stories as the present one may be numbered among the things that were. (105)

In the original, Gogol's narrator has his share of censure for prevailing mores, but he invariably expresses it ironically, especially in the first volume, and he never poses as "historian of an actual event," only as author of a *poema* (epic poem).

In keeping with the moralizing tone of such addenda, though somewhat at odds with his or her claim that this is "fact," the pirate translator augments the narration of the story with colorful irony. In the passage below, flourishes found only in the English version appear in italics:

> "Dost thou see it?" said the one to the other, "there is a wheel for you! What do you think of it, would it break or not, supposing it had to roll as far as Moscow?"
>
> "It might stand the journey," replied the other, *musingly, as he scratched himself sedulously behind the ear.*
>
> "But supposing it was on its way to Kazan, I think it would not *stand the wear and tear of such a distance?" said the first speaker again.*
>
> "It will never roll *into the ancient Tatar fastness,*" responded his friend *somewhat affirmatively.*
>
> Thus ended the learned conversation, *the scientific depth of which we will not venture to explore.* (2–3)

These additions exaggerate the peasants' uncouth ways (scratching behind the ear), dramatize the story (identifying speakers and describing their manner), and increase the narrator's role in it (note the added commentary: "said the first speaker again," "somewhat affirmatively"). Clearly, we cannot discuss this production as a translation, since it represents such a brazen reworking of Gogol's novel. It is, however, instructive with regard to English attitudes toward Russia and Russian literature: Russian society was so uncivilized to their minds that the writer of the English version could produce a seemingly factual account of its depravities by *expanding* on the satirical qualities of Gogol's style.

Even after the cessation of hostilities in the Crimea, the "informational" approach to Russian literature continued, aided by the high Victorian eagerness to define art as moral example. Davie (1990) argues that it took the more jaded late Victorians to appreciate Russian novelists. He cites a review of the 1862 translation of Lev Tolstoy's *Childhood and Youth* as an example of the puritanical, not to mention literalist, attitude that blinded early critics to the merits of Russian realism: "The world can get on very well," wrote the reviewer, "without criticisms written by a son on the behavior of his father at his mother's funeral."[9] Clearly, a work's formal merits (especially if it was to be imported from a savage land) were secondary to its "factual" or cultural content.

In subsequent decades, until the early 1880s, political and economic competition renewed British mistrust of Russia, and trade in Russian translations was slow. Booksellers and libraries had few Russian works. Courses in Russian language were rare. (Even in 1897 there was a series of letters in the London *Morning Post* complaining of the lack of Russian courses or examinations in England.)[10] In general, the 1860s were a period of insular Anglocentrism, and only between 1869 and 1874 was there a mild burst of interest, especially in Turgenev, fed by a few positive reviews that emphasized his poetic gifts and promoted his "suggestive" but neither graphic nor supernatural storytelling (Gettmann 1941, 29–30). The one serious scholar of Russian letters at this time was William Ralston, who translated works by Ivan Krylov and Turgenev, among others, and wrote articles on Russian folklore and major literary figures. Although Ralston was admired as a perceptive critic and a capable translator by Russian intellectuals, who admitted him as a corresponding member of the Academy of Sciences in St. Petersburg, no such recognition accrued to him at home (Alekseev 1964). The extent of the academic stature that Russian literature received in England at the time was that Ralston was invited to give a series of a few lectures at Oxford in 1873. His influence, however, was short-lived. By the late 1870s hostility toward Russia had reached new heights, fueled by Russia's Balkan policies and its growing reputation for domestic terrorism. Russian literature again became a source of information for the curious and fearful, and its artistic merits were almost entirely lost from view.

The American response to Russian literature followed a different chronology, as Gettmann demonstrates. There were neither the great surges of russophobic curiosity nor the periods of indifference, but rather a steady increase of interest, particularly in Turgenev. Americans had earlier access to Russian literature: in the 1870s there were probably three times as many American as British translations, and their quality was generally superior as well.[11] Many works by Gogol and Tolstoy and several novels by Turgenev, including *Dimitri Roudine*, *Fathers and Sons*, and *Smoke*, appeared in New York in the 1860s and 1870s, a decade or more before London publishers brought them out. What is more, they were reviewed in all the major American journals. Especially in the case of *Fathers and Sons* (trans. 1867), the reviews were enthusiastic about the novel's aesthetic as well as documentary merits. As Gettmann writes, the reviewer for the *New Englander* (July 1867: 592) read the novel expecting to find "insight into the workings of the Russian mind but found it as absorbing as any English or American novel" (1941, 41).

Americans' affection for Russian literature was not only more constant but more broadly based. George Sand once commented to the itinerant Russian intellectual M. M. Kovalevsky that the English praised Turgenev highly but read him little; Kovalevsky found, on the other hand, that "even middle-class Americans" knew Turgenev's works.[12] Alekseev ascribes this difference to the Americans' greater sympathy for the problems of serfdom and its abolition, which, as we have seen, Western critics had already determined to be Turgenev's great theme. There also were aesthetic differences between England and America: Bryner (1958, 5–6) indicates that the British found Turgenev's plots excessively slow, while the Americans praised him for "rapidity of movement." An obituary in the *Dublin Review* (1884) referred to several barriers to Britain's reception of Turgenev, including "neglect of plot, the poor quality of translations, and the abundance of English novels" (Gettmann 1941, 95). In contrast, American writers from Henry James to Edith Wharton adopted Turgenev as their model for the "well-formed novel." It was American writers, in fact, from whom Turgenev received his most enthusiastic promotion in his lifetime: James wrote several articles about his Russian friend, praising him in the strongest terms and recommending him as "a novelist's novelist."[13] As early as 1874 James wrote, "[Turgenev] is particularly a favourite with people of cultivated taste; and nothing, in our opinion, cultivates the taste more than to read him."[14] When English readers returned to their russophobic "informational" approach to the literature, Americans did not follow suit, continuing to assess Turgenev's writings as art. Indeed, Gettmann writes that "the English welcomed *Virgin Soil* as a social document, [while] American admirers of Turgenev were displeased with it" (1941, 102), precisely because it seemed to place information above art.

On the Continent, too, Russian literature received an earlier and warmer reception as art than it did in England. In part, this was due to closer contacts with Russian culture. Many Russian writers knew French and German, and those who had European friends often felt compelled to make their own translations of Russian poetry. Thus, P. A. Viazemskii translated Pushkin for his friend Chateaubriand, A. I. Turgenev did the same for Lamartine and for his English friends (Alekseev 1989, 272). Karolina Pavlova was a Russian poet of some note whose earliest publications were "highly successful" and influential translations of Russian poetry into both French and German in the 1830s.[15] The Collège de France had a chair of slavonic studies as early as 1840, nearly half a century before Oxford began its curriculum in "Lithu-Slavonic Languages" in 1887 (Orel 1977, 1). Versions of Gogol's and Dostoevsky's works appeared in France and Germany three decades before they came out in English. (Turgenev was Gogol's first translator into French, and he and Herzen propagandized Russian literature in their French and German writings.) A fine German translation of Turgenev's *Sportsman's Sketches* appeared very shortly after the work came out in Russian, followed by Charrière's vastly inferior, but ultimately more influential, French version, and another by Hippolyte Delaveau, who collaborated with the author (Alekseev 1989, 227). The complete works of Turgenev were available in French at least a decade before the English variants appeared in full.[16] Those English readers who were familiar with Gogol, Turgenev, Dostoevsky, or Tolstoy in the 1860s and 1870s mostly read them in French or German, or in English translations from French and German sources. Among the latter were several Turgenev works taken from the authorized French versions, and the first English edition of *War and Peace* (1882) also came by way of the French.

This is not to say that Russian literature achieved mass popularity in France or Germany before the 1880s. Hemmings shows that in France even the most significant Russian writers were known only to "the merest handful of specialists" before that time. Translations were available, he writes, but they were not read: "A perfectly satisfactory translation of *War and Peace* was produced in St. Petersburg and offered for sale in Paris as early as 1879: scarcely anyone bought it then, but six years later the book was a best-seller" (1950, 2–3). Until 1884 occupants of the much-touted chair of Slavonic studies in France were at best indifferent to Russian literature: they included the Polish poet Adam Mickiewicz, a Balkan expert, and a Lithuanian linguist (ibid., 3–4). Nevertheless, there was none of the retrenchment seen in England in the 1870s, since France looked to Russia as its ally against Prussia. By the early 1880s, the groundwork was laid in France for serious study of Russian literature. Hemmings catalogs numerous encyclopedic and comparative works on Russian culture published in France between 1875 and 1885. The most influential of these were Ernest Dupuy's *Les grands maîtres de la litterature russe* (1885) and Viscount E. M. de Vogüé's *Le roman russe*, published serially in *Revue des deux mondes* in 1885. De Vogüé's study appeared in book form in America in 1886, and in England in 1887, and these versions went through about a dozen editions in thirty years.

In addition to the weight of Continental and American opinion, there were internal pressures guiding the British toward an acceptance of Russian literature. Continuing conflicts on Russia's borders meant that there were many English military men who had spent a great deal of time in or near that country, and many of them learned Russian, as did journalists and diplomats involved in the lengthy and repeated negotiations between the two countries

(Alekseev 1944, 133).[17] Whereas almost no one in England knew Russian at mid-century, by 1880 there were dictionaries, textbooks, and means of learning Russian directly, rather than through French or German sources. Russians exhibited a growing interest in England and America at this time. It became fashionable for Russians to carry on correspondences in English. Disaffected or radical Russians began to emigrate to England and America in the late 1880s, where they found friends among intellectuals who supported their revolutionary sentiments.[18] They, in turn, taught their new friends about Russian language and culture, creating both a new audience and a new supply of potential translators. Constance Garnett, for example, learned Russian from émigré friends, by listening to their conversations and reading books they recommended (Rubenstein 1974, 360). She was aided in her early translating career by Sergei Stepniak, a fugitive Russian terrorist.

Late Victorian culture was, in general, more open to foreign influences than was the high Victorian age. Having reviled the French naturalists in the 1860s and 1870s, the English lionized them in the 1880s. There was a strong reaction, however, on the part of those who found the French writers too graphic. (This reaction culminated in the imprisonment of the publisher Henry Vizetelly in 1889 on charges of pornography.) In this context, the likes of Turgenev and Tolstoy began to seem the answer to English readers' dreams. James had anticipated this exaltation when he praised Turgenev in 1874 for rivaling French writers in storytelling while adding a religious, "*ascetic* passion."[19] Captain R. G. Burton, writing in *Westminster Review* (December 1895, 539), made this comment: "It is refreshing, in these degenerate days of the modern novel, to turn from the inane indelicacies of fashionable fiction, from the hysterical emanations of the unhealthy imagination of the New Woman and the vapid vapourings of the *fin-de-siécle* young man, to the luminous pages of a literature that has in it all the life of true realism, whilst it does not flaunt in our faces those lower phases of human nature which are best left to the imagination of the prurient." The goal of adopting a literature with "scarcely a line which could offend the most sensitive reader" (as Burton put it) was to have important consequences for the selection and stylistic treatment of Russian novels in translation. Welcomed as outsiders, Russian novelists were rapidly brought *inside* English culture, imported wholesale if they conformed to Victorian readers' expectations, or made to conform when necessary.

Thus the floodgates were open for what Davie calls the "torrent" of translations that appeared after 1885, with a "trickle" in the half-decade before that. His aquatic metaphor echoes a comment of the time, from *Literary World* (23 November 1889, 415), to the effect that the very idea of a "Russian literature" had seemed until recently an oxymoron, "But, like a sudden gulf stream, a warm wave of life flows, all at once, from this region of ice, to quicken the pulses of the whole civilized world. It is a new renaissance." Scholarship about Russian literature, much of it translated from French, began to appear in English and be taken seriously. Perhaps most significantly, literary translation was becoming a profession in its own right, and individuals began to take personal responsibility for conveying foreign literatures, especially Russian, accurately and artistically into English.

There was something strongly programmatic about all these efforts to adopt Russian literature in English, and they would have a powerful, lasting influence on the choice of works for translation and the way they would be received. It is probably not coincidental that the main focal point for the growing mania for Russian novels was de Vogüé's *Le roman russe*, for it offered an overview that would classify, explain, and evaluate these new and confusing works. It was, Hemmings argues, a polemical volume aimed at changing the course of French literature, "an attempt at utter demolishment of the naturalist aesthetic theory" (1950, 30). As such it presented Russian literature as the great alternative, a paragon of decency and truthfulness with a moral edge, qualities calculated to warm the hearts of the late Victorians. Coming out almost simultaneously with the "flood" of translations, this book did more to shape Western attitudes toward Russian literature than any other work. Edmund Gosse later called it "perhaps the most epoch-making single volume of criticism issued in France during our time."[20] A few of de Vogüé's observations achieved the status of aphorisms: "From 1886 on only a rare English critic could escape de Vogüé's notion that Turgenev's heroine characteristically possessed the iron will which Turgenev's hero lacked, or that Dostoevski was like a traveler who had visited the entire universe and who described everything he saw, but who had never travelled except by night" (Orel 1977, 3).

Alongside relatively sober accounts of the plots and themes of major works and assessments of their authors, de Vogüé gives occasional, illuminating glimpses into the stereotypes of the time. He does not hesitate to generalize about the Russian character: "The Russian people are afflicted with a national, a historical malady, which is partly hereditary, partly contracted during the course of its existence. The hereditary part is that proclivity of the Slavonic mind towards that negative doctrine which to-day we call Nihilism" (1887, 20). De Vogüé goes on to connect this doctrine to Buddhist teachings, an obvious reminder that Russia, to European eyes, was more an Eastern country than a Western one. He also expresses some dismay that Russian audiences find Gogol's *Inspector General* such a funny play: "I have often seen the 'Revizor' performed. The amiable audience laugh immoderately at what a foreigner cannot find amusing, and which would be utterly incomprehensible to one not well acquainted with Russian life and customs. On the contrary, a stranger recognizes much more keenly than a Russian the undercurrent of pathos and censure" (71). How ironic that a Western audience would supposedly "get" Gogol's message more clearly than Russians, especially when Gogol was generally agreed to be "too Russian" for Western tastes. De Vogüé himself wrote of Gogol, "[The reader] must not expect the attractive style or class of subjects of Tolstoi or Dostoevski. What *they* show is results, not principles; they tell of what we can better apprehend; for what they have studied is more common to all Europe. Gogol wrote of more remote times, and, besides, he and his work are thoroughly and exclusively Russian. To be appreciated by men of letters, . . . his works must be admirably translated; which, unfortunately, has never yet been done. We must leave him, therefore, in Russia. . . ." (87)

This patronizing tone is indicative of—and no doubt contributed to—the Western European consensus that Russia was essentially an untamed land with a great but somewhat anomalous and equally untamed (if not unwitting) genius for literature. The exception that proved this rule was, of course, Turgenev, whose death in 1884 had been the occasion for retrospective articles and lamentations about the loss of "this most Western of writers." If his death was seen as a loss to world culture, then Russian literature must have become part of that culture, providing just the combination of exotic and familiar qualities to whet the appetites of English readers.

TURGENEV AS VICTORIAN WRITER

The darlings of the English literati of the late nineteenth century were Turgenev and Tolstoy, in that order. Dostoevsky remained too foreign for even late-Victorian tastes; his moment was not to come until a quarter of a century after Turgenev's. It would seem that the order of reception of these authors was inevitable. Turgenev's understanding of Western aesthetic sensibilities, coupled with the timeliness of his appearance in print and his own propagandizing efforts, essentially spawned the very idea that Russia had a literature worthy of the name, which gave rise to a more general acceptance of Russian literature as a phenomenon in its own right and not a mere subset of European literature. At the same time, the fact that translators and readers gained their acquaintance with Russian literature through Turgenev had a profound and lasting impact on the perception *and the production* of Russian literature in English. Though British readers recognized Russian novelists as having something special to contribute to world culture, Turgenev helped them to believe that Russian literature could fit into the stylistic mainstream in England, and subsequent translations increasingly forced Russian novels into this mold.

The first legitimate translations of Turgenev's works, from Russian rather than French, appeared only in the late 1860s. Even then they did not achieve immediate acclaim. Critics patronized Turgenev, considering him unprofessional and, at best, artistic in his artlessness (Orel 1977, 2). However, as French and American intellectuals began to extol his work, and Turgenev himself made friends among the British intelligentsia, the currency of his novels and stories rose in value. They appealed to an English audience that was tired of the single-minded Victorian predilection for novels of manners, an audience that sought a more "realistic" approach to modern problems. More important to his later followers was the fact that he was a Russian author who seemed to transcend Russian backwardness, who understood the English sensibility, and whose aesthetic meshed clearly with theirs. He portrayed the evils of serfdom and exposed inequities in Russian life, but always from a genteel, liberal viewpoint. (This quality had been recognized in France as early as 1854, when Prosper Mérimée wrote that Turgenev "is not blind to the fact that evil practices flourish in his native land, but he does not denounce them with indecorous violence" [Hemmings 1950, 6].) Unlike Tolstoy, he used a small, intimate scale to portray big issues, and unlike Dostoevsky, he did so with drawing-room elegance. De Vogüé wrote, "His scenes were always Russian, but the artist's interpretation was different from Gogol's, having none of his rough humor and enthusiasm, but more delicacy and ideality. His language too is richer, more flowing, more picturesque and expressive than any Russian author had yet attained to; and it perfectly translates the most fugitive chords of the grand harmonious register of nature" (1887, 101). A reader of Russian would probably disagree with the assertion that Turgenev surpassed Gogol in "richness" and "expressiveness" of language, but to the extent that these categories accompany the aristocratic ideal of "flowing" and "picturesque" writing, they define themselves in terms of Turgenev and ipso facto exclude Gogol. That is, *richness* is here a matter of elegant language rather than mastery of dialectal nuance, for example, and *expressiveness* presumably has a lyrical connotation. Ford Madox Ford complimented Turgenev for "disappearing" into the "surrounding atmosphere," praise that epitomizes the aesthetic ideal of the late Victorians.[21]

Turgenev also appealed to literary purists, perhaps because his style was less convoluted than those of other Russian writers. Arnold Bennett felt that he was the only great novelist in the world who did not neglect technique (Bryner 1958, 17). Henry James wrote in 1896, "The perusal of Tolstoy—a wonderful mass of life—is an immense event, a kind of splendid accident, for each of us: his name represents nevertheless no such eternal spell of method, no such quiet irresistibility of presentation, as shines, close to us and lighting our possible steps, in that of his precursor."[22] James's commentary shows an appreciation for the moral message of Turgenev's work, but it also reveals a desire to fit Turgenev into American culture: while commenting that "it is the Russian type of human nature that he depicts," James nonetheless wrote that Turgenev's heroines possess "the faintly acrid perfume of the New England temperament—a hint of Puritan angularity."[23] G. Phelps argues that Turgenev may have been anointed by English and American writers because the challenge he posed was relatively gentle: "Turgenev's studies of social ferment in fact constituted less of a threat to the existing order than Tolstoy's drastic spiritual and ethical challenges, or Chekhov's exposure of inner decay" (1956, 120). It is difficult to say whether this attitude was superimposed upon Turgenev's literature by the Victorian audience, or grew out of a tendency among translators to make their versions of Turgenev as "beautiful" as possible. Constance Garnett wrote that "Turgenev is much the most difficult of the Russians to translate because his style is the most beautiful" (C. Garnett 1947, 195). (Davie [1990, 277] finds this classification of "that burly huntsman Turgenev" among "the hermaphrodites of aestheticism" amusing and "astonishing.")

To add to his appeal, Turgenev's style transcended national boundaries to some degree, reflecting his own cosmopolitan sensibilities and damping the fear of "Russianness" evident in reviews of Gogol and Dostoevsky. The critic Stuart Sherman wrote in 1912: "I will not question Turgenev here, because the almost impeccable beauty of his art seems exceptional and attributable as much to French influence as to Russian instinct for form" (323). Still, at the same time that Western intellectuals were adopting Turgenev for their own, they also delighted in the fact that he was Russian, and that he made "Russianness" accessible to them. Henry James had eulogized him thus: "His genius for us is the Slav genius; his voice the voice of those vaguely-imagined multitudes whom we think of more and more to-day as waiting their turn, in the arena of civilisation, in the grey expanses of the North."[24] The combination of familiarity and novelty was intoxicating, as Maurice Baring noted in the *Quarterly Review*, some time after the most abandoned passions for Turgenev had faded:

> One reason of the abundant and perhaps excessive praise which was showered on Turgeniev by European critics is that it was chiefly through Turgeniev's work that Europe discovered Russian literature, . . . The simplicity of Russian literature, the naturalness of the characters in Russian fiction, came like a revelation to Europe; and, as this revelation came about partly through the work of Turgeniev, it is not difficult to understand that he received the praise not only due to him as an artist, but the praise for all the qualities which are inseparable from the work of any Russian. (1909, 193–94)

Turgenev's art had everything to which the late Victorians aspired, and it was comforting to see in him the epitome of Russian culture and English good taste. Thus, Turgenev served as an ambassador in every way: by his physical presence and his writings he brought Russian literature to the English; by his graceful style he brought the English to Russian literature.

One important result of the English and American affection for Turgenev was a rise in emphasis on literary translation. Turgenev's works were translated more frequently, and more successfully, than those of any other Russian writer of his century. A concern for style appears in translations of Turgenev earlier than in those of other writers. Ralston's 1869 translation of *Dvorianskoe gnezdo* (1858), which bears the English title *Liza*,[25] was acclaimed by the author as well as the critics, one of whom declared that "unlike almost all translations, it is a pleasure to read it for its style alone."[26] Although he tended to be overly literal and had an excessive proclivity for annotations and explanations, Ralston showed enormous respect for Turgenev's artistry, and he dedicated *Liza* to his friend, the author (see Tove 1966, 139).

De Vogüé lists fifteen English translations of works by Turgenev published in the 1880s alone, and twenty-six altogether by 1886, which is twice the number of editions of Tolstoy's works and five times the number for Dostoevsky, Gogol, or Pushkin. It is probably not coincidental that his ascendance coincided with the emergence of a cadre of professional translators. True, some of them specialized in other authors than Turgenev, such as Tolstoy's champions Louise Maude and Aylmer Maude. Nevertheless, Turgenev's style became the test of a translator's skill. He also could be said to have made the name of the most famous translator of Russian literature of all time, Constance Garnett, who produced a collected edition of his works between 1894 and 1899 (fifteen volumes), plus two volumes in 1921. Moser (1988) discusses these translations in some detail, and compares them to the series translated by Isabel Hapgood, an American journalist and traveler, and published in 1903–4.[27] Although he declares Garnett's versions to be less accurate than Hapgood's, they won the loyalty of readers for their style, "reproducing in English something of the simple eloquence of the original," as a reviewer wrote.[28]

In part, Turgenev's influence on writers of English was due to Constance Garnett's efforts as a translator. Arnold Bennett congratulated her for writing such "good English, and quite apart and aloof from the ruck of translations."[29] Joseph Conrad was a loyal admirer of her work. In 1899 he wrote: "It is as if the Interpreter had looked into the very mind of the Master and had a share in his inspiration;" and in 1917: "Turgeniev for me is Constance Garnett and Constance Garnett *is* Turgeniev. . . . She has done that marvellous thing of placing the man's work inside English literature, and it is there that I see it—or rather that I *feel* it" (Conrad 1928, 248–49). This last judgment bears some consideration. For Conrad, the goal of translation was to naturalize a work, to fit it "inside" English literature, so that the reader would have a somatic affinity for it, "feel" it to belong. (As example 1.1 shows, Garnett's versions sometimes naturalized Turgenev's language to the point of blandness.) Conrad was, of course, at home in many languages and literatures, so this was not necessarily an appropriative desire. Himself a Pole, he certainly had no interest in promoting Turgenev's "Russianness," as so many of his contemporaries did, and he would later dismiss virtually all other Russian authors as "unworthy" of Garnett's efforts. His antipathy for Russian culture probably added to his glee that Turgenev, the only Russian author he truly admired, had, in effect, joined the *English* canon.[30] Whatever Conrad's own motives, the general response to Garnett's translations was appropriative: Western readers were able to understand Russia because they could

Turgenev's style was not as uniformly classical as critics and translators seemed to assume. Bakhtin has described Turgenev's style as employing "character zones" in narration "from various forms for hidden transmission of someone else's word, from scattered words and sayings belonging to someone else's speech, from those invasions into authorial speech of others' expressive indicators (ellipsis, questions, exclamations)" (1981, 316). For example, in the much translated *Dvorianskoe gnezdo* (*Nest of Gentlefolk* or *Noblemen's Nest*), narration about the old servant Anton takes on a folkloric coloring when recounting Anton's own storytelling:

Антон . . . начинал свои неторопливые рассказы *о стародавних временах, о тех баснословных временах* . . . когда во все стороны, даже под городом, тянулись *непроходимые леса, нетронутые степи.*

(191; emphasis added)

The parallelisms and compound, hyperbolic adjectives reinforce the sense that Anton is in no hurry, that he takes pleasure in the telling. They are all but gone in the Garnett and Ralston translations:

Anton . . . began upon his slow, deliberate stories of *old times, of those fabulous times* . . . when there were *impassable forests, virgin steppes* stretching on every side, even close to the town. (Garnett, 123-24)

Anton . . . would begin a deliberate narrative about *old times, those fabulous times* . . . when on all sides, right up to the town, there stretched *impenetrable forests and untouched steppes.* (Ralston, 190)

Antón would . . . begin his leisurely stories of *olden times,—of those fabulous times*—when . . . in all directions, even close to the town, stretched *impenetrable forests, untouched steppes.* (Hapgood, 123–24)

"Old" and "fabulous" are too prosaic and have too little in common to convey the parallel redundancies of *starodavnikh* and *basnoslovnykh* ("the olden days" and "the fabled days," or "days of old" and "days of story and fable" might be better). By the same token, Garnett's "impassable" and "virgin" lack the morphological similarities and the metrical consistency that give the last phrase its epic poetic quality; Ralston's choices preserve the parallel somewhat better, as do Hapgood's. The latter also has the more folkloric "olden times." Still, the effect is muted; if one wanted to bring out this aspect of the work more strongly, a possible alternative would be:

Anton would begin his leisurely stories of days of old, of the days of story and fable . . . when forests impenetrable and steppes untouched began at the very edge of town and stretched in every direction [as far as the eye could see].

The last phrase might be added to enhance the folkloric quality and also to prolong the supposedly "leisurely" narration.

---

understand Turgenev, and they could understand Turgenev largely because of Garnett's facility for English.

Critics strove to find familiar themes and images in Russian works: echoes of Walter Scott in Tolstoy's Cossacks, Henry Fielding's "wholesome naturalism" in Gogol (Orel 1954, 458–59). But in general, English readers found most Russian writers other than Turgenev to be "too Russian." Indeed, according to Orel, two conflicting attitudes coexisted within English-language criticism of the time: one, that Russian fiction could be "anglicised without serious inconvenience"; and the second, that Russian literature was unique and untouchable. In this context the attraction of Turgenev, particularly in Garnett's fluent translation, is clear: since his works fell within existing definitions of the "literary," they could retain their essentially "Russian" quality while being anglicized, thus satisfying both schools of thought. It follows that what was essentially "Russian" about Gogol or Dostoevsky was something less civilized and therefore less easy to reconcile with the critics' contradictory impulses.[31]

On the other hand, the elegant beauty of Turgenev's prose was not sufficient to sustain interest in Russian literature for long; it merely served to whet English and American appetites for those other Russian novels that were setting the Continental literary world abuzz. Thus, by the end of the century, Turgenev had served his purpose and was, it seems, no longer needed. By the time Garnett completed her translations of his works, there was little demand for them (Orel 1954, 466), but Russian literature was established as an important component of world culture.[32] And the cult of Tolstoy quickly took over.

DOSTOEVSKY AND TOLSTOY

Translations may be partly to blame for the English tardiness in accepting writers other than Turgenev. A new translation of *Dead Souls*, by Hapgood, came out in 1886, but "even then it received scant justice, for a concocted *Continuation of Dead Souls*, vastly inferior in quality, was added without explanation" (G. Phelps 1956, 17). De Vogüé (1887, 87) also expressed dissatisfaction over translations of Gogol's works into French. Dostoevsky was known in France and Germany some time before English readers had access to his works, but there, too, critics received his writing with skepticism. Commentary on Dostoevsky stressed his wildness, his uncouth qualities, his deviation from accepted literary norms. In an unguarded moment, de Vogüé expressed his "astonishment" that translations of Dostoevsky's romances "are greatly enjoyed by the French" (1887, 142).[33] Probably taking their cue from the viscount, English and American readers were slow to take Dostoevsky seriously. As Moser writes, "The first English version of a major work by Dostoyevsky (which is now usually rendered as *Notes from the House of the Dead*) did not appear until 1881, the year of Dostoyevsky's death; *Crime and Punishment* and *The Insulted and Injured* appeared in English some five years later. But Dostoyevsky remained much too Russian for the English mind even then" (1988, 435).

When more works by Dostoevsky appeared in translation in the mid-1880s, their reception was tepid, or simply patronizing. In 1884 *The Uncle's Dream* and *The Permanent Husband* appeared in translations by Frederick Whishaw. William Sharp wrote in the *Academy* (4 August 1888, 68) that they were "admirable" and commented, "Mr. Whishaw's English version is, as usual, so good that I can well believe what I have heard as to Dostoieffsky's novels being more literary in English than in Russian." Thus the reviewer is complimenting the *changes* Whishaw made in the texts. These changes included cutting several passages from the originals. Semion Rapoport commented wryly on the same translator's truncated versions of *Crime and Punishment* (1886) and *The Idiot* (1887), "I suppose because, being himself a novelist, [Whishaw] held himself a better judge of what is of interest to the reader than Dostoevsky himself" (1928, 504).[34] This condescending attitude toward Dostoevsky, as a rough-hewn writer in need of stylistic assistance, would persist for decades. Writing in 1910, some twenty-five years after the first translations appeared, Maurice Baring was able to claim: "In England, Dostoevsky cannot be said to be known at all, since the translations of his works are not only inadequate, but scarce and difficult to obtain, and it is possible to come across the most amazing judgments pronounced upon them by critics whose judgment on other subjects is excellent" (130–31).

One such critic was Henry James, who had worked so hard to promote Turgenev in America. Dostoevsky offended James's aesthetic preference for order and method, his love of objectivity, and, quite possibly, his loyalty to his friend Turgenev.[35] One of Dostoevsky's few early defenders in England was Robert Louis Stevenson, who wrote to a friend:

> Raskolnikoff is easily the greatest book I have read in ten years; I am glad you took to it. Many find it dull: Henry James could not finish it; all I can say is, it nearly finished me. It was like having an illness. James did not care for it because the character of Raskolnikoff was not objective; and at that I divined a great gulf between us, and, on further reflection, the existence of a certain impotence in many minds of to-day, which prevents them from living *in* a book or character, and keeps them standing afar off, spectators of a puppet-show.[36]

Thus Stevenson admired precisely those qualities—subjectivity and incoherence—which repelled most critics. His comments on "living in a character" anticipate Bakhtin's analysis of polyphony in Dostoevsky's novels. (It should be noted that both James and Stevenson were apparently reading the novels in French; *Crime and Punishment* appeared in English only some months after this letter was written.)

The neglect of Dostoevsky's work lasted for several decades. Publishers brought out his works sporadically, feeling "there was no real market in England for Dostoevsky," as they told Baring in 1903 (G. Phelps 1956, 156).

Scholars and critics looked askance at him, too. Phelps documents only a few articles on him before 1895, and those anything but warm.[37] While they might praise his "narrative power" and characterization, and his "evocations of poverty and wretchedness," they are disdainful of the novels' value. Phelps notes that "it was almost universally agreed that he could not write a novel that even remotely approached a work of art," and, "the truth of the matter was that Dostoyevsky's fictional methods were utterly incomprehensible to those accustomed to the traditional forms of nineteenth-century English fiction." The adjectives critics used for his writing—"unattractive," "somewhat repellent," "peculiar rather than nice," "unquestionably unpleasant"[38]— reveal the real source of the problem. Dostoevsky simply was not sufficiently genteel for the late Victorian audience. They looked on Dostoevsky, as on Gogol earlier, as a curiosity or a window onto Russian life, but not as an artist. Davie writes, "Many reviewers were still naïvely looking in Dostoievsky, as they had in Turgenev, for factual information about Russian conditions" ("and," he adds, "whenever this was not the main focus of interest, controversy turned instead on whether Dostoievsky was a Russian Emile Zola") (1965, 3). Translators, too, reflected the "informational" bias, concentrating more on the sociological content of his novels than on their artistic qualities.

Tolstoy suffered less at the hands of translators, but he was also slow to gain recognition among English readers. He himself was partly responsible, since he refused to give Ralston permission to publish excerpts of *War and Peace* in 1878—79, on the grounds that the work was of insufficient interest (Alekseev 1964). Nevertheless, Tolstoy soon overtook Turgenev as the favorite among English-language readers, who seem at first to have had room in their hearts for only one Russian author at a time. Like Turgenev, Tolstoy found earlier popularity in America. By 1889 twenty-seven editions of his novels and stories had appeared there, prompting the London *Academy* "Bookworm" to comment, "In the eighties a good many American versions had circulated in this country [i.e., England]—Vizetelly and Walter Scott being, I think, the only English publishers who saw their way to the popularisation of Tolstoy in those days."[39] Tolstoy, it seems, was too large and complex, at least at first, to win over British aesthetic opinion, which could not reconcile his religious reputation with his literary realism.[40] Even in America there was resistance to his writings, as to his philosophy. Conservative critic Maurice Thompson called him "a rich man who prefers to live in brutal vulgarity" and called his novels "as dirty and obscene as the worst parts of Walt Whitman's 'Leaves of Grass.'"[41]

Still, the weight of Tolstoy's reputation eventually won out in Britain, where the 1890s became the decade of Tolstoy. An anonymous writer in *Literary World* (1 February 1890, 39) declared: "When the present fever of admiration, which makes the judicious smile, has abated, [Tolstoy] will remain among the great novelists of the century." The Brotherhood Publishing Company was founded in Croyden in the early 1890s to publicize Tolstoy's works and those of his disciples. (In the first decade of the twentieth century, eighty-six editions of individual works by Tolstoy were published, and no fewer than six editions of his collected works appeared.)[42] Davie (1965, 6) credits the fact that Tolstoy was still alive, and that his stature as "sage and prophet" preceded his fame as novelist, for his meteoric rise in popularity in England and America.

Thus, at the turn of the century, many Russian works were available in English, but it was primarily Turgenev's personal charisma and Tolstoy's moral example that drew readers to their works. There remained a strong sense of Russia as fundamentally an alien land, which was a barrier to the acceptance of other writers. One advocate of Russian literature in the early twentieth century was Maurice Baring. Writing in *Quarterly Review*, Baring acknowledged the poetry of Turgenev's style (three quarters of which, he said, was lost in translation), but also cited its conventionality, which he did not think would stand the test of time. He hailed "the rising of Dostoievsky's red and troubled planet," which had "[caused] the rays of Turgeniev's serene star to pale" (1909, 181). Readers objected to this article as too hard on Turgenev. Baring responded to their criticism in his book *Landmarks in Russian Literature* (1910), complaining that anyone who suggested that Gogol or Dostoevsky might surpass Turgenev as a writer was accused of breaking "a cherished and holy image" (118). He reprinted his encomium for Dostoevsky in this volume, and he also lavished praise on Gogol's "rich and native" language (48), lamenting that *Dead Souls* had been allowed to go out of print.

Another champion of the lesser-known writers was Edward Garnett, husband of the translator and himself a notable critic and writer. He ascribed the English barriers to appreciation of Russian authors to conflicting cultural inclinations. For Maxim Gorky, for example, Mr. Garnett expected less success in England than in France or Germany. "The fact being that to the Russian mind it is 'immoral' to conceal the seamy facts in a world so constantly dominated by ugliness, while to the English mind it is 'immoral' not to let character and conscience have the last word in 'the battle of life'" (*Academy*, 8 June 1901, 497–98). In 1906 Mr. Garnett noted balefully that *The Brothers Karamazov* had two French versions and none in English, and that Dostoevsky's works in general were out of print in England. He hypothesized that the English fear of "morbidity" and desire for "wholesomeness" made it difficult for them to enjoy Dostoevsky's works and thus accounted for their scarcity (*Academy*, 1 September 1906, 202).

THE "RUSSIAN CRAZE"

During the Russo-Japanese War, in which English sympathies lay with the Japanese, there was a brief retreat from russophile tendencies. However, with the 1905 revolution in Russia came a renewed fervor for things Russian, building eventually to what would be known as the "Russian craze" of, roughly, 1910–25. W. L. Phelps wrote his *Essays on Russian Novelists* in 1910, calling Russian fiction, like German music, "the best in the world" (vii). In his review of Phelps's book Stuart Sherman wrote of Russian fiction, "Its influence upon contemporary writers has unquestionably been immense. And its popular vogue has been sustained along with the samovars and tea and beaten brass that entered in the wake of the Japanese war" (1912, 322). John Galsworthy called *War and Peace* "the greatest novel ever written," and Vita Sackville-West wrote, "I think myself that Tolstoy stands among novelists as Shakespeare stands among poets—head and shoulders above the rest of them" ("In Praise of *War and Peace*"). Now, when English writers made lists of the best novels in the world, the majority were Russian novels. An article in the *New York Times Book Review* in 1912 characterized contemporary British and American novels as unsuccessful imitations of the Russians' confessional mode and argued that the results were only "stupidly indiscreet" rather than simple and realistic.[43]

At its inception, the Russian craze retained some of the patronizing tendency to stereotype the "Russian character" seen in the nineteenth century. After expressing the desire to write from the inside, as if through Russians' eyes, Baring generalizes about them very much from the outside: "The Russian character and temperament are baffling, owing to the paradoxical elements which are found united in them" (1910, xiv). He finds that Russians differ markedly from natives of other countries, that they are passive but obstinate, humane, kind, never hypocritical, and tolerant of "moral delinquencies" that affect only the individual, but not those that affect the community (1–3). Thus, although he appeared to advocate broader acceptance of Russian authors other than Turgenev, he did so within the appropriative framework of his predecessors.

While the Russian craze was fed by familiarity with Turgenev and Tolstoy and by the political swing toward Russia around the time of the First World War, it was Dostoevsky who now took the English-speaking world by storm. Whereas Germans had had access to translations of Dostoevsky for over sixty years, and French audiences had had his complete works since 1890, English publishers had shown no such alacrity, and it took two decades and the weight of Garnett's reputation as a translator to make his novels available. Richard Garnett chronicles the resistance her publisher Heinemann felt, even in 1911, to bringing out *The Brothers Karamazov* in English. Having been told by a "distinguished Russian" that passages in it were "appallingly shocking," Heinemann wrote to Mrs. Garnett that he was "leaving it to you to tone down such passages as might be thought offensive in this country" (R. Garnett 1991, 260, citing an undated letter from Constance to Edward Garnett). The Garnetts themselves were so convinced that Dostoevsky would not appeal to English tastes that they accepted a reduced, flat fee rather than a royalty for the translations (ibid., 259–69).

Dostoevsky was, of course, not unknown to English intellectuals before that point. Arnold Bennett, for example, found *The Brothers Karamazov* very impressive when he read it (in French) in 1909, and D. H. Lawrence was impressed with *Crime and Punishment* around the same time. In 1910 an old translation of *Crime and Punishment* was adapted (and strangely altered)[44] for the stage as "The Unwritten Law." A new Everyman edition of the same translation increased the public recognition of Dostoevsky's name and cleared the way for further translations of his neglected novels. This passing familiarity created such an aura of expectation that when Garnett's translation of *The Brothers Karamazov* finally appeared in 1912, it caused an enormous sensation. Contemporaries were aware of its significance. "John Middleton Murry compared the Garnett translation to the 'most epoch-making translations of the past,' placing it on a level with Sir Thomas North's *Plutarch*" (Moser 1988, 435).

Garnett followed this novel with eleven more volumes of Dostoevsky's works in the next eight years. "Constance Garnett's translations of Dostoyevsky's major works was, at least in its immediate effects, one of the most important literary events in modern English literature," her biographer wrote (Heilbrun 1961, 188). Each new volume was received with great fanfare and consumed greedily by English intellectuals. A new cult soon formed, though less unanimous than that for Turgenev. Orel notes Dostoevsky's "sensational popularity" and his "message, however variously interpreted, . . . [that] consumed reams of space and almost completely distracted critics and readers from what, customarily, are the aesthetic considerations in the reading of a novel" (1954, 469). It was, however, not just a cult of Dostoevsky, but a cult of Dostoevsky *via* Constance Garnett. Amidst the general acclaim for Mrs. Garnett's translations of Dostoevsky, we can detect hints that her triumph lay partly in adapting him to the aesthetic demands of the English reader. Mrs. Garnett wrote, "Dostoievsky is so obscure and so careless a writer that one can scarcely help clarifying him—sometimes it needs some penetration to see what he is trying to say" (1947, 195). At times, such clarification is welcome, and it certainly makes the Garnett translations easy to read, compared to some more recent, more literal translations. The *Times Literary Supplement* (4 July 1912, 269) praised her translations by saying, "English readers, embarking on the huge tract of Dostoevsky's fiction, need all the help they can get in the way of clarity and comfort." On the other hand, one main result of her tendency to "clarify" was the elimination of deliberate prevarications and mutterings on the part of the narrator that give an air of intrigue and rumor to much of Dostoevsky's style, as seen in example 1.2.

In spite of Garnett's smoothing of Dostoevsky's voice, many readers still found his works challenging, even excessively so. Edward Crankshaw found them to be full of "overpowering vehemence" that "takes the thing out of the translator's hands and sweeps the reader along in an indiscriminate, headlong rush" (Crankshaw 1947, 196). John Galsworthy wrote to Edward

Early in *The Brothers Karamazov* the narrator describes the brothers in strongly subjective tones, ostensibly refuting local gossip (but, of course, reporting it at the same time). Of Alyosha he writes,

Да и все этого юношу любили, где бы он ни появился, и это с самых детских даже лет его. Очутившись в доме своего благодетеля и воспитателя, Ефима Петровича Поленова, он до того привязал к себе всех в этом семействе, что его решительно считали там как бы за родное дитя. А между тем он вступил в этот дом еще в таких младенческих летах, в каких никак нельзя ожидать в ребенке рассчетливой хитрости, пронырства или искусства заискать и понравиться, уменья заставить себя полюбить. Так что дар возбуждать к себе особенную любовь он заключал в себе, так сказать, в самой природе.

(Bk. 1, chap. 4; 14:19)

Indeed, everyone loved this young man wherever he appeared, and it was so even in his earliest childhood. When he came to live in the house of his benefactor and guardian, Yefim Petrovich Polenov, he attached everyone in the family to himself so much that they decidedly considered him, *as it were*, their own child. Yet he entered the house at such an early age that one could hardly expect in a child *any calculated cunning, or pushiness, or skill in ingratiating himself, or knowledge of how to please and how to make himself loved.* Thus he possessed in himself, in his very nature, so to speak, artlessly and directly, the gift of awakening a special love for himself. (Pevear and Volokhonsky, 19; emphasis added)

This passage reveals much about the narrator. He displays a cynical attitude toward people in general (that they can only be loved if they push or ingratiate themselves) in his somewhat bewildered acknowledgment that Alyosha was different. In Constance Garnett's version, the information about Alyosha is readily available, but that about the narrator is hidden:

Everyone, indeed, loved this young man wherever he went, and it was so from his earliest childhood. When he entered the household of his patron and benefactor, Yefim Petrovich Polyonov, he gained the hearts of all the family, so that they looked on him quite as their own child. Yet he entered the house at such a tender age that *he could not have acted from design nor artfulness in winning affection.* So that the gift of making himself loved directly and unconsciously was inherent in him, in his very nature so to speak. (14; emphasis added)

Note how she shortens the list of insinuating behaviors and eliminates the narrator's interruptions ("as it were"; syntactic breaks in the last sentence). For Garnett, these are simply the facts of Alyosha's character; for Dostoevsky's narrator, they are suspicious and, if true, astonishing.

Garnett in 1914, "I'm reading *The Brothers Karamazov* a second time; and just after *War and Peace*, I'm bound to say it doesn't wash. Amazing in places, of course; but my God!—what incoherence and what verbiage, and what starting of monsters out of holes to make you shudder" (1934, 217; see also Heilbrun 188).[45]

The most ambivalent, and illuminating, reaction to Garnett's translations came from Joseph Conrad, who called *The Brothers Karamazov* "an
impossible lump of valuable matter . . . terrifically bad and impressive and
exasperating" (1928, 240–41). Conrad commented to Edward Garnett upon
reading it: "Of course your wife's translation is wonderful. One almost breaks
one's heart merely thinking of it. What courage! What perseverance! What
talent of— interpretation, let us say. The word 'translation' does not apply to
your wife's achievements. But indeed the man's art does not deserve this
good fortune. Turgenev (and perhaps Tolstoy) are the only two really worthy
of her."[46] Here we see the translator's authority overtaking that of the author.
Garnett's style is the measure, not Dostoevsky's. The critic and his language
may be more sophisticated in 1912 than in 1884, but we still hear overtones
of wanting Dostoevsky to be "more literary in English than in Russian," or of
translators who "held themselves a better judge of what is of interest to the
reader than Dostoevsky himself" (see p. 28 above).

The passion for Russian authors during the Russian craze was not limited to Dostoevsky, but encompassed a general interest in things Russian. In
1915 Rebecca West declared, "We are deeply and affectionately familiar
with Russian life" (Orel 1977, 5). D. H. Lawrence complained of the indiscriminate nature of the Russian craze, calling Turgenev a "male old maid"
unworthy of the attention he was receiving.[47] Knopf began publishing a substantial series of translations, including some old standbys and some writers
"totally unfamiliar in English," among them Lermontov and Goncharov.[48] In
English as well as American journals there was a constant flow of literary
comment on Russian literature, and a continual call for more translations. It
being wartime, the attitude toward translation took on a patriotic flavor once
again. One anonymous critic lamented in 1915, "England's belated tribute to
the supremacy of Russian literature is not without a phase of irony, in view of
the fact that Germany was the first of the Occidental nations to welcome this
literature, through a wealth of immediate translations of all the Russian mas-
terpieces."[49] For this critic, Russian literature is tainted by virtue of having
been translated into German first. Such a view hints at a bidirectional influence between original and translation: not only does the translation represent the original, it affects the original by association.

Two translations of *Dead Souls*, which had long been out of print in
English, appeared in 1915. Stephen Graham's version demonstrates, however, that the impetus for its publication had more in common with the "informational" trends of the 1850s than with the literary fervor of English intellectuals. He wrote in his introduction,

> At this time, when knowledge of the Russian life and character is so necessary for
> the British people, it is important that the great Russian classics be accessible.
> Ideas of Russia gleaned from books on Russia written by English people should be
> checked either by personal observation in Russia or by the reading of the great

Russian novels. The works of Dostoieffsky and Tolstoy and Turgeniev have done much for Anglo-Russian friendship and mutual understanding. Gogol, who has been strangely neglected, can take his share. (1915, 10)[50]

This translation has little literary merit (see C. Proffer 1964, 420), but perhaps more than the other translation, by C. J. Hogarth, published in the same year and thoroughly criticized by Rapoport: "Mr. Hogarth has a very poor knowledge of Russian but a rich fancy (I believe he, too, is a novelist), and decorates Gogol with such ornaments of style as to make him unrecognisable.... It would be necessary to copy out practically his whole translation of Gogol's work to point out all the absurd additions and errors which it contains, as one meets them on every page" (1928, 505).

Not all were fully sympathetic to the Russian craze. Puritan and Victorian prejudices remained in opposition to it. C. T. Hagberg Wright (1921, 106) lamented the "curious lack" of "influence, both as to form and matter, exercised by the Russian bible" in works by Russian authors or their critics. Sherman recognized that Tolstoy, Dostoevsky, Gorky, and others were valuable not for their beauty but for their "virtue," but he wondered whether the latter was of a type worthy of emulation: "[Whether] their predominating excitement makes in the main for that sober wisdom which is the comeliest countenance of virtue, for that inner poise and serenity which is indispensible [sic] to high leadership and right action—this is another question. For my part I pray to be delivered from envisaging life through the nervous asceticism of the old age of Gogol and Tolstoi, as through the epilepsy of Dostoevski" (1912, 323).

The Dostoevsky cult, which was largely restricted to intellectuals, waned as the last of Garnett's volumes appeared in 1920. Walter Neuschäffer, in his review of Dostoevsky's influence on English writers, concluded that he "remains alien, almost incomprehensible, to the English spirit" (1935, 10). This was not the end of the Russian craze, however, for Garnett led her contemporaries to another Russian writer who sparked in them some of the same affections that Turgenev had once enjoyed: Chekhov. Chekhov was popular during his lifetime in Russia, but he never achieved the status or lasting influence at home that he was accorded in England. As with Turgenev and Dostoevsky, Garnett did not limit herself to a few of Chekhov's works but heaped upon the English reading public thirteen volumes of stories, two of plays, and one of letters, thereby creating a rich humus within which the cult could develop. And develop it did. The appearance of Garnett's Chekhov collection has been likened in impact to her *Brothers Karamazov* (Heilbrun 1961, 192). Robert Morss Lovett wrote in 1925, "The interest in Tchekhov does not wane. Since his death in 1904 the translation of his stories has gone steadily on in the capable hands of Mrs. Constance Garnett, and his reputation has increased, until he stands with Turgenev, Tolstoy, and Dostoevsky as one of the four Russians of incontestably first rank in the literature of the latter nineteenth century" (286).

Response to the Garnett versions of Chekhov is eerily reminiscent of the Turgenev period. Edward Crankshaw cites Conrad's reaction to her versions of Turgenev and comments, "And we should add to Turgenev, Chekhov. Chekhov, for us, is Mrs. Garnett, and Mrs. Garnett is Chekhov— for better or for worse. These were the two great writers whom Mrs. Garnett made supremely her own" (1947, 196). Indeed, it is difficult to say where Garnett's style begins and Chekhov's leaves off. Chekhov's writing lends itself to translation in much the same way as Turgenev's: it has simplicity and grace, it tends to use a single perspective and little extraneous detail. (In fact, D. S. Mirsky argues that Chekhov's style improves with translation. His Russian, says Mirsky, is "fluid and precise" rather than "melodious," and it is easy to translate because its language is "colorless," "lacks individuality," and is "devoid of all raciness and nerve.")[51]

Cult status did not suit the unpretentious and inconclusive work of Chekhov, as it did not suit Turgenev's before him. Both writers' works possessed a piquant combination of familiarity and difference that made them especially ripe for popularity in translation, but that popularity was to some degree independent of the inherent merits of the works. G. Phelps's comment on the Chekhov cult in England shows its appropriative quality: "The majority, failing to appreciate the fundamental realism and sanity of Chekhov's vision and purpose, handed themselves over to a cult which they had created more in their own likeness than in that of Chekhov himself" (1956, 188). Looking back at the end of the "Russian craze" period, in 1925, Virginia Woolf commented on Chekhov's importance in terms that illumine both his influence on English style and the inappropriateness of the worship of his work: "Where the tune is familiar and the end emphatic—lovers united, villains discomfited, intrigues exposed—as it is in most Victorian fiction, we can scarcely go wrong, but where the tune is unfamiliar and the end a note of interrogation or merely the information that they went on talking, as it is in Tchekov, we need a very daring and alert sense of literature to make us hear the tune" (247). Nevertheless, it was the spare and simple language of Chekhov that most attracted Western readers. He offered them something at once alien and familiar, a sure antidote to their uneasy feelings about Dostoevsky and Tolstoy. One reviewer even took some comfort in the fact that Chekhov found a more loyal following among Western audiences, who had "become more sensitive for nuances," than among the less subtle Soviet readers.[52] It would seem that, for all their appreciation of Russian culture, Western critics retained a sense of superior sophistication: recall de Vogüé's 1886 assertion that Western audiences could better appreciate the pathos underlying Gogol's humor.

CONSTANCE GARNETT

Chekhov may have found his perfect interpreter in Constance Garnett. It is worth lingering over her particular contribution to Russian literature in English, because so many readers throughout the English-speaking world hear Russian literature in her voice. A reviewer in the *Times Literary Supplement* wrote in 1912 (4 July, 269): "We owe it mainly, indeed we owe it almost entirely, to her that Russian novels may now be read in sound and native English." Tove (1958, 193) points out that she has reached audiences in Australia, China, India, Egypt, and other former colonial areas, as well as England and North America. As Carolyn Heilbrun, who has chronicled the Garnett family, writes, "From 1912 probably until the Second World War, her name was for most people synonymous with translations from the Russian" (1961, 185). As we have already seen in the cases of Turgenev and Chekhov, this identification occurred not only because of her prolific output but because people equated her voice with those of Russian writers.

Constance Garnett brought Russian literature within reach of English readers, and the popularity and longevity of her works is testament enough to their value. The most common adjectives applied to her by sympathetic critics have more to do with the quantity than the quality of her work. They refer to her "achievement" (Moser), her "courage" (Conrad), her "great pioneering work" (anonymous reviewer). D. H. Lawrence once visited her home and marveled at how fast she worked, producing an impressive stack of translated pages in one sitting. He admired this "constant, rapid, all-absorbing work" as the hallmark of a true artist (Heilbrun 1961, 164). One could view such comments another way, however, as exhibiting a patronizing attitude toward translation. In this view, the translator is the servant of the receiving culture, essentially a soldier called to heroic battle ("yeoman service," as Moser says of Garnett) in the cause of transporting, or importing, another culture. Individual words, individual pages become unimportant in the massive campaign to absorb a nation's literature.

Indeed, assessments of Garnett's contribution repeatedly argue that it is wrong to quibble over her individual translations, for after all she chose a herculean task, translating seventy-two volumes in half as many years. Heilbrun states, "Because [Garnett] continued steadily to translate Russian literature, to maintain a supply of readable, readily available, and inexpensive editions of Russian works, it was to her translations that people automatically turned. Though there were other competent translators, . . . taken as a whole her translations were, at the time they were made, easily the best" (1961, 185). Individual translations might be better, but Garnett's oeuvre was what was important. She did not simply produce some good translations, she made virtually all the works of the most significant authors available in reliable English versions. Heilbrun's suggestion that we should look at Garnett's work "as a whole" is intriguing: it points to the notion that readers wanted a single mediator for Russian literature, one who would standardize it and make it familiar. As the reviewer in the *Times Literary Supplement* put it, "English readers, embarking on the huge tract of Dostoevsky's fiction, need all the help they can get in the way of clarity and comfort" (4 July 1912, 269). This meant, on the one hand, domesticating or "taming" the works to English tastes, and on the other, unifying Russian literature so that readers could understand it, too, "as a whole."

It would seem, from comments like Conrad's (that only Turgenev—and possibly Tolstoy—were "worthy of her"), that Garnett's contemporaries were delighted to find someone of the cultural stature of Constance Garnett as their mediary for Russian literature.[53] Clearly they felt that they could trust her in this role, for they accepted her versions unconditionally. Kornei Chukovsky makes it clear that this reverent attitude did no favor to her or to her loyal readership: "I repeat: her translations would have been considerably better if they had been submitted at the time of their publication to the intense scrutiny of critics. . . . But there was no criticism" (1984, 222). Constance Garnett was the arbiter, and for most English-speaking readers, Russian literature was what she made of it.

In the introduction to their recent volume, *Translation, History and Culture*, Susan Bassnett and André Lefevere (1990, 2) describe the phenomenon of reader loyalty to translations. They reflect on Marcel Proust's comment about his grandmother's aversion to new translations of classics, which turn the familiar Ulysses and Minerva into the obscure Odysseus and Athena. "Proust's grandmother, therefore, does not really like or dislike a translation; rather, she trusts or distrusts a translator. The translator whose work she is familiar with is, to her, a 'faithful' translator." Thus, once someone like Garnett becomes established as the canonical translator of Russian literature, it becomes increasingly hard to unseat her.

Why would anyone want to unseat her, if she is so beloved, so well established, so unquestioned? One answer is that she only went unquestioned because she suited the needs of her time so well that no one knew what questions to ask. Later critics, faced with different cultural conditions and presenting new demands—for psychological complexity, for example, or for stylistic nuance—have been less ready to accept her at her word. Affection for Garnett's work, as for Russian literature in general, has tended to go in waves, with periods of worship followed by periods of reaction. Nabokov called her Gogol translations "dry and flat, and always unbearably demure," but more careful "and thus less irritating than some of the monstrous versions of *The Overcoat* and *Dead Souls*" (1944, 38). Chukovsky, who tended to be more restrained than Nabokov in slinging barbs (who isn't?), finally dismissed all Garnett's translations but her Turgenev, calling them "insipid, pale, and—worst of all—trivial" (1984, 222).

Chukovsky's complaints may seem extreme, given that generations have been swept up by Garnett's versions of Russian classics. However, some

An example of the sort of unquestioning acceptance Constance Garnett's translations received, even long after other translations had become available, is seen in Augusta Tove's analysis (in Russian) of the various English versions of Chekhov's works. Of Garnett's translation of "The Steppe" (1888), Tove remarks, "Constance Garnett has re-created all the charm of the original, its fragrant [*blagoukhannyi*] style. . . . [She] retains the personifications [of nature], the epithets, and the musical quality of the intonation. She has found the exact equivalent for the author's simple but expressive words" (1963, 146–47). Yet a close look at the passage Tove cites in support of these claims also reveals certain omissions, which smooth out the syntax and make the narrative more impersonal and omniscient:

Но вот наконец, когда солнце стало спускаться . . .

(Chekhov, "Step'," 28)

But at last, when the sun was beginning to sink . . . (185)

Оно переглянулось со степью — я, мол, готово — и нахмурилось.

(28)

It exchanged glances with the steppe, as though to say, "Here I am" and frowned. (185)

Еще бы, кажется, небольшое усилие, одна потуга, и степь взяла бы верх.

(29)

One effort, one struggle more, and it seemed the steppe would have got the upper hand. (187)

In the first phrase, the deictic *vot* 'here,' 'there,' or 'Look!' is omitted in English, taking away the sense of a narrator who is alive to every nuance of the scene at the moment it is occurring: "*But now, at last* . . . " In the second, the inserted "as though to say" (in place of the simple indicator of direct address *mol*) makes the whole statement part of the narrator's regular exposition, rather than a sudden exclamation in another voice. (I suggest: *The sun and the steppe looked at each other. "I'm ready," frowned the sun.*) And finally, "it seemed" is far less personal than the present tense *kazhetsia* 'it seems', for the Russian implies "it seems *to me* (the narrator)." This could be achieved with another indicator of subjectivity, such as *perhaps*. While it may be true that Constance Garnett does a better job than the other translators reviewed by Tove in the areas of "idiomatic language, the finest nuances of meaning, the emotional coloration of the words, and expressions from different linguistic registers" (1963, 146), her treatment of narrative voice leaves something to be desired.

---

specific criticisms recur in writings about Garnett's translations. One is that she still had a Victorian prudishness about language. Her son, David Garnett, later wrote that, though she held liberated attitudes about free love and women's sexual needs, his mother "was prudish in speech and disliked, or rather did not understand, bawdy conversation."[54] Russian classics tend to be anything but bawdy, which was something the Victorian readers appreciated about them, but Garnett tamed them further, changing even such expressions as "my God" to "my Goodness." We can dismiss this, perhaps, as an inevitable dating of the language of a translation. However, when it adds a veneer of respectability to every page, it becomes more than a simple matter of age; it becomes an active force within the works. It becomes, as Chukovsky wrote, a matter of turning the Russians' "volcanoes" into "a smooth lawn mowed in the English manner" (1984, 221).

Many commentators have noted a more serious flaw in Garnett's writing: her tendency to smooth over the stylistic differences among the various authors she translated. C. Proffer says of her *Dead Souls*, "Gogol's style becomes indistinguishable from that of Turgenev, Tolstoj, Dostoevskij, or Čexov" (1964, 425–26; see also Chukovsky 1984, 220–21; Heilbrun 1961, 193 n. 2). As we will see in later chapters, this particularly meant erasing those idiosyncrasies of narrative voice and dialogue that different authors possessed. Gogol's pounding repetitions, Dostoevsky's constant interruptions of the text or his tendency to put one character's words in another's mouth, Tolstoy's interminable sentences, Turgenev's tendency to allow his narrator's voice to echo the dialect of the character being described—all were smoothed over, brought closer to an ideal of good English. Given the general acceptance of this criticism of Garnett's stylistic homogenizing, one wonders what it means to say that her style was so close to Chekhov's and Turgenev's. At which end was the merging of styles occurring? (Or, to paraphrase Conrad, was she doing justice to them or they to her?) The Garnett case seems to point to a danger of endowing a translator with too much authority. Her work becomes so definitive that the author is lost, or the original is ignored. How else could we explain the hubris of V. S. Pritchett, who wrote a biography of Chekhov without knowing any Russian? He based his interpretations on the Garnett translations, explaining, "They appeared in a haphazard chronology, inaccuracies have been pounced upon, but her voice is close to Chekhov's period" (1988, ix). It is true that she and Chekhov were roughly contemporaries, but that is scarcely sufficient reason to rely blindly upon her translations. (It stretches credulity even farther to read a similar claim about her translation of *Dead Souls*. L. J. Kent comments in his preface to the revised edition of her translation that "the language has not been converted into the contemporary idiom because, as far as possible, the intention has been to preserve the tone of the original" [1964, xi]. Not only must we believe that Garnett *is* Turgenev and Chekhov, but now her version of Gogol becomes the "original.")

Many Garnett translations have now been revised for definitive modern editions of Russian works, such as Norton Critical Editions. Here, too, the editors show an almost irrational loyalty to Garnett. In one of the more sober editor's prefaces, L. J. Kent explains his decision to revise and update her translations for *The Collected Tales and Plays of Nikolai Gogol* because "eminent scholars of Russian literature with whom I consulted agreed with my point of view that, despite occasional errors and the often debilitating effects of Victorianism, her work remains a remarkably competent and wonderfully conscientious accomplishment. Too many more recent translators confuse sheer verve with scholarship." This is straightforward enough, and

Kent goes on to cite the need to spruce up the style and "bring Gogol in English closer to the spirit of Gogol in Russian" (1964, xi). In other words, Garnett needs stylistic modification. However, for many editors it is precisely the style that attracts them to Garnett's versions, and they seem less able to explain the changes they introduce. Ralph Matlaw chooses the Garnett versions of Chekhov's stories, *Fathers and Sons*, and *The Brothers Karamazov* for the Norton editions, revising them all for "accuracy and readability." However, for each he finds serious stylistic flaws ("the subtleties of Chekhov's style are lost in translation" [1979, xi]; sometimes "Mrs. Garnett followed [Turgenev's] Russian too closely, to the detriment of English style" [1966, vii]). Most interesting is his claim that Garnett's "eminently readable version has [sometimes] modified [Dostoevsky's] repetitions for the sake of a facile elegance" (1976, 736). He cannot seem to decide whether readability is a flaw or an asset.

After World War II new translations of Russian classics began to appear, but readers and critics often remained loyal to Constance Garnett. The following review, of David Magarshack's 1954 version of Dostoevsky's *The Possessed*, shows the degree of affection Garnett inspired:

> Several generations of English readers have come to know Dostoevsky's *Besy* through Mrs. Constance Garnett's translation, *The Possessed*. But the perfect translation is an unattainable ideal, and it is only natural that in every second or third generation a new translator should feel impelled to offer a fresh interpretation of an original masterpiece in the light of his own time. Nor is it a denigration of Mrs. Garnett's great pioneering work on the Russian nineteenth century novelists to say that Mr. Magarshack has now produced a new version of *The Possessed* which is tauter and basically more accurate than its predecessor.[55]

It is a testament to Garnett's staying power that a new translation required such an elaborate defense for superseding hers, even forty years later.

Recently a well-known college president dismissed my question about alternative translations of Russian classics, saying essentially, "We use Garnett in our classes because we see no need for any others." I hope that the analysis in the next three chapters will offer a counterweight to such arguments. I do not deny the value of Garnett's translations, but even the most canonical translations can accomplish only a few things at most, and there is often room for other translations that serve other purposes. In the case of Russian literature, the importance of twentieth-century schools of criticism, based on the narrative styles of the likes of Dostoevsky and Gogol, has placed new requirements on literary translation that Garnett did not have to meet (in fact, that she virtually had *not* to meet). Many teachers continue to use Garnett's versions in college courses because they are canonical or familiar, because critical vocabularies are based on her renditions of particular words and phrases, or simply because they like them best. I have no interest in discouraging them; I only hope that they will recognize that these rationales often have more to do with the place of Garnett's translations in *English* literature than with their success at representing *Russian* literature.

THE SOVIET PERIOD

The Russian craze died out in England toward the end of the 1920s. Virginia Woolf wrote, in Series One of the *Common Reader,* that "the most elementary remarks upon modern fiction can hardly avoid some mention of the Russian influence, and if the Russians are mentioned one runs the risk of feeling that to write of any fiction save theirs is a waste of time" (1925a, 216–17). By Series Two, however, she was less enthusiastic: "Our prolonged diet upon Russian fiction, rendered neutral and negative in translation, our absorption in the convolutions of psychological Frenchmen, may have led us to forget that the English language is naturally exuberant, and the English character full of humours and eccentricities" (1935, 235). (This was, incidentally, partly a reaction to the English dependence on translations, for which Woolf had already expressed some mistrust in 1925.)[56]

Chekhov was the last Russian writer whom English readers were able to appropriate for their own. Russian literature of the early Soviet period offered fare that was less palatable to English tastes. Most of the stylists and experimental prose writers of the 1920s and 1930s, who were tolerated but essentially ignored by the Soviet regime, were also neglected by translators and Western audiences. One notable exception was Zamiatin's *We,* which for political reasons appeared first in English, not in Russian.[57] Even this novel appeared only in the United States, not in England; George Orwell, who drew upon it for his *1984,* had to read it in French (Struve, 1964). Literary journals in the United States and Britain published regular commentary on the current state of Russian literature, voicing especially high praise for Isaac Babel's *Konarmiia* (*Red Cavalry*) and Yuri Olesha's *Envy.* (See, for example, Tobenkin [1928, 541] and Mirsky [1931, 477–80].) However, they seem to have reached a limited audience and the selection of works was "arbitrary and haphazard" (Struve 1964, 137). Gleb Struve claims to have offered the first course on Soviet literature at a Western university in 1932, but for the most part, few people were interested in the topic or read the anthologies and surveys he and others produced (139).

In general, it was the sociological aspects of Soviet literature that captured English and American interest. Many of the new socialist novels caught reviewers' attention, and a good number were translated fairly quickly into English. Fyodor Gladkov's *Cement* (1925; trans. 1929), Alexander Fadeev's *The Nineteen* (*Razgrom,* 1927; trans. 1929), Nikolai Ostrovsky's *The Making of a Hero* (*Kak zakalialas' stal',* 1932-4; trans. 1937), and Mikhail Sholokhov's *The Quiet Don* (1934–40; trans. 1943) are some examples. Tobenkin credited *Cement* with "profound narrative sweep" and called it the "first big psychological novel of the new order" (1928, 541). By 1931 Mirsky, noting that Russian works were appearing in German, French, "and even English," was able to assert that "Bolshevik authors can no longer complain of being neglected by the West." He praised Sholokhov's and Fyodor Panferov's successes in 1930, but admitted there were no "imaginative works of the first magnitude" in Soviet literature at that time. And to the extent that attention was being paid, it was more to the sociological or political value of the works than to aesthetic criteria. Mirsky advocated this sociological approach in 1931; Ernest J. Simmons echoed his comments in 1952, when he compared Soviet prose to the novels of Horatio Alger in their value to the social historian.

It took World War II and its aftermath to spark more widespread interest in Russian language and culture. In 1944 Simmons wrote a description of a new intensive course at Cornell University in Russian language and civilization. The course had been criticized as "communistic" by the New York *World-Telegram*. Simmons struck back, assailing the nation's ignorance of the Soviet Union:

> Over the last twenty-five years our colleges and universities have sadly neglected formal education on Soviet Russia. Before the war fewer than a dozen institutions offered courses in Russian language, literature and history, and very rarely were such efforts concerned with developments after the 1917 Revolution. Courses in the social sciences devoted almost no solid instruction to Soviet Russia, and graduate students considered such a concentration a professional liability. The unfortunate result today is a shocking lack of properly trained teachers in the Russian field, which, under the impact of the war, is coming to be regarded as of the utmost importance. (1944, 674)

By 1958 the number of American universities and colleges offering Russian had increased by an order of magnitude, but there was still a shortage of teachers and virtually no precollege instruction in Russian.[58]

In the meantime, however, the numbers of specialists on Russian language and culture had grown enough to change attitudes toward translation dramatically. New translations of earlier Soviet works began to appear: Bely's *Petersburg* came out in English in 1959, four decades after its Russian appearance; Fedin's *Cities and Years* (Russian text 1924) appeared in 1962. There was also a renewed interest in Russian classics at this time, perhaps because of increasing numbers of college and university students of Russian, and publishers began to bring out new translations. Most notable among the new popularizers of Russian literature was Magarshack, whose translations, mostly for Penguin Books, became almost as ubiquitous as those of Garnett. Magarshack's approach, which still shows some tendency toward clarification and simplification of style, is more sympathetic than Garnett's to psychological complexities in the various characters. He allows their syntax to

David Magarshack's translations of Russian classics are more attentive to the stylistic idiosyncrasies of the various authors and to the voices within the texts. For example, in the opening chapter of Dostoevsky's *The Idiot* we meet Rogozhin, a distracted young man who employs a coarse colloquial manner. His father has died, still angry at him, while Rogozhin was away and no one had alerted him in time to return home and make amends:

— Рассердился-то он рассердился, да может, и стоило, — отвечал Рогожин, — но меня пуще всего брат доехал. Про матушку нечего сказать, женщина старая, Четьи-Минеи читает, со старухами сидит, и что Сенька-брат порешит, так тому и быть. А он что же мне знать-то в свое время не дал? Понимаем-с! Оно правда, я тогда без памяти был. Тоже, говорят, телеграмма была пущена. Да телеграмма-то к тетке и приди . . . . Только Конев, Василий Васильич, выручил, всё отписал. С покрова парчового на гробе родителя, ночью, брат кисти литые, золотые, обрезал: «Они, дескать, эвона каких денег стоят». Да ведь он за это одно в Сибирь пойти может, если я захочу, потому что оно есть сватотатство.

(Bk. 1, chap. 1; 10)

"Angry he certainly was, and perhaps with reason," answered Rogozhin, "but it was my brother's doing more than anything. My mother I can't blame, she is an old woman, spends her time reading the Lives of the Saints, sitting with old women; and what brother Semyon says is law. And why didn't he let me know in time? I understand it! It's true, I was unconscious at the time. They say a telegram was sent, too, but it was sent to my aunt. . . . Only Vassily Vassilitch Konyov was the saving of me, he wrote me all about it. At night my brother cut off the solid gold tassels from the brocaded pall on my father's coffin. 'Think what a lot of money they are worth,' said he. For that alone he can be sent to Siberia if I like, for it's sacrilege." (Garnett, 9)

"Angry? I should think so; and with good reason!" cried Rogozhin. "But it was that brother of mine who got my goat. Mother's all right. She's an old woman. Reads the lives of the saints, sits with her old women, and what my brother says goes. And why didn't he let me know in good time? Aye, why not, indeed? Mind you, it's quite true I was lying unconscious just then. Besides, he did send a telegram. He did that. But, you see, the telegram arrived at my aunt's. . . . It was Konyov, a friend of mine, who came to my rescue. Sent me a full account of everything, he did. That brother of mine cut off the tassels from my dad's coffin at night; solid gold they was. No use wasting them, he thinks; cost a fortune, they does. Why, damn him, I could send him to Siberia for that, so help me, for it's sacrilege, it is!" (Magarshack, 33)

Garnett's version stays closer to the meaning of the words but strays much farther from their effect. Her Rogozhin speaks in complete, grammatical sentences, with apparently impeccable logic. Magarshack's is more impetuous in his speech, less grammatical—(possibly too much like a London barfly)—and far more believable. Can you imagine a delirious, angry young man quoting his brother this way: "'Think what a lot of money they are worth,' said he"? Lest Garnett's stilted version merely be attributed to archaisms, the reader should compare Whishaw's 1887 rendering of the last sentences:

It's only thanks to Konief that I heard at all; he wrote to me all about it. He says my brother cut off the gold tassels from my father's coffin, at night, "because they're worth a lot of money!" says he. Why, I can get him sent off to Siberia for that alone, if I like; it's sacrilege. (11)

remain confused, breaks up their sentences with exclamations and repetitions, and otherwise avoids smoothing out their language (see example 1.4).

One significant change that appears in Magarshack's translations is a new sensitivity to scholarship about Russian authors. Magarshack himself wrote a number of biographies (of Chekhov, Turgenev, Gogol, Pushkin) and other scholarly works, including ones on Chekhov and Dostoevsky. In this, he stands in stark contrast to Constance Garnett, who wrote only an occasional, very brief introduction to a translation. Although his writings are almost purely biographical, saying little about stylistic questions, they do explain why Magarshack might have been more sensitive to idiosyncracies of different writers' styles. There was also a change in translation criticism in the postwar period, especially after Joseph Stalin's death. This was due to the new, relatively large cadre of specialists who knew both Russian and English and could measure translations against the originals. Whereas Garnett's versions generally appeared unchallenged by critics, now translations were compared (if only to Garnett's) and given more detailed examination. A new self-consciousness arose about the nature of the English-speaking world's exposure to Russian culture. Indeed, of the essays on translation history and on the impact of Russian literature on England and America used in this chapter, many came out in the 1950s and early 1960s.

Not all who tried their hand at translating in this period were as gifted as Magarshack or as accurate as Garnett. The most egregious flaws are found, perhaps, in the works of Andrew MacAndrew, whose versions of *Dead Souls* and other classics have received ample criticism. Proffer (1964), for instance, calls MacAndrew's version of Gogol's "epic poem" incomplete, inaccurate, and dull. MacAndrew's example provides clear testimony to the value of an "old reliable" such as Constance Garnett; one could trust that her work was "conscientious" (this was the adjective most frequently used for her works, apparently to mean "accurate and readable"). Other notable failures in this period were the Max Hayward–Manya Harari *Doctor Zhivago*, of which more later, and the first translation, in 1959, of Andrei Bely's *Petersburg*. As subsequent translators of the same work wrote, "Apart from gross misreadings, it makes numerous cuts, which eliminate, among other things, virtually the entire persona of the narrator, whose presence is essential to any real understanding of what Bely is up to. The translator, John Cournos, deserves our respect as a pioneer, but his work conveys little of the intricacy and subtlety of the original" (Maguire and Malmstad 1978, xi).

As in earlier periods of international tension, the politics of fear and mistrust again colored the selection of works for translation and the quality of the translations. Works from the earlier Soviet period were revived, or brought out for the first time, primarily if they had "informational" value in the fight against communism.[59] New works by unofficial or dissident writers were rushed into print, while others languished. Robert Maguire and John Malmstad explain this phenomenon as follows:

Our far more open societies [in the West] have shown themselves curiously prone to ape the Soviets by allowing political criteria to determine what belongs in the canon of "interesting" Russian literature and what does not. Attention focuses on "acceptable" writers like Leonid Leonov or Valentin Kataev for the picture they supposedly provide of Soviet life, and conversely, on writers who are completely unacceptable, like Solzhenitsyn and the Pasternak of *Doctor Zhivago*, for their exposure of the gross defects in the moral fabric of their country. Those writers of real talent whom the Soviets have simply neglected tend to suffer the same fate here. (1978, x)

Of writers from the early Soviet period, they list Babel and Olesha as examples; one could add most of their talented contemporaries. Writing in 1971, Priscilla Meyer lamented the neglect of writers of the twenties in scholarship, particularly in the realm of style (420).

The bias toward information and away from art in the Khrushchev and Brezhnev years was even more pronounced with regard to contemporary works. Scholarship said little about stylistic matters, much about the sociopolitical implications or complications of various works. In a 1957 discussion of the thaw in Soviet publishing, George Gibian noted the reemergence in print of Anna Akhmatova, Mikhail Zoshchenko, and Boris Pasternak but declared that the appearance of Vladimir Dudintsev's and Daniil Granin's novels critical of social class stratification in the Soviet Union was far more important (18). The informational attitude took its toll on translations; not only were works selected according to political criteria, they were translated so as to highlight content at the expense of style. This was especially true of the few sensational books that promised to be best-sellers, a phenomenon that has never been conducive to thoughtful or careful translating. Foremost among these were Pasternak's *Doctor Zhivago* (1958) and Alexander Solzhenitsyn's *One Day in the Life of Ivan Denisovich* (1962). (Mikhail Bulgakov's *The Master and Margarita* also came out quickly in two English translations after it appeared in Russian in 1967; their relative merits and shortcomings are discussed in detail in Appendix 1.)

Pasternak's novel, published only abroad at that time, was rushed into print. Vladimir Markov faults the translators for replacing Pasternak's vivid language with their "pedestrian" prose: "We cannot blame the translators too much for this pale, monotonous, and timid translation. They probably did not have enough time. Those who read the novel in English have no idea of the rhythmic variety, stylistic virtuosity, and striking beauty of imagery of the original" (1959, 21). Harari responded to attacks on the stylistic shortcomings of the translation as follows: "Max Hayward and I took only about six months to translate the Russian text because we believed that, once the book was outside Russia, the sooner it was published, widely known, and (as we hoped) appreciated as a literary work, the better it would be for Pasternak. . . . As we said in our 'Translators' Note' to the Collins edition, both Max

Hayward and I were deeply conscious of our failure to do justice to [his] style" (1959, 51–52). In other words, the literary qualities of the work had to take a back seat to its political importance. Curiously, despite the universal dissatisfaction with this translation, no other version has yet appeared. In 1978 Munir Sendich put the negative reviews to a test with a close analysis of the translation. He concluded ruefully, "One wonders what kind of impact Pasternak's novel might have had on English readers over the past twenty years had its image not been maimed and defaced in a thousand places" (249).

Solzhenitsyn's prison camp novella has had a different fate. Four separate English translations appeared within a few months of the work's publication in the Soviet Union in 1962. Yet all, to one degree or another, sacrificed the raw camp language, which had been the first thing to shock Russian readers, for something far more ordinary. Lauren G. Leighton calls the style of *One Day* "the first venture towards a determined return to the most basic colloquial Russian as a literary standard" (1978, 119). Yet he finds even the best translations guilty of failing to convey this style and the personalized *skaz* narration underlying it. This quality of Solzhenitsyn's language has also eluded the most recent translator, H. T. Willetts, but he has at least managed to preserve the subjective quality of the narration, much of which takes the prisoner Shukhov's own viewpoint (see example 1.5).

Less sensational works of the Soviet period have received more careful treatment in translation, especially when the translators were prominent specialists on the period or the author. Foremost among them may be Malmstad and Maguire, whose 1978 version of *Petersburg* is both a scholarly and literary delight. There is a fine edition of Babel's short stories, translated by Walter Morison and others, in 1955. And Maria Gordon and Hugh McLean have made valiant efforts to reproduce Mikhail Zoshchenko's impossibly convoluted prose.

Translations of Soviet (that is, nondissident) prose of the 1950s–1970s are relatively few and far between. Despite the heroic efforts of Ardis and other small presses, the market for Soviet writers was simply too small to justify large numbers of translations. A handful of writers made it into English, including Vasily Shukshin, Fyodor Abramov, Valentin Rasputin, Vladimir Tendriakov, Yuri Trifonov, Chingiz Aitmatov, Fazil Iskander, and Andrei Bitov. Of these, only Aitmatov's *The Day Lasts More than a Hundred Years* has stayed in print consistently enough to be used in college courses, which is the main method for promoting such works. As before, criticism has been scant and little attention paid to translations from this period.[60]

The translation of prose of the Brezhnev era appears to have been a labor of love. Most translations are by scholars, who generally receive more credit and professional recognition for critical works than for translating. In recent anthologies, the translators are almost never mentioned, and translators' introductions are extremely rare. In part this is because questions of style have been overshadowed by more superficial political considerations.

According to the preface to Willetts's 1992 translation of *One Day in the Life of Ivan Denisovich*, the main raison d'être of this new translation is the fact that earlier ones were based on an incomplete text, the expurgated version printed in *Novyi mir* in 1962. The preface, by Alexis Klimoff, refrains from criticizing the earlier translations on the basis of style, although plenty of such criticism has appeared in the past. It does offer a description of the stylistic challenges of the work, and says that Mr. Willetts has met them, particularly the challenge of colloquial language that has foiled every other translator. In fact, Solzhenitsyn's slang and camp jargon are only weakly represented in Willetts's version (see chap. 2); it is, rather, in the realm of narrative voice that the new translation represents a vast improvement over its predecessors. Solzhenitsyn's work is a tour de force of narrated monologue and only Willetts is daring enough to capture it:

Испыток не убыток, не попробовать ли в санчасти *косануть*, от работы на денек освободиться? Ну прямо все тело разнимает.

И еще — кто из надзирателей сегодня дежурит?

(*Odin den'*, 10)

(a) Maybe Shukhov would try to get himself on the sick list so he could have a day off. There was no harm in trying. His whole body was one big ache.

Then he wondered—which warder was on duty today? (Hayward and Hingley, 4)

(b) There's never any harm in trying, so why not have a go at the dispensary and get a few days off if you can? After all, he did feel as though every limb was out of joint.

Then Shukhov wondered which of the campguards was on duty that morning. (Parker, 20)

(c) Might as well give it a try—wander over to sick bay and wangle a day off. Every bone in his body was aching.

Ah, but who's warder on duty today? (Willetts, 6)

The first two versions here distance the narration from Shukhov in various ways. They use his name and third-person pronouns for him; they refer to the events in the past tense. The final paragraph, which is simply an unmediated question in Russian, becomes narrated direct speech in (a) and simple indirect speech in (b), thereby destroying the identification between narrator and character (and, perhaps, reader). The change between the 1960s style of translation for this work and the 1990s version is dramatic, and it serves as a fine example of the rise in so-called abusive translation—translation that does not scruple to violate normal English usage to serve stylistic needs.

In part, perhaps, it is because publishers want audiences to think they are getting "the real thing." Then again, it may simply be because there are so many translators, translating short stories or novellas, and very few of them have names that resonate with readers. It is interesting to compare the introductions to the two anthologies of Russian literature from the early 1980s compiled by Carl Proffer and Ellendea Proffer. The first, *Contemporary Russian Prose* (1982), which presents seven works by the most prominent Russian writers (Soviet and émigré) of the 1970s, has a very brief general introduction by both editors, followed by biographical sketches of the authors. It says very little about style or language, except to characterize works as various forms of realism, fantasy, or surrealism (more labels of content than of form), and nothing about the translations or the ten translators.

The second, *The Barsukov Triangle* (1984), representing thirteen writers from the Soviet Union, some less well known, has a much longer introduction by Carl Proffer, discussing particular questions of Soviet publishing politics and literary trends. This is partially by way of justifying of the editors' choice of authors and explaining why their works may not seem particularly innovative. Mr. Proffer writes of formal restrictions imposed by the censors, including the rejection of stream of consciousness and "Proustian detail and self-analysis," the restriction of grotesque and fantastic elements, the need for clear chronology, and the imposition of a standard lexicon:

> Form, language—what does this leave us with? With one area of acceptable innovation. . . . When country prose came in, the pale, polluted bureaucratese, and the hackneyed plain vocabulary of the socialist realist classics were supplanted by something that was at least *realistic*. Indeed, the very fact that it was realistic and from the "folk" (*narod*) made it acceptable in principle. So for the first time in decades, the rich dialects of many areas of the Soviet Union were reflected in literature. (1984, xiv-xvi)

One would expect, then, some discussion of the strategies used for translating this one important formal "innovation" their anthology illustrates, but not a word is said. Once again, the sixteen translators receive credit only in the tiniest print in the table of contents, and otherwise the volume is silent about them and their work. Thus, in the century and a half since the early pirated editions of Gogol, Lermontov, and Turgenev, translation from the Russian seemed to have come full circle: the new efforts were more legitimate, more scholarly, but primarily a means for readers to find out more about Russia rather than a literary force in themselves.

RECENT TRENDS

In the era of glasnost' the vogue for Russian literature shifted once again. Now Soviet writers were at the forefront of the changes in the communist system and became the darlings of the West. Books that had long remained in authors' drawers came out, sensationally, in Russia, but most had long since appeared in English. More recent works began to appear, largely in anthologies of short stories and excerpts. Suddenly it was next to impossible to find a publisher for works by former dissidents (publication of my own recent translation, with Larry P. Joseph, of Abram Tertz's important novella *Little Jinx* was stalled for years, largely for this reason).

The advent of "alternative prose" in Russia appears to have loosened strictures in the United States as well, at least with regard to the nature of acceptable translations. Glasnost' and the demise of Soviet censorship have allowed political readings of literary works to recede into the background, bringing formal and stylistic questions to the fore. At the same time, the idea of "abusive" writing has become more acceptable in both languages, for original works and for translations. The anthology *Glasnost* (1990), edited by Helena Goscilo and Byron Lindsey, presents some good examples of "alternative prose" and its "alternative" treatment in the West. Refreshingly, style and language constitute a large part of the editors' discussion, replacing the content-oriented introductions of earlier anthologies, and the translations reflect this concern. In her introduction, Goscilo describes Liudmila Petrushevskaya's "well-known penchant for chatty first-person narration" (xli), and Goscilo's translation conveys this quality admirably, as in this passage from "Our Crowd":

> At first, then, it was like this: Serge and Marisha, their daughter in the other room, I in my superfluousness, my husband Kolya—Serge's faithful, devoted friend; Andrei-the-Stoolpigeon, first with one wife, Anyuta, then with various other women, then with the constant Nadya; also Zhora, who's half-Jewish on his mother's side, which nobody besides me ever mentioned, as if that were a vice of his: once Marisha, our divinity, decided to praise our plain-looking Zhora and said that Zhora had large eyes—what color were they? Everybody spoke up, some said yellow, others light brown, and I said Jewish, and for some reason everyone got embarrassed and Andrei, my eternal enemy, snorted. (5)

The whole story reads like this—a narrator who can never shut up and leaks out all the important information around the edges of the story.

Goscilo also gives a nuanced description in the introduction of the narration of Victor Erofeyev's "The Parakeet," which she calls an "orgy of rhetorical devices, full of vulgarisms, political slogans and clichés, [and] elevated diction. . . . The rapid swings in tone and the various clashing voices discernible in an externally monological text owe an incalculable debt to Dostoevsky's *Notes from Underground* and Albert Camus's *The Fall*" (xl). The translation, by Leonard J. Stanton, copes well with this challenge, here depicting the end of an inhumanly brutal torture session:

> But we came, via a roundabout way, to the truth, arrived, in the bitter end, at the shared opinion that your boy, Yermolai Spiridonovich, wanted to resurrect the parakeet in order to prove the superiority of the overseas bird over our own sparrows and thereby to diminish our pride, to hold us up to the world in a ridiculous and incorrect light. When Yermolai Spiridonovich and I came to share that common opinion, we embraced in our joy: a job well done, I say, is its own reward, bring us, my stalwarts, wine and viands, and we shall make merry! And my stalwarts bring us white salmon, suckling pigs and lambs, sundry souffles and a wine that has the playful name, Madonna's Milk. We ate and then shot the breeze. . . . (375–76)

In a few sentences we hear the echoes of political clichés ("the superiority of the overseas bird," "a ridiculous and incorrect light"), pompous bombast

Translation Example 1.6: A Change in Translation Style

In part, the increased attention to stylistic devices in translation is a result of their increasing importance in the original works. What Goscilo calls "alternative prose" distinguishes itself largely on the basis of stylistic innovation and rejection of the formal strictures of earlier times, and translators go out of their way to emphasize this fact. The work of the prolific translator Antonina Bouis is a case in point. Her translations of Valentin Rasputin from a decade ago tend to neglect any stylistic nuances of his text, as the next chapter will show, in favor of conveying the plot and normalizing the diction. More recently she has translated Tatyana Tolstaya's stories, where the narration moves in waves through various characters' conscious and unconscious minds, making Rasputin's efforts at quasi-direct narration pale in comparison.

А дядя Паша — муж такой страшной женщины. Дядя Паша — маленький, робкий, затюканный. Он старик: ему пятьдесят лет. Он служит бухгалтером в Ленинграде: встает в пять часов утра и бежит по горам, по долам, чтобы поспеть на паравичок. Семь километров бегом, полтора часа узкоколейкой, десять минут трамваем, потом надеть черные нарукавники и сесть на жесткий желтый стул.

(Tolstaya, "Na zolotom kryl'tse sideli," 42)

Here, Bouis has no hesitation about breaking the rules of English diction:

And Uncle Pasha is the husband of this scary woman. . . . An old man: he's fifty. He works as an accountant in Leningrad; he gets up at five in the morning and runs over hill and dale to make the commuter train. Seven kilometers at a run, ninety minutes on the train, ten minutes on the trolley, then put on black cuff protectors and sit down on a hard yellow chair. ("On the Golden Porch," 43)

Incomplete sentences, shifts of tense, omission of subject—all are hallmarks of Tolstaya's style, and they appear here in spite of English norms. Compare the use of such devices in Rasputin's *Zhivi i pomni* (1978), translated by Bouis as *Live and Remember* (1980). An old man has left his ax in his favorite hiding place:

На другой день хватился — нет топора. Обыскал все — нет, поминай как звали.

(7)

The next day he reached for it—no ax. Searched high and low—gone, nothing but a memory.

Bouis translates this as follows:

The next day he noticed that the ax was gone. He searched everywhere—it was gone, vanished into thin air. (3)

Note how the translator has unified the first sentence grammatically and replaced the old man's voice in *net* 'not there, no' with a more objectively narrated complete sentence, "it was gone." And yet a more literal rendition of the syntax would still have left this passage more stylistically normal than the one from Tolstaya.

("bring us, my stalwarts, wine and viands"), and slang ("shot the breeze").

It is curious that even in this collection, with such lofty stylistic goals set in the introduction and achieved in the translations, the translators themselves receive no attention. Their names appear only at the end of the stories they translated; they are collectively saluted by Lindsey in the editors' preface as "our super colleague-translators" who "deserve the primary credit for the realization of this collective endeavor"—but, it would seem, who receive none of it. It is remarkable that commentators can write in great detail about narrational devices and take for granted that translators have captured them. Paradoxically, as translations bring more obvious innovations into English, translators seem to be becoming more anonymous. The supposedly "invisible" translation strategies of earlier times, that smoothed and packaged the work for general consumption, made celebrities of the translators, while the much more daring translations now appearing are the work of unassuming scholars and writers who are willing to bring language out into the open in all its materiality while themselves "disappearing" behind it. Perhaps one clue to this paradox lies in the changing role of the author, and changing attitudes toward authority, in recent literature. As Goscilo writes,

> Authorial attitudes and allegiances, which are trumpeted forth in both standard Soviet fiction and in the exposé branch of glasnost literature, are challengingly elusive in alternative prose. . . . [The] multiple perspectives, unexpected shifts in tone and lexical levels, startling juxtapositions, and frequent compression of material in alternative fiction tend to dialogize or obscure even tentatively implied values and hierarchies. Whereas monologists wishing to "speak out" conceive of text as soapboxes to be mounted, dialogists strive to distance themselves from their works. (1990, xxxix–xl)

If the authors are stepping back and letting the words speak for themselves, then perhaps it is fitting that the translators do the same, although one could hope that they would receive more credit, not less, for their efforts.

One major factor in the rise of "abusive" translations, in addition to the increasing "abusiveness" of original Russian (and other) literary works and the new cachet of translation studies, is the increasing importance of literary theory and criticism in the production and reception of literary works. Scholarly translators such as Maguire and Malmstad, McLean, Willetts, and Goscilo and her contributors are thoroughly conversant with the critical literature about the works they translate, and it shows in their translations. In particular, Russian literature has been at the forefront of experimentation with narrative voice, a key element in Russian literary theories as well. For a century and a half translations were shaped largely by centripetal forces alien to Russian literature: Victorian prejudices, political stereotypes, ignorance, hostility, or neglect. Now the people shaping translations are increasingly conscious of centrifugal forces at work within the literature—nuances of narrative language, formal technique, inter- and intratextual reference—and the meeting of outer and inner forces is beginning to show in translation.

The most dramatic realization of the new equilibrium between inner and outer forces in translation is seen in the new translations of Dostoevsky's works by Richard Pevear and Larissa Volokhonsky (*The Brothers Karamazov* [example 1.2]; *Crime and Punishment* [see chap. 3 below]) and Jane Kentish (*Notes from Underground* [example 3.9] and "The Gambler"). Consider example 1.7 from *The Brothers Karamazov* (bk. 5, chap. 6), in which Dostoevsky's polyphonic pyrotechnics appear to great advantage. This is the scene in which Smerdyakov accosts Ivan Karamazov and confides in him the outlines of the tragedy to come.

The saturated ambivalence of the original text, captured well by Pevear and Volokhonsky, dissipates in Garnett's translation (which, incidentally, has become so canonical that it serves as the basis for the Norton Critical Edition and even for the translation of Bakhtin's discussion of Dostoevsky's narrative art). Note how much shorter her version is, avoiding as it does numerous qualifications (*finally, somehow, already, as it were*). Apart from the substitution of the euphemism "goodness" for "God," her affinity for a single viewpoint appears in the interjection "—goodness knows why!" By setting it off with dashes and an exclamation point, Garnett marks it clearly as a separate voice interjected into the narrator's exposition, rather than merging the voices as Dostoevsky does. This artificial narrative distance asserts itself again when Garnett refers to the men as "those two." Thus, where one might read other versions, including the Russian original, as expressing Ivan's own confusion as Smerdyakov's moral relativism penetrates his thoughts, this is nearly impossible in reading the Garnett version.[61] By its very elegance, her language *obscures* the obscurity of this encounter (which occurs in a chapter entitled, "For a While a Very Obscure One"). Unintended meanings are beginning, here, to take over Ivan's discourse and thoughts, and later they will burgeon into the Devil that haunts him.

Caryl Emerson points out, in her approving review of the Pevear-Volokhonsky translation, "What Bakhtin valued in Dostoevsky was a special way of using language to release human potential, such that each character could communicate maximally with others and make their voices part of himself" (1991, 312). Garnett's practice, endorsed by Joseph Conrad and other contemporaries, was instead to subsume the voices under her own in the interests of "clarity." The obscurity was thus reanalyzed as *Dostoevsky's* confusion, rather than Ivan's, and the exchange of voices became external to the novel (one between author and translator) rather than internal to it (between Ivan and Smerdyakov). For Pevear, on the other hand, the intertwining voices in *The Brothers Karamazov* are part of the novel's explicit challenge to the reader or translator. As he said in an interview: "Aesthetically, [Dostoevsky] was not understood at the turn of the century. . . . The older translations reflect misunderstandings; the translators would smooth out the writing,

Но главное, что раздражало наконец Ивана Федоровича окончательно и вселило в него такое отвращение, — была какая-то отвратительная и особая фамильярность, которую сильно стал выказывать к нему Смердяков, и чем дальше, тем больше. Не то чтоб он позволял себе быть невежливым, напротив, говорил он всегда чрезвычайно почтительно, но так поставилось, однако ж, дело, что Смердяков видимо стал считать себя бог знает почему в чем-то наконец с Иваном Федоровичем как бы солидарным, говорил всегда в таком тоне, будто между ними вдвоем было уже что-то условленное и как бы секретное, что-то когда-то произнесенное с обеих сторон, лишь им обоим только известное, а другим около них копошившимся смертным так даже и непонятное.

(Bk. 5, chap. 6; 243)

But in the end the thing that finally most irritated Ivan Fyodorovich and filled him with such loathing was a sort of loathsome and peculiar familiarity, which Smerdyakov began displaying towards him more and more markedly. Not that he allowed himself any impoliteness; on the contrary, he always spoke with the greatest respect; but nonetheless things worked out in such a way that Smerdyakov apparently, God knows why, finally came to consider himself somehow in league, as it were, with Ivan Fyodorovich, always spoke in such tones as to suggest that there was already something agreed to and kept secret, as it were, between the two of them. . . . (Pevear and Volokhonsky, 267)

But what finally irritated Ivan Fyodorovich most and confirmed his dislike for him was the peculiar revolting familiarity which Smerdyakov began to show more and more markedly. Not that he forgot himself and was rude; on the contrary, he always spoke very respectfully, yet he had obviously begun to consider—goodness knows why!—that there was some sort of understanding between him and Ivan Fyodorovitch. He always spoke in a tone that suggested that those two had some kind of compact, some secret between them. . . . (Garnett, 247)

---

thinking, 'Oh, he means this . . . He's just being careless.' [But] he really was extremely careful. . . . [There] are 20,000 ways to say anything, but the author wrote it only one way" (Emerson 1991, 316).

The new attention to nuance is laudable, but there is one further step to take in conceptualizing the translation of polyphony. Pevear's inclination, like that of nearly all translators, is to view each word as Dostoevsky's careful choice, while for Bakhtin, the words also come from the characters. The Pevear and Volokhonsky translations, as Richard Lourie has pointed out,[62] suffer from a mannered, even stilted quality of language that may be the result of excessive attention to the author's words, and too little to the characters' voices. For Lourie the goal is language that sounds "natural" (and he favors Garnett's versions on this score). In the guise of acknowledging the characters' voices, Lourie actually circles back to the traditional reliance upon a broader cultural voice, to what "sounds right" under rather rigid assumptions about language propriety. But a translator who attaches validity to Bakhtin's ideas would need to filter out static from abstractions about both the author's voice and the social voice, and listen to the characters themselves.

This prescription smacks of a mystical notion of the author as medium rather than creator, but it acknowledges an aspect of Dostoevsky's works that is gaining currency. Dale Peterson compares Dostoevsky and other literary exponents of the Russian "soul" to African-American literary "soul talk," claiming for both an inevitable, even uncontrollable diglossia, a "counter-language" that is "necessarily reactive to the pressure of an imposed cultural norm" (1992, 751). This norm, for Russian writers, is imposed less by the powers that be in Russia than by "modern Europe's philosophy of history," or "the standard literate discourse of European humanism" (752). It is, therefore, the close relative of the translation norm that flourished earlier in this century. Literature of the "soul" includes a dichotomy between oral and literate culture and an exaltation of the most devalued features of the vernacular language. Peterson writes, "In more than one sense, the literature of the 'soul' justifies the margin, constructing an unsuspected richness of meaning in spaces that were taken to be blank and without significance" (751). Bakhtin, for one, recognized the energy fields present on the margins and in the "blank" spaces of Dostoevsky's prose. Given Peterson's argument, one might claim that these fields intensify with translation, since the clash with European culture (Peterson's "powerful master narrative of cultural evolution") becomes more internal to the translated work, a centrifugal as well as centripetal force. The next chapters turn to some of the supposedly "blank" spaces in literary works, the boundary lines between oral-type language and literary language, between narrator and character, between a period mark and the next sentence, to observe more closely the role inner and outer forces play in Russian-English translation.

Chapter Two

Narrator and Translator

> You must know that for the most part Akaky Akakievich
> expresses himself in prepositions, adverbs, and, finally, the
> kinds of particles of speech that have positively no meaning
> whatsoever.
>
> —Nikolai Gogol, "The Overcoat"

THE PERSONAL NARRATOR

Little words that have "positively no meaning whatsoever" abound in human speech and, often, in literary narration. These are the fillers and signals of register; terms of endearment, respect, condescension, or disrespect; markers of phatic and conative functions; or simple idiosyncracies that distinguish living speech from expository prose. Generally defined as lacking semantic content but fulfilling some communicative function, these elements of language rarely advance a plot but immeasurably increase the richness of the telling. Unlike the pristine diction of expository prose, prose with an abundance of "meaningless" sounds and phrases suggests palpable human voices and allows them to interact and interpenetrate one another's spheres. As a literary device, they have had great proponents in many languages (William Faulkner, Laurence Sterne, Mark Twain, to name some anglophone examples). But nowhere have they had so rich a flowering as in Russian literature, where they are used to set up layer upon layer of meaning within the narration and between narrator, character, and reader. Why "must we know" that Akaky Akakievich used meaningless particles in his speech? First, because they establish the insecurity and insignificance of his character, but also because they identify the narrator with this pathetic creature. After all, the narrator, too, uses an abundance of fillers (*you must know; for the most part; and, finally; positively; whatsoever*). Thus Akaky Akakievich becomes Everyman, his voice merely a somewhat less articulate echo of the generalized voice that tells of his miserable condition.

Unfortunately, translators tend to consider semantics first, and

(a) Akaky's speech:

Нужно знать, что Акакий Акакиевич изъясняется большею частью предлогами, наречиями и, наконец, такими частицами, которые решительно не имеют никакого значения.

("Shinel'," 149)

The reader should know that Akaky Akakievich spoke mainly in prepositions, adverbs, and resorted to parts of speech which had no meaning whatsoever. (Wilks, 80)

It might be as well to explain at once that Akaky mostly talked in prepositions, adverbs, and, lastly, such parts of speech as have no meaning whatsoever. (Magarshack, 243)

(b) Gogol describes Akaky Akakievich as a

... чиновник ... низенького роста, несколько рябоват, несколько рыжеват, несколько даже на вид подслеповат ...

(141)

... a bureaucrat ... of shortish height, somewhat pock-markedish, somewhat reddish-haired, somewhat even to the naked eye nearish-sighted ...

... he was short, somewhat pockmarked, with rather reddish hair and rather dim, bleary eyes ... (Garnett, 3)

... he was shortish, rather pock-marked, with reddish hair, and also had weak eyesight, or so it seemed. (Wilks, 71)

He was in fact a somewhat short, somewhat pockmarked, somewhat red-haired man, who looked rather short-sighted ... (Magarshack, 233)

"meaningless" phrases suffer as a result. Of all Gogol's translators, David Magarshack seems to have been most attentive to the qualities linking his narrators to his characters. Compare Magarshack's version of the description of Akaky's speech style to that of Ronald Wilks (example 2.1a). Both translations are less saturated with superfluous language than the original, but Magarshack calls attention to the narrator in his opening phrase ("It might be as well to explain"), while Wilks seems to shun such attention. The distinction between the various translations is more stark in another descriptive passage from "The Overcoat" (example 2.1b).

Here, the translators' temptation to remove redundancies and repetitions leads to an almost complete leveling of narrative style. The Russian repetitions of *neskol'ko* 'somewhat' and *-ovat* '-ish' create a pounding cadence of mediocrity that is important to the characterization. Magarshack is the only one who keeps the monotonous hammering of "somewhat," but he then eliminates the patently redundant (and therefore stylistically significant) "-ish" morphemes. Garnett allows one redundancy ("rather reddish") but eliminates the rest. Otherwise the translations clearly emphasize the meaning of the passage at the expense of the more significant manner of speaking. It seems that for translators, too, the adverbs and particles that distinguish the narrator's speech "have positively no meaning whatsoever."

When translators' prefaces or critical reviews discuss Russian style, they usually confine themselves to matters of dialect and register, or to peculiarities of certain characters' speech. These matters appear to fit into the perceived "content" of prose fiction: they contribute to our understanding of character or setting. And translators sometimes work to reflect such particularities in their English prose. But when the individualities of speech do not belong to a character, when they are offering a generalized sense of the narrating voice, then they most often disappear altogether in translation.

Lawrence Venuti (1992, 4), among others, argues that it is a given of translation that it will shift attention away from the "materiality of language," which may account for some of the loss of narrative intrusions. But what about those frequent cases in which translators neglect the simplest, most literal solutions, substituting a more expository style for subjective narration at every turn? All too predictably in translation, colloquial language becomes more standard, interjections and other interferences disappear, and interior monologue loses its immediacy. This occurs, as this chapter will show, in translations by many different translators, of books by many different authors. I believe that it points to a deeper cause than the passive trends already noted, that it is evidence of two forces, one outer and one inner, acting upon translation itself. The first is a result of clashing cultural attitudes toward narrative style in the original and target languages. The second is an internal struggle between translator and narrator for control of the text's language.

OUTER FORCES: THE POLITICS OF STYLE

It is hard for someone raised in a Western democracy to conceive of a political battle over literary devices. Censorship is not unknown in America, but it is based upon content rather than style. Social critics may have squirmed over Holden Caulfield's subjective bitterness, but they could not make a federal case of it, so to speak, and the U.S. Congressional Record is unlikely to contain a word on such a topic. In Russia, on the other hand, literary style has long been considered a matter of national significance, debated at high levels as a political question. Nearly every Russian leader since Peter the Great has had something to say about literature: what form it should take, what issues it should address, what should and should not be published. For centuries Russian writers had censors looking over their shoulders, and the censors, in turn, gave readers cause to scrutinize works closely for what might have been left unsaid. For translators, this disparity between the two cultures presents a problem at least as difficult as any grammatical or lexical discontinuities. The debate on multiculturalism in America is bringing out the notion that every literary choice has political undertones, but traditionally readers of mainstream literature in English have not considered stylistic or lexical concerns to have political significance. As a result, translators cannot easily convey in English the emotional and social force that certain literary devices possess in Russian. The prevalent solution to this dilemma (it may be a glorification to refer to this essentially tacit or even unconscious process as a "solution") has been to ignore narrative devices altogether in translation, replacing them with a more neutral form of standard literary English. In keeping with our traditional political values regarding literature, we give primacy to "factual" content and explicit commentary in translating and promoting Russian literature in English.

On the whole, Russian literary scholars study the *language* of literature more closely than do their counterparts in any other country. The English term *philologist*, which once denoted a "lover of language and literature," now refers primarily to classical scholars interested in textology.[1] Otherwise it has become virtually pejorative, signifying those who get bogged down in studying (or, worse, counting) words instead of appreciating literature. In Russia, *filolog* has been the term of choice for literary scholars, whose contributions to our understanding of the relationship between form and content in literature are immeasurable. This greater emphasis on formal matters, especially on stylistics, helps to explain the strong political taboos associated with formal innovation in the Soviet period. It also offers some reasons for the existence of a highly developed, serious, and organized school of literary translation in Russia, because translation depends on analysis and recognition of the thematic role of formal elements in literature.[2]

Written Russian has always been part of a system of di- or heteroglossia. The earliest writers used Old Church Slavic for some genres, vernacular Russian for others. Over the centuries borrowings—whether of Greek stylistic flourishes or of German or French lexical or syntactic turns of phrase— carried particular social, cultural, and even political meaning. In the mid-eighteenth century Mikhail Lomonosov codified the various registers of the written language, based upon their relations to vernacular Russian and Church Slavic. He saw the literary language not only as the basis for literature but as "the thread connecting old and new, Ancient Rus' and post-Petrine Europeanized Russia" (Sakharov 1987, 282). By the end of that century, Europeanization was so rampant that a reactionary movement developed, led by Admiral Shishkov, to purify the Russian lexicon and grammar and restore increasingly archaic (or even previously nonexistent) Church Slavicisms to active use. It was Aleksandr Pushkin's triumph to incorporate what had formerly been considered separate *languages* as stylistic strata within one literary universe, using archaisms, neologisms, colloqui-

alisms, and borrowings to create contrasts of mood or character, to humorous or tragic effect. The novelists who followed him further exploited the
nuances of Russian stylistic stratification.

In the twentieth century, there was a return to diglossia in the literary
language. Symbolist poets asserted a division in the language, some reviving
archaisms, others explicitly delineating the poetic from the mundane. The
Bolshevik reaction to "formalism" eventually inverted the hierarchy, declaring florid or mystical language off-limits for true writers. Far from rejecting
the formalist claim that literary devices were the repositories of textual
meaning, Soviet ideologues insisted on controlling and manipulating these
devices, deciding which were compatible with the new dogma of socialist
realism and which were not. Even colloquial language came to be considered
unworthy of the great Soviet people. Vladimir Lenin complained in *Pravda*
(3 December 1924) that foreign words were "perverting" the Russian language, and Lev Trotsky declared in *Problems of Life* that "the fight against
bad language is also part of the struggle for the purity, clearness, and beauty
of Russian speech."[3] (Advocates of a standard literary language were not
unknown in the English-speaking world, but they tended to be deeply conservative, if not reactionary, critics who argued on purely aesthetic rather
than political grounds.)[4] Maxim Gorky wrote in 1933, "We should demand
from each word maximum effectiveness, maximum inspirational power. We
will achieve that only when we develop respect for language as our material,
when we learn to shuck off its empty hull, when we cease to distort words
and make them incomprehensible and deformed. The simpler, the more
accurate, the more correctly situated a word is, the more power and conviction it imparts to a phrase" (1953, 403). Gorky's "respect for language as our
material" is the opposite of Venuti's "respect for the materiality of language":
for Gorky, language is the invisible building block of literature; for Venuti,
the blocks are necessarily visible, the stuff of art.[5]

Galina Belaia describes a movement in the 1930s and 1940s toward
euphemism and away from popular (*prostonarodnyi*) or folk (*narodnyi*) language, with a concomitant "narrowing of the concept of 'literariness' to mean
'neutrality'" (1983, 65). Even dialogue in fiction adopted this "neutral" style,
which, in turn, reinforced the idea that folk elements were unacceptable. By
the postwar period this straightjacket was so tight that critics vied to find
unacceptable examples of colloquial speech in literature. Efim Dorosh wrote
a review of G. Medynskii's story "Mar'ia" in which he upbraided the author
for allowing the chairwoman of a collective farm to go by the peasant nick-
name of the title, instead of her formal name, Mariia Karpovna.[6] As Fyodor
Abramov later wrote in his scathing critique of postwar literary distortions of
peasant reality, "Mar'ia and Semyon speak in the novel in simple, vernacular
Russian, sometimes even using local expressions. And once again the critic is
indignant. How can this be! That remarkable supervisor of kolkhoz production, Mariia Karpovna, and 'a former brigade leader, until recently a warrior

in the victorious, eminently cultured Soviet Army'—and suddenly they are allowing themselves to sin against the literary language!" (1954, 228). Ironically, the original works upon which the doctrine of socialist realism was based, such classics as *Cement* and *The Quiet Don*, masterfully mixed "literary" and vernacular language, whereas the later, "high" socialist realist works fell almost completely out of touch with the way people talked or lived.

In addition to deviations from the lexical norm, other literary devices came under official scrutiny. Idiosyncracies of narrative voice were high on the list of undesirable literary devices in the Stalin era. In a lecture in the early 1920s Evgenii Zamiatin had commented approvingly on the trend toward narrative intrusions in Russian literature. He compared it to English literature of the time, in which "you now find interjections from the author, scenes and descriptions of characters in colloquial rather than 'typical' narrative language [*tipichno-povestvovatel'nyi iazyk*], and addressed directly and personally to the reader."[7] But a decade later there were strong attacks on skaz and interior monologue for their excessive "subjectivity." In 1933 Gorky reviewed Fyodor Panferov's important socialist realist work about the peasantry, saying: "The first pages of his *Bruski* are written in a pure language, realistically descriptive, precise, and firm. But after that he leaps into the insipid, verbose, and viscous 'skaz' tone, which, unfortunately, many writers have adopted" (1953, 403). As examples Gorky lists a number of cases of alliteration, calling them unnecessary and inharmonious, and criticizes the author for verbosity.

Interior monologue was similarly discouraged by Soviet ideologues. G. Schaarschmidt (1966) maintains that this device violated the hard-line Marxist demand for a dualism of content and form. The novels of James Joyce and Faulkner were held up as examples of excessive subjectivity, unsatisfactory as to both content and form, as Karl Radek's speech to the first Congress of Soviet Writers in 1934 makes clear: "But even if one could grant for a moment that the Joycean method is useful for depicting small, insignificant, pointless people, their doings, thoughts, and feelings,—though tomorrow these people might take part in great things,—still it is patently obvious that this method would become bankrupt at the moment when the author turned his movie camera on the great events of the class struggle, on the gigantic clashes of the modern world."[8] After this, Soviet writers shunned the works of their Western counterparts and interior monologue was officially banned. Sholokhov and Konstantin Fedin, who had used it frequently in their early works, retreated from it after the mid-thirties. Schaarschmidt (1966, 146–48) indicates that the device did not disappear from Soviet literature, but it became incidental rather than central to a writer's style.

Around the time of Stalin's death in 1953 the strictures on writers began to loosen. The first critical portrayals of rural life and collective farm administration appeared in 1952.[9] By 1954 there was full-fledged revolt against the standards to which Soviet prose had been kept, particularly the

Régine Robin writes that "the prose of the 1920's in its entirety was obsessed with . . . stylistic orna-mentations. Gladkov's *Cement* relies on them, and the first volumes of *The Quiet Don* constitute an epic written in ornamental prose" (1992, 179). The earliest volume of Sholokhov's eight-part epic is full of colloquialisms, telegraphic descriptions, and parataxis:

Аксинью выдали за Степана семнадцати лет. Взяли ее с хутора Дубровки, с левой стороны Дона, с песков.

За год до выдачи осенью пахала она в степи, верст за восемь от хутора. Ночью отец ее, пятидесятилетний старик, связал ей треногой руки и изнасиловал.

— Убью, ежели пикнешь слово, а будешь помалкивать — справлю плюшевую кофту и гетры с калошами. Так и помни: убью, ежели что... — пообещал он ей.

(Bk. 1, pt. 1, chap. 7; 2,38–39)

They married Aksinia off to Stepan at seventeen. Found her in Dubrovka village, on the left side of the Don, in the sands.
A year before they gave her away she had been ploughing in the steppe, eight miles or so from the village. In the night her father, an old man of fifty, tied up her arms and raped her.
"Squeal about this and I'll kill you, keep your mouth shut and I'll get you a velvet jacket and gaiters with boots. Don't forget, keep quiet or else..." he promised her.

Pronouns are used only when absolutely necessary, and rough, terse dialogue takes the place of description at the most dramatic moments in the story. In contrast, the last book (bk. 4, pt. 8) uses col-loquialisms sparingly, as if merely to add color, and the characters speak in full sentences, when they speak at all:

Каждый день, стряпая, она готовила что-нибудь лишнее и после обеда ставила чугун со щами в печь. На вопрос Дуняшки — зачем она это делает, Ильинишна удивленно ответила: «А как же иначе? Может, служивенький наш нынче прийдет, вот он сразу и поест горяченького, а то пока разогреешь, того да сего, а он голодный, небось...»

(Bk. 4, pt. 8; 5:310)

Every day, over her cooking, she prepared something extra and put a pot of cabbage soup in the oven after dinner. To Duniasha's question, why she was doing that, she answered in amazement, "And what else should I do? What if our soldier boy comes back today, this way he'll get something hot to eat right away, otherwise while you're heating it up, what with this and that, he's there hungry, maybe . . . "

Apart from the ludicrous content, given the rural starvation of wartime, and the contrast between the brutality of the earlier story and the sentimentality here, the language has become flat and unconvinc-ing. In the first volume, Duniasha's question would have interrupted the narrative, and in more collo-quial terms (*chego ty*). Very rarely did the earlier narrator paraphrase characters' speech. And that nar-rator had no need for precious phrases (*sluzhiven'kii nash* 'our soldier boy'; *togo da sego* 'with one thing and another') to inject local color into the story. Socialist realism, it seems, went directly from idolizing its own precursors to producing its own epigones, with scarcely any stylistic contribution of its own in between.

"rose-tinting" of reality and other restrictions on content. While these arguments, for the most part, simply revised the emphasis of socialist realism away from didactic visions of socialist ideals and toward a more realistic view of Soviet life, articles such as Abramov's indicated resistance to stylistic dogma as well. Abramov, who was a specialist on Sholokhov and admired his portrayals of life from the peasant point of view, criticized the inaccurate picture of peasant life writers had presented and assailed critics such as Dorosh for their excessive attachment to standard Russian. His own language, however, demonstrates a lingering insecurity about anything that might undermine the purity of Russian: "We should note that linguistic purity and correctness are dear to us as well. And we believe that our literary language is sufficiently rich to provide all necessary expressive means. But does that really imply that in characters' dialogue (and sometimes even in authorial speech) we cannot use everyday, even dialectal words and phrases to artistic benefit?" (Abramov 1954, 228). Thus peasants in literature of the fifties became free to reassume their popular names and colloquial speech, but their narrators could not stray far from literary standards.

Abramov's anger at the "whitewashing" of rural life was symptomatic of an important shift in the emphasis of literature in the post-Stalin era. The underlying goal of socialist realist restrictions on language variation and style had been to eliminate a sense of class differences in literature. This had underlain Gorky's lament about skaz narration in the 1930s as well as Dorosh's argument against giving peasant women peasant names. But not only had class differences not been wiped out by Soviet rule, they had been exacerbated by repressive policies toward the peasantry, by the deep sense of shared hardship within particular social strata, and by the nomenklatura system in the cities. Thus George Gibian, reviewing Soviet literature in 1956, hailed the appearance of Dudintsev's *Not by Bread Alone* and Granin's *Personal Convictions*, which lashed out at "an entire Soviet social class, a social attitude, a system and an ideology" (18). The use of an unseen but personal narrator, as well as of colloquial language for narration, was one of the subtlest and most interesting expressions of this reemergent class-consciousness among Soviet writers. These devices, after all, use oral-type language cues (and therefore markers of class) to differentiate the narrator from some objective, omniscient voice, to show allegiances, and to suggest either identification with or condescension toward the social group being portrayed.

Among the writers who pioneered the use of colloquial language and oral-type syntax in post-Stalin literature was a group that came to be known as the *derevenshchiki*, or village prose writers, as well as some who were known, for contrast, as "urban" or "youth" writers. Abramov himself was a leading *derevenshchik*, who set about "correcting" the picture of peasant life seen in postwar fiction. His tetralogy, *The Priaslin Family* (1958–78), depicted the events of the war, postwar reconstruction, and the dissolution of village life in the 1960s and 1970s through the eyes of one family. Self-consciously styling himself after the early Sholokhov, he used extensive narrated monologue, peasant dialect, and a narrating voice very close to the villagers themselves. (The second book of the tetralogy, *Two Winters and Three Summers*, has two English translations; the rest has yet to be translated.) The most vivid example of colloquial narration in prose of the post-Stalin decade was Aleksandr Solzhenitsyn's *One Day in the Life of Ivan Denisovich* (1962), which brought prison camp jargon and rural dialectalisms together in raw narrated monologue. While not strictly a *derevenshchik*, Solzhenitsyn shared their goals for the revitalization of the living language.[10] By the late 1960s village prose was evoking, according to Belaia, "the coloring of folk-colloquial language . . . not by the use of a specially chosen lexicon but with the entire structure of their texts, imitating the traditional style of epic narration, with its details from daily life and unhurried meditation [on events]" (1983, 72). The most accomplished of its proponents was Valentin Rasputin, author of several deeply psychological explorations of peasant women's lives. To convey their profound connection to their villages and their families, as well as their complete alienation from bureaucracy and technological development, Rasputin also relied heavily on narrated monologue and colloquial narration. Other authors who took a psychologically intimate approach to class conflicts were Vladimir Tendriakov and Yurii Trifonov, the former depicting working people in many different settings, the latter concentrating on the urban intelligentsia and the moral compromises it was forced to make. All these writers exploit the same narrative devices to express the social rifts at the core of their stories; for this reason, and because their works have been translated by many different translators, we can use them to make general observations about what happens to narrative voice on its journey from Russian into English.

INNER FORCES: TOWARD A GRAMMAR OF TRANSLATION

In a literary work written in the third person, narrative voice may range from the supposedly neutral, nonevaluative, omniscient narrator in two directions: toward a much more personal, intrusive quality, or toward a more elusive identification with characters within the story. The two poles are not very distant from each other, and they may even be indistinguishable in those cases, as with some village prose, when the entire milieu seems personified and a generalized voice speaks both through the characters and through the narrator. Nevertheless, they are worth observing separately in the translation context, since they make use of different linguistic strategies that pose distinct problems for the translator. The intrusive narrator uses deictic expressions ("here" and "now"), evaluative terms, and interjections to define his or her worldview. These devices are generally as available in English as in Russian. The elusive narrator primarily uses interior or narrated monologue, which is similar to indirect speech but without the *verbum dicendi*. As the next chapter will demonstrate, the normal formation of narrated monologue in Russian differs from that in English and creates a particular problem for the translator. Narrative intrusions, on the other hand, are generally explicit and readily translatable. The fact that English translators routinely neglect them, therefore, raises questions about the very nature of translation as a communicative act.

Deixis

The most obvious sign of a narrator's worldview is the use of deixis, which orients the speaker in space *and* time with respect to the action and the audience, thereby highlighting the addresser-addressee relationship.[11] When used in third-person narration, such expressions as "now," "here," "many years ago" pinpoint the narrator as present at the scene. They also suggest that the audience is physically accessible to the narrator and that it has a definite viewpoint. The effect is to imitate the oral speech situation, in which a gesture is enough to establish a place and time. Although English has most of the same deictics as Russian, this is a feature of narrative language that is often omitted or changed in translation.

All of the examples in 2.3 have a third-person narrator who seems to be present on the scene. The first three are descriptions of remote towns and villages, and the narrator seems to be among their long-suffering inhabitants. In (*a*) and (*b*) the translations eliminate this sense, removing the word "here" and replacing ambiguous phrasings with more specifically objective ones. (For example, the verb *uznali* 'learned [pl.]' could mean either "they learned" or "we learned," in this context.) In (*c*) and (*d*) the English versions preserve some sense of narrative presence, but the Russian originals have much stronger voices. In (*c*) Jacqueline Edwards and Mitchell Schneider have "for years now"; D. B. Powers and Doris C. Powers have a dash and a colloquial phrase that suggests subjectivity ("—and for a number of years"), but neither is as strong as the desperate interjection "oh, how many years now." The narrator in (*d*) is even more expressive, using deictics ("look how soft"; "there, up above") and colloquial emphatics ("look how soft"; "who wants to go inside?"), as well as the syntax of one who is carried away with the description.

The last three examples in 2.3 have in common one Russian deictic term that does not have an English equivalent. The Russian word *vot* is defined as indicating proximity or immediacy or adding expressiveness to a phrase. It can mean "right here," or "there," or even "look" or "see," or it can simply be emphatic. Twice I have used "now" in its place, to reflect the sense of immediacy *vot* imparts. This term is so common in Russian and so difficult to approximate in English that translators tend to ignore it. The evidence seems to show, however, that along with it they discard other deictic expressions and the entire sense of a narrator's presence. In isolated instances translators are probably right to omit it, because the English alternatives

Translation Example 2.3: Deictics

(a) Даже о войне здесь узнали только на другой день.

(Rasputin, *Zhivi i pomni*, 11)

[They/we] even found out about the war only on the next day.

They even heard about the war a day late. (Bouis, 8)

(b) Но вот уходят они из города, исчезают так же внезапно, как и появились, и уже никогда не увидеть их здесь.

(Kazakov, "Arktur—gonchii pes," 117)

But now they're leaving town, disappearing just as suddenly as they came, and they'll never be seen around here anymore.

—then, just as suddenly as they came, they vanish, never to be seen again. (Harari and Thomson tr., 270)

(c) ...пинежские подзолы да супеси вот уже который год подкармливают отощавший город.

(Abramov, *Dve zimy i tri leta*, 280)

How many years already have the sterile soil and sands of the Pinega been feeding the withered city.

. . . for years now it had been the sandy, barren soils of the Pinega that had been feeding that withered city. (Edwards and Schneider, 4)

The sandy Pinyega loam had in fact been feeding the emaciated city—and for a number of years. (Powers and Powers, 3)

(d) Когда идет снег — вот такой мягкий, пушистый, словно где-то там, наверху, теребят диковинных снежных птиц, — не очень-то хочется идти домой.

(Rasputin, "Rudol'fio," 318)

Lit.: *When it is snowing—look what soft, fluffy snow, as if somewhere, up there, they were plucking fantastic snowbirds—[one] doesn't much want to go home.*

When the snow is like this—soft and fluffy, as if somewhere above fantastic snowbirds were being plucked—it's hard to go inside. (Heinemeier and Valova, 113)

---

often sound stilted. But when *vot* is used as part of a larger tendency to personalize the narrative voice, translators need to plumb the expressive resources of English.

Possible alternative translations to the four examples, which would preserve the narrator's identification with the scene, would be:

(*a*) Even news of the war didn't get here until the next day.

(*b*) But now they leave town just as suddenly as they came, never to be seen around here any more.

(*c*) It's been how many years already that the sterile soil and sands of the Pinega have had to feed the withered city.

(*d*) When the snow is like this—so soft and fluffy, as if somewhere up there fantastic snowbirds were being plucked—who wants to go inside?

These all strive for some ambiguity as to who is talking, including the elimination of third-person references to the villagers. They also attempt to include all deictics from the Russian or replace them with colloquial interjections or emphatic stress if necessary (*vot* leads to "It's been how many years" and "*so* soft").

Deictics may be used for a different type of personalized narration. In the 1960s and 1970s Yurii Trifonov wrote novels about social climbers in Moscow. Some criticized the author at the time for being "too objective, too alienated from the characters, [and] showing only the ugly side of contemporary life" (Proffer and Proffer 1982, xiii). Yet the narration uses deictics that suggest, at least, that the narrator has been an eyewitness to the events. The overall effect is not one of identification with the protagonists so much as deep sympathy for their plight.

The House on the Embankment (*Dom na naberezhnoi,* 1976), Trifonov's important work about growing up in a corrupt system, opens with a lament that none of the protagonists is still alive (Example 2.4*a*). This beginning is striking for its casual, personal tone, as if the reader were sitting with the narrator and looking at an old school photograph. The English translation neutralizes this personal effect by calling the protagonists "those boys" instead of "these boys," and changing the colorful phrase "[they] are nowhere in the wide world" to "not one . . . is alive."

The same interested narrator appears at the beginning of another Trifonov novella, *The Long Goodbye* (*Dolgoe proshchanie,* 1971; example 2.4*b*). Here, the translator has done a better job of capturing the personal tone, except that she has replaced the deictic "this spot" with the more objective "the spot where the butcher shop now stands." The following alternative solutions lend a more colloquial tone to the opening lines:

Not a one of these boys is still among the living. If it wasn't the war, it was illness that took them, except those that just vanished into thin air.
Back then, eighteen years ago or so, this spot was covered with lilacs. . . . But all that, of course, was long ago.

Interjections and Parentheticals
Trifonov's narrator's use of *vprochem* ("however" or, here, "of course") is an example of another set of intrusive elements available to authors wishing to

(a) Никого из этих мальчиков нет теперь на белом свете. Кто погиб на войне, кто умер от болезни, иные пропали безвестно.

(*Dom na naberezhnoi*, 363)

Not one of those boys is alive today. Some were killed in the war, some died from sickness, some disappeared without a trace . . . (Glenny, 189)

(b) В те времена, лет восемнадцать назад, на этом месте было очень много сирени. . . . Но, впрочем, все это было давно.

(*Dolgoe proshchanie*, 131)

In those days, about eighteen years ago, the spot where the butcher shop now stands was covered with lilac bushes. . . . But of course this was all a long time ago. (Burlingame, 203)

---

personalize narrative voice. These include such signals of subjectivity as modal particles, parentheticals, interjections, and some qualifiers (the last three are known, collectively, in Russian as *vvodnye slova*, or "parenthetic words"). Usual definitions of this category stipulate that they modify whole utterances, as opposed to single words or phrases, and that they can be omitted without surface semantic loss. In the case of the unseen personal narrator, however, such terms do not just modify utterances but constitute an entire perspective, and the meaning of the work loses greatly by their omission. Walter Arndt describes the role of modal particles as expressing "the objective relationship or subjective attitude of the speaker to the actuality of the phenomena and relationships in nature and society with regard to their likelihood, possibility, inevitability, etc." (1960, 325). V. V. Vinogradov (1986, 605–6) stresses the role of *vvodnye slova* in presenting subjective thought processes as opposed to logical sequences of ideas. As Uwe Hinrichs notes, "By maintaining/restricting the social/individual identity, *vvodnye slova* can contribute to the regulation of interactional nearness and distance, but they also affect the definition of communicative relationships" (1983, 202). Thus, they are all essential to narrative voice. However, because many of the modal particles appear frequently in prose without any apparent semantic content, it is common practice in translation simply to omit them. In isolated instances their omission makes little difference, but if they disappear throughout a text this can have profound effects on "the definition of communicative relationships."

We have already seen how Gogol's style loses in translation when these elements are neglected (example 2.1). Often they are a primary source of humor in his works, as in those of Fyodor Dostoevsky, and their loss is one reason why English-speaking readers tend to think of Russian literature as essentially humorless. The fact that Russians use modal particles (such as *ved', uzh, zhe, -to, a, i*) and parentheticals (*mozhet byt'* 'maybe,' *znachit* 'that is' or 'I mean,' *kstati* 'by the way,' *odnim slovom* 'in a word,' etc.) in speech

Но все-таки огромное большинство держало *несомненно* сторону старца Зосимы, а из них очень многие *даже* любили его всем сердцем, горячо и искренно; некоторые *же* были привязаны к нему почти фанатически. Такие прямо говорили, не совсем, *впрочем,* вслух, что он святой, что в этом нет *уже и* сомнения, и, предвидя близкую кончину его, ожидали немедленных *даже* чудес и великой славы в самом ближайшем будущем от почившего монастырю.

(Bk. 1, chap. 5; 14:28; emphasis added).

But all the same *the vast majority* undoubtedly *took Elder Zosima's side, and very many of them* even *loved him with all their hearts, ardently and sincerely; some,* though, *were almost fanatically devoted to him. These said directly—not entirely,* however, *aloud—that he was a saint, that there was not* even *the slightest doubt of that, and, seeing that his end was near, anticipated prompt miracles,* even, *and great glory to the monastery in the very near future from the departed.*

But the majority were on Father Zosima's side and very many of them loved him with all their hearts, warmly and sincerely. Some were almost fanatically devoted to him, and declared, though not quite aloud, that he was a saint, that there could be no doubt of it, and, seeing that his end was near, they anticipated miracles and great glory to the monastery in the immediate future from his relics. (Garnett, 23)

The attitude of sarcastic condescension comes out most clearly in the almost paradoxical phrase, "These said directly—not entirely, however, aloud—that he was a saint." All translators replace *vprochem* in this phrase with a simple connector ("though," "if," "although") which diminishes the narrator's role in the telling. Several published translations also work to smooth over the contradiction between saying *outright* but not *aloud*, either by having them speak in soft voices or not speak openly:

These openly declared, though not in a very loud voice, that he was a saint. (Magarshack, 30)

Some said, although not quite openly, that Zosima was a saint. (MacAndrew, 34)

The French version by Henri Mongault follows the same pattern:

Ceux-là disaient, mais à voix basse, que c'était un saint. (28)

Translators seem to take upon themselves responsibility for making the narrator sound rational, or at least intelligible, in spite of his native proclivities.

---

without thinking and in literature without advancing the plot does not mean the terms are simply empty. On the contrary, it means that these terms carry the rhythms, even the character of the speaker. They may imply insecurity, as with the description of Akaky Akakievich above, or they may express sarcasm, secrecy, or any number of other underlying motives. Early in *The Brothers Karamazov*, when Father Zosima is on his deathbed, tensions at the monastery build, rifts between long-standing factions are exacerbated, and (*a*) ...измочаленные елки и березы — вповалку, крест-накрест, как, скажи, поверженные в бою солдаты.

(Abramov, "Oleshina izba," 410)

... shredded pines and birches—side-by-side, criss-cross, like, say, soldiers fallen in battle ...

... birches and firs, shredded and split into fibers, lying side-by-side and piled over one another, like soldiers fallen in battle ... (Gorgen, 129)

(*b*) Никакой, поди, разницы, когда уезжать...

(Rasputin, *Proshchanie s Materoi*, 246–47)

It makes, perhaps, no difference when one leaves ...

It made no difference when they left ... (Bouis, 57)

---

rumors fly. The narrator is quick to reassure the reader about these problems, but at the same time, using language peppered with emphatics or oppositional particles, he fans the flames and spreads the rumors still further (example 2.5). His account is rife with hyperbole ("vast majority," "undoubtedly," "very many," "with all their hearts," "almost fanatically," "in the very near future"). The constant qualifications and restatements make the narrator ludicrous and simultaneously provide rather ominous foreshadowing of the role of rumor and shifting allegiances in the lives of the main characters. The Garnett version eliminates all the qualifiers that are emphasized in this passage. It evokes well the atmosphere of gossip and mistrust within the monastery but eliminates the sense that the outside world—egged on by the narrator, perhaps—has a similarly wary, even condescending attitude toward the monks.

Modal particles, such as *dazhe* 'even' or *uzhe* 'already,' frequently disappear in translation, partly because of their relative invisibility, or their inability to stand on their own. They seem to take with them more autonomous words and phrases that are equally outside the syntactic core of the sentence, and therefore do not contribute directly to its semantic content. We have seen a number of instances of their omission in translation, especially of the loss of *vot* and *vprochem*. Even when such terms are set off conspicuously by commas, obviously interrupting the flow of the sentence or calling attention to its telling, they still may disappear. In both passages in example 2.6 there is in the Russian sentence a phrase set apart by commas which either calls attention to the process of the telling (as in the first case, "say") or expresses some attitude toward the content on the part of the speaker (as in the second case, "perhaps"). In English, the personal and ironic metaphor of the first sentence comes to seem purely literary, while the

И вот утром в выходной день наш артист, получше принарядившись, попорол на это свидание.

А надо сказать, что в трамвае у него случился небольшой эпизод и столкновение с соседом. Ну, вообще легкая перебранка, крики и так далее. В результате чего наш артист, как человек несдержанный немного более, чем следует, погорячился....

(Zoshchenko, "Zabavnoe prikliuchenie," 140)

And so, on the morning of his day off, our actor got himself all dolled up and sallied forth to his rendezvous.

But we must relate that in the trolley car he had a little altercation, a conflict with his neighbor. Just a little argument, some shouting, and so on. As a result of which the actor, as a man with a little less self control than was desirable, lost his temper. (Gordon and McLean, 220)

second becomes a simple statement of fact rather than a cry of despair at the characters' helplessness to stop the destruction of their island.

Pragmatic Connectors

Closely related to the modal particles are the syllables that are used to link sentences, paragraphs, or other pieces of discourse together. It is very common, especially in spoken discourse and written dialogue, to begin Russian sentences or signal each participant's turn in a dialogue with introductory *a* and *i*. These roughly mean "and" or (in the case of *a*) "but." However, their semantic weight is often negligible compared to their role in establishing a storytelling rhythm. Students of Russian regularly learn simply to overlook them in interpreting oral statements, to listen for the second syllable, not the first. But in written prose, when they sit prominently at the front of a sentence, capitalized, often repeated in sentence after sentence, they seem to carry a greater burden.

Pragmatic connectors are a prominent feature in the prose of many Russian authors, especially of those who adopt a colloquial tone or *skaz* narration. Mikhail Zoshchenko used them especially liberally, both in first- and in third-person narration. In his "An Amusing Adventure" (1935), the narrator is ostensibly third-person, but he is highly intrusive. He calls the various characters *"our* lady," *"our* ballet dancer," etc., and begins paragraph after paragraph with *I vot* 'And so,' which does not further the story but calls attention to the teller. Zoshchenko's narrative language has been the subject of much study, and translators have been quite conscientious in replicating it wherever possible. The translation in example 2.7 by Maria Gordon and Hugh McLean takes great pains to make the language colloquial and to retain the humorous syntax. The only concession to "smoothness" is in the third sentence, where "You know, basically a little argument" becomes simply "Just a little argument," with the narrator's casually gossipy tone somewhat effaced. Otherwise, this is a good example of the value of pragmatic connectors in English as well as Russian narration.

Pragmatic connectors in the Zoshchenko example establish a relationship of banter and good humor between narrator and reader. Above all, they stress a quality of personal communication. This quality has a somewhat different effect in the bricklaying scene in Solzhenitsyn's *One Day* (example 2.8). The careful description of the steps involved in laying a brick rings of a master's explanation to an apprentice. Each step is marked off by some expression with *i*, which underscores the importance of each successive action but also shows its crucial place in the orderly sequence:

i na to mesto brosaet 'And throws it down where it belongs'
I khvataet 'And picks up'
I eshche rastvor . . . razrovniav 'And smoothing out the cement'
I seichas zhe 'And right away'
I uzh on skhvachen 'And it's already set.'

The exception to this pattern is the most important step, laying on the brick (*Shlep tuda shlakoblok!* 'Slap on that brick!') which has, instead, the combination of a dash and an exclamation point to give it emphasis (the impact would, in fact, be lessened by the presence of *i*).

Solzhenitsyn makes use in this passage of other interesting devices that do not fit within the usual framework of sentence analysis. Two comments are set aside in parentheses; these are particular tricks of the trade, passed on lovingly, as if whispered to the eager novice. The penultimate sentence forms an especially complex imperative. It begins with two infinitives that carry an urgent imperative force (*podrovniat', podbit'*). As if that were not enough, the sentence ends with three repetitive, cautionary commands with *chtoby* 'be sure that,' as if to make absolutely certain that the apprentice has understood.

In translation, Solzhenitsyn's pragmatic connectors receive short shrift. Ralph Parker (*b*) faithfully retains Solzhenitsyn's sentence structure and punctuation,[12] but he eliminates the step-by-step impact of *i* and reinterprets the narrative as a description of a single event rather than as a generalized process. The result is less personal and less generalizable than the original. The other two translations (*a* and *c*) use an effective substitute for *i* by starting sentences or phrases with *then*. (*Then he'd pick up a brick; Then he'd level off the mortar; and then they froze in place.*) However, they neglect to highlight several steps in this fashion, including some very important ones: throwing on the mortar, straightening out the brick, and, in (*c*), the brick freezing in place. In addition, both (*a*) and (*c*) eliminate virtually all extraordinary punctuation, including parentheses, the exclamation point, dashes, and colons, and turn the imperative sentence into a simple declarative (*He had to even it out fast; Then, quick as quick, he squared it up*). These changes

Мастерком захватывает Шухов дымящийся раствор — и на то место бросает и запоминает, где прошел нижний шов (на тот шов серединой верхнего шлакоблока потом угодить). Раствора бросает он ровно столько, сколько под один шлакоблок. И хватает из кучки шлакоблок (но с осторожкою хватает — не продрать бы рукавицу, шлакоблоки дерут больно). И еще раствор мастерком разровняв — шлеп туда шлакоблок! И сейчас же, сейчас его подровнять, боком мастерка подбить, если не так: чтоб наружная стена шла по отвесу, и чтобы вдлинь кирпич плашмя лежал, и чтобы поперек тоже плашмя. И уж он схвачен, примерз.

(Solzhenitsyn, *Odin den'*, 43–44)

Shukhov takes up the steaming mortar in his trowel—and throws it down in the right place and commits to memory where the lower seam ran (that seam is where the center of the upper brick belongs). He throws on just enough mortar for one brick. And he grabs a brick from the stack (but grabs it with care—wouldn't want to tear a sleeve, bricks can really scratch). And then with the mortar good and smooth—clap the brick on! And right away, right away level it, knock it in with the side of the trowel, if it's off: the outer wall must be straight, and the bricks must lie even length-wise, and also even widthwise. And now it's set, frozen in place.

(*a*) He'd scoop up some steaming mortar with his trowel, throw it on, and remember how the groove of the brick ran so he'd get the next one on dead center. He always put on just enough mortar for each brick. Then he'd pick up a brick out of the pile, but with great care so he wouldn't get a hole in his mitten—they were pretty rough, those bricks. Then he'd level off the mortar with a trowel and drop the brick on top. He had to even it out fast and tap it in place with his trowel if it wasn't right, so the outside wall would be as straight as a die and the bricks level both crossways and lengthways, and then they froze in place. (Hayward and Hingley, 109)

(*b*) Here was one. Shukhov took up some of the steaming mortar on his trowel and slapped it into the appropriate place, with his mind on the joint below (this would have to come right in the middle of the block he was going to lay). He slapped on just enough mortar to go under the one block. He snatched it from the pile—carefully, though, so as not to tear his mittens, for with cement blocks you can do that in no time. He smoothed the mortar with his trowel and then—down with the block! And without losing a moment he leveled it, patting it with the side of the trowel—it wasn't lying exactly right—so that the wall would be truly in line and the block lie level both lengthwise and across. The mortar was already freezing. (Parker, 95)

(*c*) He scooped up a trowel full of steaming mortar, slapped it on the very spot, making a note where the blocks in the row below met so that the middle of the block above would be dead-center over the groove. He slapped on just enough mortar for one block at a time. Then he grabbed a block from the pile—he was a bit careful, though, he didn't want a hole in his mittens, and those blocks were horribly scratchy. Then he smoothed the mortar down with his trowel and plopped the block on it. Then, quick as quick, he squared it up, tapping it into place with the side of his trowel if it wasn't sitting right, making sure it was flush with the outside of the wall and dead-level widthwise and lengthwise. Because it would freeze on and stick fast right away. (Willetts, 99) significantly alter both the nature of the description, with its emphasis on quick timing and precision, and its communicative force: gone is the sense of the master-apprentice relationship, of the delight of the master craftsman who can share—and show off—his expertise.

Pragmatic connectors gain their storytelling force by repetition, and by virtue of their position at the beginning of sentences. Some writers use them even in absolute initial position. Here, their role as connectors makes them point outside the text, to some implied context or preexisting world.[13] Absolute initial *i* is especially common in modern works that emphasize themes of continuity and interconnectedness, such as the psychological dramas of Rasputin and Trifonov (example 2.9), or Chingiz Aitmatov's 1981 novel, *I dol'she veka dlitsia den'* (And the day lasts longer than an age). Aitmatov uses the connector to begin his title, foreshadowing the mixture of memory and perseverance, folklore and futuristic fantasy of his novel. (The title of the published translation is *The Day Lasts More than a Hundred Years*, which forfeits this effect.)

Rasputin (example 2.9*a*) begins his novella about an interruption of the circular rhythms of rural life, *Farewell to Matëra* (1976), with the phrase "And again . . . " This sentence, he suggests, is not a beginning but a continuation of an "endless" story. The unusual use of the reflexive possessive pronoun *svoia*, in the nominative case and without an apparent referent ("it's own spring"), is another indicator of unspecified, structural interconnection. The translator, Antonina Bouis, eliminates both these signals. Faithful to the original's semantic assertion of circularity, the English sentence nevertheless omits all structural reflections of the theme. Contrast her version to one more attentive to the colloquial storytelling voice:

> *And so spring came once more, yet another in this endless cycle, but for Matëra it was the last.*

Here, the strong opening connector and the self-referential "this" imply a deeply sympathetic narrator. Such a narrative presence is consistent with the introduction, later in the story, of the island's mythical consciousness in the form of "the Master" (*Khoziain*).

Yurii Trifonov (example 2.9*b*) uses the identical opening words for his novel *Another Life* (1975). Like Rasputin's, Trifonov's use of the pragmatic connector in opening position emphasizes that this is but one event among many, and his translator, like Rasputin's, retains the emphasis semantically but not structurally. In addition to the initial *i*, Trifonov makes repeated use of pragmatic connectors and copulae in the opening chapter of this work. The first four paragraphs begin as follows: *I opiat'* 'And again'; *Odnako* 'However'; *A on, byvalo* 'And/But he, at times'; *A inogda on* 'And sometimes he . . . ' The Michael Glenny translation retains only the second of these ("Yet she found it easy"). Significantly, this is the only paragraph that begins with a (*a*) И опять наступила весна, своя в своем нескончаемом ряду, но последняя для Матеры.

(Rasputin, *Proshchanie*, 203).

And again came spring, its own in its own unending chain, but the last one for Matera.

Once more spring had come, one more in the neverending cycle, but for Matyora this spring would be the last. (Bouis, 1)

(*b*) И опять среди ночи проснулась, как просыпалась теперь каждую ночь . . .

(Trifonov, *Drugaia zhizn'*, 219)

And again [she] woke up in the night, as she was waking up now every night . . .

Again she woke up in the middle of the night, just as she had lately been waking up every night . . . (Glenny, 11)

---

copula other than *a* or *i*; *odnako* 'however' has more semantic independence and therefore, it seems, receives greater respect from the translator. Otherwise he has "Again she woke up," "At other times," "Sometimes he would wake up . . ." These more standard time expressions diminish the stream-of-consciousness quality of the heroine's ruminations, the sense that she is communicating with herself. As in the examples above, the *telling* of a story (even in the heroine's own head) loses out to the story itself when a work is translated.

Tense shifts

In addition to lexical items that carry a phatic function, the use of present and future tenses allows the narrator to simulate direct address to the reader. The rich possibilities available in Russian for tense shifts and ambiguous use of tense will be treated in detail in our discussion of interior monologue. One example will suffice of their use with third-person narration. The opening chapter of Rasputin's *Farewell to Matëra* contains, among various deictics and other indicators of personal narration, the phrase, "[The name] Podmoga makes sense" (example 2.10). By changing it to "Podmoga . . . *made* sense," the translator suggests that this was the villagers' assessment, whereas the present-tense Russian version refers at least as much to the narrator's viewpoint and represents an attempt to persuade the audience. It is, admittedly, awkward in English to shift tenses in mid-narration, but there are other means of signaling the narrator-reader relationship, such as "Podmoga, for obvious reasons . . ." or "Podmoga, clearly, because . . ." The translator's temporal distancing of the narrator from the village is confirmed in the final

... другой остров, который называли то Подмогой, то Подногой. Подмога — понятно: чего не хватало на своей земле, брали здесь, а почему Поднога — ни одна душа бы не объяснила, а теперь не объяснит и подавно.

(Rasputin, *Proshchanie*, 204)

... another island, which they called now Podmoga ['helper'], now Podnoga ['underfoot']. Podmoga makes sense: what was lacking on [their] own land they got here, but why Podnoga—not a soul could explain; and now it will be that much harder.

... another island ... which they called Podmoga, and sometimes Podnoga. Podmoga, made from the word "to help," made sense: what they lacked on their own land they got there. But why they called it Podnoga—no one could have explained it back then and now it was hopeless. (Bouis, 3)

---

phrase, "now it was hopeless," in place of the Russian "now it will be that much harder [to explain it]."

Colloquial Register

The most colorful signal of a personal narrator is the use of colloquial language. In contrast to standard "literary" Russian, the colloquial register carries the suggestion of an oral, speaking storyteller. Soviet literature of the post-Stalin era essentially reintroduced this register into Russian literature after a long hiatus, and as an innovation it had both artistic and political import. However, it has been one of the hardest features of this literature to capture in translation. Kornei Chukovsky lamented the loss of *prostorechie* (common or substandard speech) in translations of Solzhenitsyn's *One Day*: "As you see, it's a pattern. It turns out that not only Ralph Parker but all, positively all the translators flatly refused to translate *prostorechie*. And their Italian colleagues joined them in this" (1988, 394; my translation).

The communicative impact of such an omission is profound. A good example of colloquial usage in otherwise "omniscient" narration in English is John Nichols's third-person narrator in *The Milagro Beanfield War*, who adopts a folksy tone, filled with slang and regionally distinctive expressions:

[Amarante] contracted tuberculosis. He hacked and stumbled around, hollow-eyed, gaunt and sniffling, and folks crossed themselves, murmuring Hail Marys whenever he staggered into view. At twenty, when he was already an alcoholic, scarlet fever almost laid him in the grave; at twenty-three, malaria looked like it would do the job. (1974, 16)

The narrator's presence appears in such colloquial phrases as "folks crossed themselves," "he hacked and stumbled around," "almost laid him in the grave," "looked like it would do the job." There is a definite sense that someone is telling this story, someone who has mastered the local idiom, someone who understands Amarante's milieu. The reader need not infer a particular personality or allegiance for this narrator, but it is impossible to ignore his or her presence. Especially when used for otherwise "omniscient" narration, such language establishes a direct avenue of contact with the audience that so-called transparent or objective narration lacks.

Village prose writers were particularly fond of colloquial narration, using their works as a forum for reviving folk idioms and peasant dialects. Rasputin, Abramov, Vasilii Belov (whose novel *Pryvychnoe delo* [*So It Goes*] is so saturated with dialect that no one has managed to translate it), and others made wide use of oral-type constructions, creating the impression of an omniscient narrator with a peasant world view. In example 2.11a and b the tendency to use a peasant lexicon is obvious. The terms *muzhik* and *baba*, referring to a peasant man and woman, respectively, have taken on derogatory connotations in the standard language but are still the neutral terms in the countryside. In village prose they are not only acceptable but flaunted as an expression of the narrator's identification with the local perspective.[14] (They are extremely difficult to translate, sometimes given in transliteration; I have used "fellow" in (a) for *muzhik*, a weak substitute, and "grownup women" for *baba* in (b), not a substitute at all but intended as a contrast to "small fry.") In addition to these two words, many other dialectal and substandard words are in evidence here: *rebiatishki* and *devki* for peasant boys and girls; *nadumal* 'took it into his head'; *vygadlivyi* 'on-the-ball, resourceful'; *syskat'* 'to hit upon, find'. Moreover, the syntax has the distinct ring of unconstrained, oral speech ("three hundred years and more," "was a far-seeing man," "he couldn't find a better," "hadn't seen in ages"). Altogether, the use of various markers of oral speech results in a sense that someone is *telling* the story, someone who is not a character but a sympathetic, omniscient narrator.[15]

The published English translations in (a) and (b) make an effort to retain the deictic expressions ("that," "this"), but otherwise they all but erase the colloquial narrator. This is even more striking in (c), which is an explanation of Atamanovka village's excellent location for highway robbery. Here, the colloquial expressions, strongly marked in Russian, have clear English equivalents: "couldn't be more convenient," "no two ways about it" or "there's just no way," "like it or not." They are conspicuously absent in the translation, although alternatives are simple to craft:

The village couldn't be more conveniently situated for this: the mountain ridge comes almost flush up against the Angara here and there's just no way to stay clear of the village. Like it or not, you have to come out on the road.

The kinship between this narrator and that of Nichols's novel is clear: both

(a) Тот первый мужик, который триста с лишним лет назад надумал поселиться на острове, был человек зоркий и выгадливый, верно рассудивший, что лучше этой земли ему не сыскать.

(Rasputin, *Proshchanie*, 204)

It was a far-seeing and shrewd fellow that first thought to make his home on this island, some three-hundred-odd years back; he judged rightly that he'd never find a better place anywhere.

That first peasant who decided to settle on this island over three hundred years ago was a far-sighted and clever man, who had judged rightly that he would find no better land. (Bouis, 3)

(b) Но давно-давно не видал пекашинский берег такого многолюдья. Ребятишки, девки, бабы, старики — все, кто мог, выбежали к реке.

(Abramov, *Dve zimy*, 209)

But the Pekashino riverbank hadn't seen such a turnout in ages. Small fry, grownup women, old folk—every last one who could had come running to the river.

But it had been a long time since the Pekashino riverfront had seen such a throng. Little children, girls, women, old folk—everyone who could was running down to the river. (Edwards and Schneider, 4)

Still, it had been a long time since so many people had been seen on the Pinyega river bank. Children, girls, women, old men, everyone who could had hurried down to the river. (Powers and Powers, 3)

(c) Деревня для этого стоит куда как удобно: хребет здесь подходит почти вплотную к Ангаре, и миновать деревню стороной никак нельзя, хочешь не хочешь, а надо выходить на дорогу.

(Rasputin, *Zhivi i pomni*, 11–12)

The village sits ever so conveniently for this: the ridge here comes almost right down to the river, and there's absolutely no way to get around the village, like it or not, you have to come out on the road.

The village was situated very conveniently for that: a mountain ridge comes right up against the river here and you can't bypass the village; you have to take the road. (Bouis, 8–9)

---

are affectionately deprecating of the place, bent on showing its remoteness, its prejudices, but also its humanity. A translation in standard English misses an entire layer of meaning in the work.

Apart from colloquialisms per se, authors frequently use syntactic or "intonational" devices to approximate the quality of oral narration. This phenomenon is most challenging to translators, since intonation patterns in oral language are perceived largely subconsciously and vary greatly from language to language, and our writing systems do not reflect them well. However, the problem is real. Lauren G. Leighton observes about Solzhenitsyn's

(a) «Ой, лють там сегодня будет: двадцать семь с ветерком, ни укрыва, ни грева!»

(*Odin den'*, 25)

God, it'd be hell there today, with a temperature of sixteen below and the wind and no cover at all! (Hayward and Hingley, 30)

Oh, it'd be cruel there today: seventeen degrees below zero, and windy. No shelter. No fire. (Parker, 38)

Oh, it'd be hell there today: -27 and a wind, and no shelter and no fire! (Aitken, 28)

Oh, but it would be ferocious out there today—a windy 17 below and no shelter, no fire! (Whitney, 40)

It would be murder out there—twenty-seven below, and no hope of a warm! (Willetts, 29)

(b) В любой рыбе он ел все, хоть жабры, хоть хвост, и глаза ел, когда они на месте попадались, а когда вываливались и плавали в миске отдельно — большие, рыбьи глаза — не ел.

(16)

He didn't leave anything—not even the gills or the tail. He ate the eyes too when they were still in place, but when they'd come off and were floating around in the bowl on their own he didn't eat them. (Hayward and Hingley, 17)

He ate everything—the gills, the tail, the eyes when they were still in their sockets but not when they'd been boiled out and floated in the bowl separately—big fish eyes. Not then. (Parker, 29)

He ate every bit of every fish, gills, tails, even eyes if they were where they should be, but if they had boiled out of the head and were floating loose in the bowl—big fish eyes goggling at him—he wouldn't eat them. (Willetts, 17–18)

One Day and three of its translations, regarding the sentence in example 2.12a: "The syntax is . . . important for its intonation. The exclamation has to be delivered in a quick, sing-song rhythm with marked pauses for the two commas and full colon. This intonation has been erased in all three of these translations" (1978, 120). Considering the variations in 2.12a, the fact that translators could choose such different rhythms as equivalent to one original is indicative of how elusive the notion of intonation can be. Leighton did not include the Max Hayward–Ronald Hingley variant in his comments, but it does not appear to meet his standards, either. Presumably, Leighton would be happier with the recent version by H. T. Willetts, since it keeps the break and some of the singsong quality of the latter part of the sentence. In general, though, his criticism runs afoul of the fundamental circularity of the very concept of intonation, which depends on the way an individual reads a passage.

Solzhenitsyn's work also serves as an example for T. G. Vinokur, who calls its lexicon entirely literary but says it "overlays . . . a low-colloquial syntactic structure" (1965, 23). He cites as an illustration the passage about fish soup in example 2.12*b*. The Russian sentence is broken several times in imitation of oral speech; the phrase *khot' zhabry, khot' khvost* 'be it gills, be it tail', and the repetition of *el* 'he ate' create an intonational rhythm suggesting both the extraordinary and the mundane quality of this information. The interjection about "big fish-eyes" shows how close the narrator's perspective is to Ivan's own. Hayward and Hingley primarily use contractions and one dash as their concessions to colloquialism. Parker is more bold with syntax, and his added emphatic sentence (Not then.) gives the narrator weight. Willetts captures the narrator's presence with syntactic literalism, adding perhaps too much explanation but otherwise keeping the voice intact.

Admittedly, discussions of "intonation" in written prose are prone to subjectivity. Vinogradov's criticism of Boris Eikhenbaum for "listening to" and not "reading" literary works is not without foundation (Vinogradov 1966). However, it would seem that one important locus of interaction between oral speech and written language lies in the way punctuation and vocabulary are used to capture the way speech sounds, and this is a legitimate realm of concern for translators. (Punctuation itself as a stylistic feature will be discussed in chap. 4.) That these qualities are often lost in English translation may be, in part, an assertion of the priority of written-type over oral-type narrative language, a conviction about the crystallization of a literary work that is stronger in English and American culture than in Russian.

The English language contributes to this trend because it lends itself less well to approximating oral speech in writing. The absence in English of an equivalent for *vot*, for example, removes an essential tool for expressing immediacy. Russian shifts tenses and even person more easily than English does, making for a more natural range of interjections and syntactic breaks. And there is evidence that the colloquial register is more accessible to Russian writers, since Russian has a more live sense of the distinction between oral and written styles.

The interaction of oral and literary traditions and high and low styles has long been a source of play and tension in Russian prose. A serious literature based on the spoken language as opposed to the church language (or an otherwise artificial, elevated language) is a relatively new phenomenon, shocking in the *Life* of Archpriest Avvakum in the seventeenth century, still unsettling in the early nineteenth century. In the Soviet period the spoken and written languages have, theoretically, been the same, with the same dictionaries and grammar. However, there is still a divergence in vocabulary and structure between the language as spoken and the language as written. In Russian this is far more noticeable than in English, which has never had a separate literary language (equivalent to Old Church Slavic) or even an Academy invested with the power to set literary standards.

The Russian "literary," or standard, language is what is taught in the schools and used in official speech and educated writing. There exists alongside it an everyday, spoken language, also quite standardized (that is, not dialectal or idiosyncratic) but stylistically marked when it appears in written form.[16] Thus the *Great Soviet Encyclopedia* (1975 ed.) refers to "colloquial elements which bear the function of spontaneity and a certain low quality in written form and are neutral in everyday speech" (s.v. *"Russkii iazyk"*). A favorite topic for Soviet philologists is the difference between the Russian "literary language" and the "language of literature." Only the latter, they stipulate, is open to colloquialisms and to *prostorechie* (substandard, "common" language or vulgarisms).[17] Such elements are extremely numerous and can easily delineate a stylistic register. A typical page from a Russian dictionary has frequent notations of register, with nearly a third of the definitions or examples marked "colloquial" or "common."[18] In sum, the colloquial register is well recognized and readily available to Russian writers who wish to create a casual atmosphere for their narration without using idiosyncratic or regionally distinct terms; it is possible to evoke a generalized storyteller who imparts a sense of oral narration but does not interfere personally in the story.

By contrast, English has a rich dialectal system but generally lacks a *standard*, or at least standardly acknowledged, colloquial vocabulary. (We even lack a satisfactory term for *prostorechie*, since "vulgar" has come to mean "obscene.") The *Oxford English Dictionary* does not distinguish colloquial from literary terms, combining them all under the rubric of "common words" ("which belong to the language *common* to literature and everyday speech").[19] Slang, dialectal, and specialized terms may be singled out, but the register of unconstrained speech is not recognized. This may explain, in part, why translators often do not seek to use it (although English is by no means incapable of creating a colloquial effect in narration, as is clear from the Nichols example above). The importance of the dictionary norm in this regard is enhanced by a certain peculiarity of colloquial style pointed out by A. N. Vasil'eva (1976, 86): whereas other styles are determined by their central, dominant elements (for example, scientific language is dense with specialized terminology and complex sentence structures), colloquial style depends upon occasional, peripheral elements, especially key words and phrases. Thus, a pervasive effect such as colloquial narration can be reinterpreted in a linguistic or translational approach to a work as "peripheral." As many of the italicized translations above demonstrate, these changes are not required by English, they are chosen by translators.

It is worth closing with a few examples of translations that do not shrink from unusual use of lexicon and punctuation, to show how much "intonational fidelity" can add to a work's power, in English as well as in Russian.

They drove the old men, worn out from work, they took the teenagers from their studies, and runny-nosed girls—they put them all to work on the firs. And the women, women with babies, what had they to survive during these years! Here there was no allowance made whatever for age or for anything else. If you die in the woods, don't come back to the barracks without having produced your quota. Don't you dare! Give us cubic meters! The front demands it! And there would have been some excuse for it if they at least could have been eating their own rations, but in fact they were not. They had first to silence the hungry mouths of the children. (Abramov, *Two Winters*; Powers and Powers, 69)

Shukhov was wearing only camp issue anyway: go ahead, he told them silently, have a feel, nothing here except a bare chest with a soul inside it. But a note was made of Tsezar's flannel vest, and Buynovsky—surprise—had a little waistcoat or cummerbund of some sort. (Solzhenitsyn, *One Day*; Willetts, 35).

In both cases exclamations and interjections are freely used. The shift from third-person to second-person entailed by these interruptions ("don't come back," "—surprise") does disrupt the narration, but it also adds a lively fluidity to the narrator-reader relationship.

THE PERSONAL NARRATOR AND THE TRANSLATOR

There is, then, ample evidence that translators until very recently have tended to neglect signs of the intrusive narrator. This trend has been explained by Venuti (1992), for example, as a neglect of the materiality of language. It also may be evidence of the divergence between anglophone and Russian cultural interest in style and language. Many of the above examples, however, lend themselves to simple, almost literal solutions in English, which suggests that their disappearance is not a passive or inadvertent phenomenon but an active intervention in the texts.

Bakhtin's analysis of *skaz* narration holds that there are no words that belong to no one (1975, 212). The evidence given in this chapter demonstrates a general inclination among translators, at least until very recently, to seize possession of the words from the speaking narrator and give them to a more neutral, "objective," translator-narrator. They soften or eliminate marked colloquial language, saving only some deictic expressions or other semantically unmistakable indicators of the folk narrator. When deictics appear as the primary indicators of the narrator's involvement in the story, they generally fall by the wayside. Finally, interjections and parenthetical expressions of the narrator's point of view either disappear altogether or are reevaluated as simple adverbs. Language that reaches its tendrils outside the world of the story—to the folk milieu, to the narrator-addressee relationship, or into the narrator's prejudices—gets pruned into shape by translators who wish to present their readers with a well-ordered product. This trend is partly attributable to a universal tendency for translations to explain and neutralize simply by virtue of the dislocations that a change in language and receiving culture entails. But there seems to be a further motivation at work here, a tendency to assert what I. R. Titunik (1971, 93) has called "authorial authority."[20]

By constructing a local or individualized third-person narrator, the author effectively cedes some authority to that narrator, allowing the milieu or the events to speak for themselves. (This is especially the case among village prose writers, most of whom are themselves urban dwellers who feel some guilt about abandoning their rural roots.) When the characters speak, their dialogue is distanced from the reader by its formal identification as dialogue; we understand them to be speaking to one another. But when they speak through the narrator, or when elements of direct address permeate the narrator's discourse, then they seem to address the reader directly. Such interjections as *podi* 'perhaps' and *skazhi* 'say' (example 2.6) are ossified imperative forms; although they no longer act as true imperatives, they still retain a conative function. So do such emphatic expressions as *vot takoi miagkii* 'look how soft' or *vot uzhe kotoryi god* 'how many years now' (example 2.3). The message itself becomes important here, not because we focus on the "materiality of language," to use Venuti's term, but because we experience the illusion of a direct communicative act.

Translation shifts a work's frame of reference. The author's "here" and "now" are not the translator's. However, the narrator's "here" and "now" are defined within the work, wherever it is published—even if the narrator has no name or definite individuality. And although a translation addresses a different audience than the original does, it presumably need not adjust the text's conative functions, because, as Yuri Tynianov would argue, the personal narrator brings the reader into the story. Yet translators make deictic shifts all the time. Two different translations of *Dead Souls*, for example, have the narrator's *u nas* 'among us' as "in Russia."[21] While this may have some explanatory value (although it is hard to believe that one could have reached chapter 5 of Gogol's novel without knowing in what country it takes place), it sacrifices a strong example of personal narration. Here, as in many of the previous examples, the translator appears not to trust the narrator-reader communication to work.[22] Even in otherwise excellent translations of narrative voice there is a temptation to skirt around the moments of direct address to the reader (see example 2.13).

Thus, in many cases, the translator takes over the role of narrator and imbues it with greater omniscience than in the original. Perhaps the explanation lies not in linguistic difficulties or even in the cultural context of literature and its translation, but in the more personal relationship of the translator to the text. All of the translation examples above exhibit a trend toward a single, central consciousness in the works. The original authors had chosen to share possession of the narrative act with an unseen, even inauthoritative speaker. Thus they identify the act of narration with its context in the story and allow for a degree of dialogic fluidity or give-and-take between narrator and read-

---

Translation Example 2.13: Vasilii Shukshin

Vasilii Shukshin wrote dramatic short stories about criminals and other forgotten elements of Russian society in the 1960s and early 1970s. His style was marked by colloquialisms and an abrupt cadence, which the Ward and Iliffe translations capture well. But the directness of the narrative voice sometimes eludes them:

Воровал ли он со складов? Как вам сказать…

("Vybiraiu derevniu na zhitel'stvo," 146)

Did he steal from the warehouse? You see, it's like this (lit: *How to tell you*) . . .

The reader will be wondering whether he stole from his warehouse. (Ward and Iliffe, 73)

Note how the translators have substituted a less personal term ("the reader") for the original *you*, and a standard statement for the original question-answer form. The result is far more literary (emphasizing the *reader*) and less an imitation of oral storytelling.

---

er. This complex network of transmission and exchange becomes even more complex with the addition of a new player, the translator, whose accountability for and authority over the work come into conflict. Editors and readers look to the translator precisely for some sense of authority and clarity. Yet the translator's real "authority" within the textual and contextual network is highly ambiguous. As Eberhard Pause writes, "This is the paradox of translation: In uttering his translation, the translator is a *speaker*, but in this very same situation he is not *the speaker*. His utterance is not really *his* utterance. It will be understood as the utterance of someone else, it has no original status" (1983, 391). Thus, the translator is supposed to convey *more* authority than the author while possessing far less. The intrusion of another mediating voice, especially one as covert and potentially inauthoritative as the narrator described above, cannot be a welcome event for the translator who sees her or his job as bringing author and reader together with a minimum of interference.

Peter Brooks writes that "the relation of teller to listener is inherently part of the structure and the meaning of any narrative text" (1986, 55). The normalizing translator internalizes that relation and produces a new teller-listener relationship, much as the psychoanalyst does in Brooks's discussion of the analytic process:

The analyst must treat the analysand's words and symbolic acts as an actual force, active in the present, while attempting to translate them back into the terms of the past. He must help the analysand construct a more coherent, connected and forceful narrative discourse, one whose syntax and rhetoric are more convincing, more adequate to give an interpretative account of the story of the past than those that are originally presented, in symptomatic form, by the analysand. (57)

Lacking their own authority or their own "I" from which to speak, translators may lose the sense of the words as an "actual force, active in the present." Thus, the space left open by the author for interpretation and transference, or for what Brooks calls "movement of reference," is now filled by the translator, who presents a new—and, usually, narrower—set of possibilities to the reader. All the original constitutive communicative possibilities are now enclosed in that new whole. The text loses its open-ended *signifying* qualities and becomes a *signified*, a completed communication between author/text and translator, which is then passed on whole to the reader. Roman Jakobson describes most acts of translation as being equivalent to reported speech.[23] To take that idea a step farther, the translator's reporting of the speech appears to supersede the speech of another unseen mediator, replacing that voice with the neutral translator-narrator. One irony of this shift is that it enhances qualities of realism in a text: univocality, a single perspective, and referentiality. It moves the style in the direction Gorky advocated in 1934— away from the materiality of language and toward language-as-material. Post-Stalin prose, however, was intriguing to Soviet readers partly because it stretched the boundaries of socialist realism. Village prose, for example, introduced nonomniscient narrators and the sense that the village itself was speaking.[24] Translations have thus emphasized its informational content [the hardships of peasant life, the breakdown of the rural family] at the expense of its aesthetic significance. The effect has been as if to reassert Stalinist strictures on language and style.

Recent theory and—little by little—translation practice have begun to offer a new role to the translator. Building upon Walter Benjamin's argument for translations as "the latest and most abundant flowering" of literary texts, theorists have come to see translation as a locus for the celebration of difference.[25] The translator, then, becomes a creative contributor to the larger cultural phenomenon of text *plus* translations, part of what Benjamin calls the "afterlife" of the work. Douglas Robinson's recent book is aptly named *The Translator's Turn*, to signify this new sense of translational authority. The notion of abusive translation put forward by Philip Lewis, Lawrence Venuti, and others, is also an assertion of translators' rights: no longer should deviations from the literary norm be attributed to translational errors. The translator now has fuller latitude to experiment with stylistic devices outside the standard literary repertoire. And there is evidence that translators are asserting just such prerogatives, as was shown in chapter 1. Curiously, while many of the new translators freely bend English usage to allow the text's voices to speak, they still exhibit a tendency to assert some translatorial control by adding explanatory material. Note, for example, the additional information in the Willetts translation of *One Day* (example 2.12 above): boiled *out of the head*; big fish eyes *goggling at him*. And some of the new Dostoevsky translations are almost absurdly saturated with footnotes.[26] Such material may make the work more accessible to readers, and often it is unavoidable. But it should also be recognized as tendency to encapsulate a work in translation, to assert a translator outside the text, and to deliver the work as a *signified* rather than a *signifier*.

Walter Benjamin advocates a pure syntactic literalism in translation that "completely demolishes the theory of reproduction of meaning and is a direct threat to comprehensibility"(1968*b*, 78). Since this would quickly put translators out of work, it hardly seems a reasonable prescription. Some degree of literalism does, however, prevent the wholesale elimination of the narrator, who often exists only in those peripheral devices of syntactic "intonation" or speech register. Evidence from published translations shows that, at some unconscious level, a translator smooths and trims a work out of fear of being lost among the various voices in the text. But the beauty of recent theories of "abusive" translation is that the translator gains a role rather than losing one: the stretches and distortions of the target language "belong" to the translator at least as much as to the author. A translator who is expected to remain "objective" is forced into a paradoxical, dual stance, partly outside the text, encapsulating its meaning for the reader, and partly inside the narration, retelling the story in more analytical terms. A more humane and artistically acceptable approach is to cast the translator as equivalent to an orchestra conductor, who brings out the various voices in a work to best advantage and receives due credit for doing so. Thus, ideally, the translator's role is to harmonize rather than stifle the multiple voices in literary conversation.

Chapter Three

Narrated Monologue: Translating a Shifting Viewpoint

AT THE OTHER end of the spectrum from the intrusive narrator is the device of narrated monologue, in which the narrator cedes authority to the characters themselves. This may take the form of interjections in a character's voice into an otherwise "objective" passage, or it may be more generalized, permeating the narration. Variously known as *style indirect libre, erlebte Rede, nesobstvenno-priamaia rech'*, quasi-direct discourse, interior monologue, or narrated monologue, this device appears frequently in English literature. However, certain features of Russian syntax create an especially welcoming environment for it, and it has flourished on that soil. This chapter will address these syntactic features and the problems they pose for translators.

INTRODUCTION

The definitions of this device are at least as numerous as its appellations. Most scholars agree that narrated monologue shares with direct speech the lexicon, deictic positioning ("here" and "now" as opposed to "there" and "then"), and emotive modulations of the supposed speaker, and with indirect speech the shift from first to third person (plus tense shifts in English, French, and German, for example). Dorrit Cohn (1966, 105), who coins the term "narrated monologue" (which I will use, it being the most descriptive and least unwieldy of the lot), adds to this the distinguishing feature of the absence of a *verbum dicendi*.[1] In sum, Richard Luplow defines quasi-direct discourse as "a type of represented . . . discourse which has distinct characteristics of the spoken language of a given character, although the character is referred to in the third person. . . . Such discourse is not linked to the character-referent by direct grammatical connectives [but] simply by sentence contiguity or implication" (1971, 400).[2]

Discussion of the purpose of this style has revolved around the questions of where it comes from and whose speech it represents. V. N. Voloshinov (who may have been borrowing from Mikhail Bakhtin's ideas) traces the history of the debate in the late nineteenth and early twentieth centuries. It was not until the 1920s, according to Voloshinov, that critics, such as Jean Etienne Lorck, began to recognize its role as a separate, deliberate, and useful stylistic device for expressing two points of view at once (the author's and "the other's" [*chuzhaia rech'*]).[3] Lorck saw it as the most direct depiction of the experience of another's speech, because it is the way a listener would process it for him- or herself. Voloshinov (1929, 157) himself brings a sociological viewpoint to the debate, objecting to those who would psychologize the style and interpret it as a form of individual expression; instead, for him, the fact that there exist syntactic parameters for such a style in a language signifies that the society has constituted this style as a means of social interaction, expressing not "a material position of reasoning" but an "accidental, subjective condition." Roy Pascal (1977, 26–27) adds to this that there is always an authorial presence in this voice, signaled by some contextual "bridge," or nearby indicator of direct or indirect speech.

Whatever the interpretation, the linguistic mechanisms for establishing narrated monologue represent a breaking down of normal boundaries between voices. Rather than setting up a specific character-voice, narrator-voice, or authorial voice, narrated monologue merges them and allows for a kind of fluid interaction between them. Bakhtin writes: "This form introduces order and stylistic symmetry into the disorderly and impetuous flow of a character's internal speech (a disorder and impetuosity would otherwise have to be reprocessed into direct speech) and, moreover, through its syntactic (third-person) and basic stylistic markers (lexicological and other), such a form permits another's inner speech to merge, in an organic and structured way, with a context belonging to the author" (1981, 319). Like Pascal, Bakhtin recognizes this style as simultaneously "structured" and fluid: the language provides certain structures that allow the reader, in effect, to witness the breakdown of boundaries between voices.

The question of fluid boundaries is particularly significant for our discussion of translation. Many of the translation effects noted elsewhere in this book are the outgrowths of an excessive concern for boundaries: boundaries of sentences, of literary diction, of cultural acceptability. When translators neglect narrated monologue, it appears to be out of a desire to assert clear boundaries among voices. Cohn suggests that this is not simply a translation phenomenon but one endemic to the larger literary-critical culture: "The virtual neglect of *erlebte Rede* in Anglo-American criticism would seem to indicate that in the study of fictional technique boundaries of language still have a tangible existence" (1966, 100).[4] Thus there is social resistance to the translation of this device, based on a critical neglect of its importance and the natural inclination of translators to cling to safely delineated boundaries. Furthermore, narrated monologue encounters linguistic problems in translation into English, which by its analytical structure encourages divisions of subject and object and distinctions of person and tense that are more complete than those in Russian.

Voloshinov (1929, 121) breaks literary history into four periods: authoritarian dogmatism (in the Middle Ages), rational dogmatism (seventeenth and eighteenth centuries), realistic and critical individualism (late eighteenth and nineteenth centuries), and relativistic individualism thereafter. Narrated monologue appeared, according to him, only in the last two periods, with the admission of alternative points of view. He attributes the strong development of this device in Russian literature to the language's weakness in the realm of indicators of indirect speech, such as sequence of tenses or the subjunctive mood. This is due, he claims, to the fact that Russian culture never passed through the "Cartesian, rational period, when a reasoned, self-confident and objective 'authorial context' analyzed and parsed the substance of 'the other's speech' and provided complex and interesting means for expressing it indirectly" (123). As a result, he concludes, the Russian language offers exceptional possibilities for the artistic manipulation of "the other's speech."

Voloshinov laments that it is difficult in Russian to mark the boundaries between the author's speech and that of another. Others consider this an advantage, however. L. Sokolova explains that the device of narrated monologue was central to the development of Russian realism in the nineteenth century because it gave the author a conversational style and because realism could not have developed "without erasing the boundaries between written and oral speech" (1968, 210).[5] The desire to erase boundaries was especially strong in the post-Stalin Soviet Union, where narrated monologue flourished as a subtle protest against the didactic tone of earlier Soviet prose (Hughes 1977, chap. 8).

NARRATED MONOLOGUE IN RUSSIAN LITERATURE

Interjections and Unambiguous Shifts in Perspective

Since Russian has so much fluidity built into its structure, it is not surprising that Russian literature avails itself of rapid-fire shifts in person and tense. We have seen some examples in chapter 2, where the unnamed narrator was able to interject oral-type comments and exclamations into otherwise ordinary third-person narration. Such interjections are also a feature of narrated monologue (in fact, it is often difficult to tell which interjections belong to a narrator and which to the characters). They may be reproducible in English, but, as example 3.1 shows, translators frequently reanalyze even the most apparent interjections from characters as third-person commentary.

In example 3.1*a*, Yurii Trifonov allows the heroine's anger to speak for itself ("She got so angry!" or "How furious it made her!"). The interjection is (*a*) Тогда, на веранде, она почувствовала вдруг бурное отвращение, как приступ тошноты, — и к нему, и к людям за столом, глазевшим на него с веселым, пьяным дружелюбием, как в ресторане. *Как же она разозлилась!*

(Trifonov, *Drugaia zhizn'*, 233; emphasis added)

At that moment on the veranda she suddenly felt a wild revulsion, like a wave of nausea,—both toward him and toward the people around the table, gazing at him with cheerful, drunken amiability, as if in a restaurant. She got so angry!

At that moment on the veranda she suddenly felt a fierce wave of revulsion toward him, like an attack of nausea, and toward the people around the table staring at him with cheerful, boozy amiability. . . . *she completely lost her temper and said angrily* . . . (Glenny, 28)

(*b*) Ух, как лицо бригадирово перекосило! Ка-ак швырнет мастерок под ноги! И к Дэру — шаг! Дэр оглянулся — Павло лопату наотмашь подымает.
   Лопату-то! Лопату-то он не зря прихватил... (Solzhenitsyn, *Odin den'*, 45)

Oh, the look on the brigade leader's face! And how hard he threw down his trowel: Take that! Up he stepped to Der. Der looked around—Pavlo was raising his shovel to strike.
   That shovel! It wasn't for nothing that he'd brought it . . .

God, the way the boss's face twitched all over. The way he threw his trowel on the floor and went over to Der. Der looked around. Pavlo was standing there with his shovel up.
He hadn't brought it up with him for nothing . . . (Hayward and Hingley, 115)

Ugh, what a face Tiurin made. He threw down his trowel and took a step toward Der. Der looked around. Pavlo lifted his spade.
He hadn't grabbed it for nothing. (Parker, 99)

Shukhov had never seen the foreman look so ugly. He threw his trowel down with a clatter. Took a step toward Der. Der looked behind him—there was Pavlo, shovel in the air.
Of course! He'd brought it up on purpose. (Willetts, 104)

(*c*) Грузная розовая Купчиха заворочалась, с усилием поднялась, . . . Вяло повизгивали у ног ее сосунки, им, *считай*, уже по месяцу, а каждый не больше рукавицы — вечно зябнущие, серые, жалкие, не растут, *хоть плачь*. Настя сразу заметила — двое не двигаются . . .

(Tendriakov "Podenka," 362; emphasis added)

Kupchikha, the heavy, pink sow, stirred herself and lumbered to her feet . . . The sucklings squealed wanly beneath her; just imagine, a month old already and none any bigger than your mitten— pathetic, gray creatures, constantly shivering, and they just won't grow, no matter what you do.

The pink, corpulent brood sow known as Goldy rolled to her feet with an effort. . . . Her piglets lay about her feet, squealing feebly. They were about a month old, but still no bigger than so many mittens: cold, gray, miserable creatures that would not grow, *however much one tended them*. Now Nastya saw at once that two of them were motionless . . . (Falla, 170) in the third person, but it is unmistakably from her point of view, as the exclamation point shows. The translation not only eliminates the expressive punctuation but appropriates the entire sentence as part of the omniscient narration ("she completely lost her temper").

The elimination of exclamation points may simply be a response to English literary convention, but it often goes hand in hand with a more general neglect of emotive speech. In example 3.1*b* the first two translations assume that it is enough to open with an expletive ("God," and "Ugh") to establish this as Shukhov's point of view. However, Aleksandr Solzhenitsyn has chosen to sustain this effect through punctuation (dashes as well as exclamation points), phonetic spelling (*Ka-ak*), repetitions, and incomplete or colloquial expressions (*I k Deru—shag* 'And up he steps to Der'; *lopatu-to* 'that shovel'). This is not simply a matter of perspective but one of attitude: it is a very dramatic moment, a display of real heroism from Tiurin. H. T. Willetts takes more risks with English syntax, and his last line is especially apt as a way of incorporating the exclamatory punctuation into English prose style ("Of course! . . . "). However, he characteristically explains to the reader more than is necessary ("*Shukhov* had never seen the foreman look *so ugly*") instead of trusting the reader to understand the source of this perspective.

The preceding examples are clear cases of changes in narrative perspective. Sometimes, however, first- (and second-) person interjections may simply seem to be set phrases, and therefore translators overlook them. Such, for example, seems to be the case in the passage from Vladimir Tendriakov's "Podenka—vek korotkii" ("The Mayfly—a Short Life," 1965) in example 3.1*c*. Like much of the story, this passage is told from the heroine's viewpoint. Two signals of her perspective are the phrases *schitai* 'count them' and *xot' plach'* '[lit.] even if you cry' ("no matter what you do"). Both are imperative forms, although as common interjections they have lost some of the force of direct address. Nevertheless, these phrases do contribute to an overall pattern of shifting perspective in Tendriakov's story. Throughout, the narrator seems to be a voice in Nastya's head, speaking to herself, or her own voice pleading her case before those who would condemn her for failing to care properly for her piglets. The translator eliminates the first interjection ("they were about a month old") and reanalyzes the second as an impersonal clause ("however much one tended them"). The result is a more detached, less desperate voice. Another possible translation of the last two sentences is:

There were the sucklings, squealing feebly underneath her; believe it or not, *already a month old, and no bigger than your mitten: always chilled, gray and pitiful, and* no matter what, *they just will not grow.*

Nastya seems to be justifying herself to an unseen interlocutor, or—more likely—to herself. The published translation reads as more a simple statement of fact.

Interjections can represent a contained shift in perspective, in which the sentence as a whole belongs to a more omniscient narrator but that one word or phrase enters as a reminder that this is a character's point of view. Another obvious localized signal of perspective shifts is the use of first or second person. Sometimes such shifts pervade whole sentences or passages in Russian, seeming to challenge the boundaries between consciousnesses within the text. Several scholars have called attention to the passage from Solzhenitsyn's *One Day* in example 3.2a, which T. G. Vinokur calls an example of "a direct collision between indirect and direct speech within the framework of a single sentence . . . or episode" (1965, 18; see also Hosking 1980, 45). Solzhenitsyn's shift here from third to first person is distinctly marked. Vinokur calls it "a case of the highest order of merging of character and author, which allows [Solzhenitsyn] to underscore especially urgently the mutuality of their experience and to recall again and again his own direct involvement in the events he is depicting. The emotional impact of this merging is exceptionally effective: it gives an added sharpness, an extreme starkness to the bitter irony [of this scene]" (1965, 18). Despite these strong effects, the translators have eliminated or reduced the shifts in perspective, choosing instead to use third-person narration throughout (Hayward and Hingley) or to change perspective only after a paragraph break and some intervening dialogue (Parker; the dialogue is omitted in the example). These changes are not motivated by language differences, since English is perfectly capable of producing the same pronouns as Russian. In fact, the English versions are rather more confusing than the Russian: Hayward and Hingley use "these fellows" and "those others" to refer to the same group, and Parker's "across their course" (for the Russian "across our path") is rather ambiguous.

The trend in example 3.2a is not only toward unifying the perspective of each sentence or paragraph but toward the third person in general, perhaps to unify the overall narration still further. This trend is especially visible in 3.2b and c. The Russian versions could all be read as second-person address, either as Nastya speaking to herself or as the narrator warning her. (The narrator does speak directly in a few places in this story, most notably in the concluding paragraph: "Good people, save Nastya!" [430].) The translator changes both passages cited in the example to third person, smoothing over all ambiguities. It is true that English requires some attribution of such terms as *heart, husband, life*, but it is interesting that Paul Falla chooses to eliminate all direct address here, including the use of Nastya's name ("It's them or you, Nastya, stifle your pity"), replacing it with third- person commentary ("It was them or her this time, and pity must go to the wall"). The evidence of these examples demonstrates an unmistakable translation effect, in the direction of a more unified narrating voice.

(a) Как хвост на холм вывалил, так и *Шухов* увидел: справа от *них*, далеко в степи чернелась еще колонна, шла она *нашей* колонне наперекос и, должно быть, увидав, тоже припустила. Могла быть эта колонна только мехзавода. . . .

Дорвалась *наша* колонна до улицы, а мехзаводская позади жилого квартала скрылась. . . . Тут-то *мы* их и обжать должны!

(Solzhenitsyn, *One Day*, 54; emphasis added)

When the end of the line came over the hill, Shukhov *saw what was up: to* their *left, far away on the steppe, another column could be seen; it was heading across the path of* our *column and, most likely, had also speeded up, seeing [us]. It could only be the column from the tool factory. . . .*

Our column had reached the street, but the one from the tool factory had disappeared behind a housing block. . . . This is where we should catch them!

Shukhov could see what it was all about when the column cleared a rise *they'd* been passing. Way over on the plain there was another column heading for the camp, right across *their* path. These fellows must've spotted *them* too and put a spurt on.

This must be the fellows from the tool factory. . . .

Their column was now on one of the streets that led into the camp and *they'd* lost sight of the guys from the tool works behind a housing block on another street. . . . *They* were bound to beat those others to it! (Hayward and Hingley, 142–43)

When the rear of the column spilled over a rise *Shukhov* saw to the right, far away across the steppe, another dark column on the move, marching diagonally across *their* course. They, too, seemed to be forcing their pace.

It must be from the machine works, that column. . . .

Now *our* column had reached the street, while the other had passed out of sight behind the blocks of houses. . . . This was where *we* ought to gain ground. (Parker, 117–18)

(b) Тугая петелка — не вырвешься.

Тугая петелка, сама на себя накинула.

(Tendriakov, "Podenka," 420)

A tight noose—you won't break out of it.

A tight noose—[I/you/she] put it on [my/your/her] own head.

No, the noose was drawn as tight as it could be—and she had tied it round her own neck. (Falla, 239)

(c) Свиней жаль — нянчила, выкармливала. Не изверг же *она*, душа кровью обливается. Но или они, или *ты*, *задави* жалость, Настя. За мужа, за дом родной, за всю жизнь свою, если не *хочешь* потерять, — одна спичка...

(Tendriakov, "Podenka," 427; emphasis added)

Sorry for the pigs, after nursing and feeding them for so long. She is no monster, after all; [her] heart bleeds for them. But it's them or you now, Nastya, so stifle your pity. For husband, home,— for life itself: if you don't want to lose them,—just one match . . .

Of course *she* was sorry for the pigs—*she* had nursed them and brought them up, *she* wasn't a monster, *her* heart bled for them. But it was them or *her* this time, and pity must go to the wall. For the sake of *her* husband, *her* home, *her* whole life—if *she* were not to lose all these, *she* must light that match. (Falla, 247)

Tense Shifts and Narrated Monologue

So far, we have looked at examples of narrated monologue which have corresponding English forms, even if translators do not use them. However, Russian also possesses several syntactic features that English does not share, and that aid greatly in the implementation of this style. English sentences usually must commit to an orientation by stipulating person and tense, but Russian can often omit or disguise these markers. In particular, pronouns—and especially possessive pronouns—can often be omitted, leaving room for ambiguity (*mat'* could refer to "my mother," "his mother," or just "the mother;" *govorili* 'spoke [pl.]' can have *we*, *you*, or *they* as the implied subject). The referent is determined by context, which in the case of narrated monologue is a matter for inference anyway. Russian also allows for a breadth of impersonal constructions not available in English: we can say "It's cold" to mean "I am cold," but not "It's sleepy" or "It has to leave." Again, Russian leaves the referent open for inference from the context ("I am sleepy" or "She is sleepy"). Most important for narrated monologue is Russian's different treatment of relative tenses. Narrated monologue generally uses the tense of indirect speech (direct: He said, "I can't believe it!"; indirect: He said he couldn't believe it; narrated monologue: He couldn't believe it!); Russian does not backshift tenses in indirect speech, and thus the narrated monologue has much greater immediacy ("He can't believe it!" Or, more likely, the impersonal *Ne veritsia* 'It's unbelievable', which could be a direct exclamation in the first person as well).[6]

The Russian tense system in general is extremely fluid, so much so that scholars of the nineteenth century rejected the idea that Russian had any tense at all. The *-l* form for past tense is historically a deverbal adjective or past participle, while some "so-called future verb forms are independent of tense."[7] (That is, they could be used to denote past and present actions as well as future ones.)[8] V. V. Vinogradov writes of a mid-nineteenth-century philologist, "N. P. Nekrasov proved that any Russian verb form was capable of expressing the whole range of tenses. . . . In Professor Nekrasov's opinion, tense was but an abstract, subjective category of the speaker and addressee."[9] Later grammarians did not accept this radical view; they revived the theory of three tenses, "although subjecting it to strong psychologization" (1986, 442). Vinogradov discusses at length uses of the various forms of the verb which do not correspond to the tense they seem to denote, especially the use of future perfective forms to express a time relatively later than a given past action or "the sudden, swift onset in the past of some momentary action."[10] (English verb tenses are not entirely rigid, either. Present tense forms may have future or past time reference [*The plane leaves at eight; John tells me you've been abroad*]. Present progressive forms may signify narration in past or future [*I'm putting on my hat and he says to me . . . ; the orchestra is playing Mozart tonight*]. Past tense forms may signify a relative future tense [*I was meeting him the next day; he was later to regret it*]. But the range of pos-

(*a*) Сроду Настена не помнила, чтоб в сельпо продавали свечи, а тут, как
по заказу, *лежат, горюют.*
(Rasputin, *Zhivi*, 37; emphasis added)

Nastena did not remember ever before seeing candles for sale in the village commissary, but as if by
special order, here they sit, they pine *away. . . .*

Nastyona could not remember a village store ever selling candles, and now here they *were*, made to
order . . . (Bouis, 38)

(*b*) Насте . . . шел шестой год, когда началась война. Она хорошо помнит
— в избу ворвалась мать . . .   (Tendriakov, "Podenka," 356; emphasis added)

Nastya was five years old when the war began. She remembers *well—her mother burst into the cot-*
tage . . .

Nastya had been five years old when the war broke out. She *could still remember* clearly how one
day her mother had rushed into the cottage . . . (Falla, 164)

---

sibilities is far narrower than in Russian [Quirk et al. 1972, 86–90].)

Thus, a Russian narrator may shift into present or future when reflecting the thoughts of a character, but in English the past is usually maintained.
Example 3.3 illustrates this shift. The literal translations given in italics show
how difficult it is in English to avoid shifting into the past tense in these
cases. The shifts to past tense in these translations are automatic—anyone
would do the same. It requires a conscious manipulation of English to produce the present-tense effect. For example, a present-tense variant for 3.3*a*
might be, "and now come these, as if made to order." An alternative would
be to increase the other signals of narrated monologue in the passage to com-
pensate for the loss of this one in Russian. A more colloquial and emotive
version would be: "and now here were these beauties, just sitting there as if
especially for her, pining away." In 33*b*, the translator compensates for the
tense shift within the sentence by replacing the simple imperfective past of
the opening sentence (*shël*) with a past perfect ("had been"), which allows
for a forward shift to preterite ("could remember"). Another option would be
to emphasize Nastya's point of view with an exclamation: "How well she
remembered her mother rushing into the cottage!"

In some instances tense shifts in narration are made even simpler in
Russian by the fact that the verb *to be* has no present tense. Although there
are past and future forms of *to be*, their absence only weakly implies a present tense. Grammatically as well as logically, an equation is essentially time-
less, and thus many Russian descriptive sentences are virtually exempt from
the need to show tense.

The examples in 3.4 illustrate the effect of tenseless expressions in (*a*) И лишь когда Рыбная осталась позади, она попридержала Карьку и опустила вожжи. *Теперь недалеко.*

(Rasputin, *Zhivi*, 37; emphasis added)

And only after Rybnaya was behind her [Nastena] did she stop Karka and release the reins. *Now it was close.* (Bouis, 39)

(*b*) Хлип-чав, хлип-чав, хлип-чав . . .

Это под ногами, а сверху все льет и льет. И так две недели подряд.

У Анания Егоровича болели зубы, и он шел . . . держась рукой за правую щеку.

(Abramov, "Vokrug da okolo," 194)

Slop-chock, slop-chock, slop-chock. . . .
That is from underfoot, while from above it just pours and pours. And it's been that way two weeks straight.
Anany Egorovich had a toothache, and he walked . . . holding his right cheek.

Flip-flap, flip-flap, flip-flap. . . .
That's what it was like underfoot. And from above it *just kept on* pouring down. It had been like that *now* for two weeks running.
Anany Yegorovich had tooth-ache and he was . . . keeping his hand to his right cheek as he went along. (Floyd, 25; emphasis added)

Russian. The comment in 3.4*a*, *Teper' nedaleko* 'Not far now,' has no verb to orient it in time, so the words can belong equally to Nastena and the narrator. "Now it was close" introduces a new element of time: this is the narrator approximating Nastena's viewpoint; the words cannot belong equally to her. There are few other possibilities in English: the elliptical "Not far now" or "Not much farther" sound stranger than the Russian, and inserting a present-tense verb seems stilted. One option might be to make the sentence more colloquial, to highlight its closeness to her thoughts rather than to the narrator's: "It wasn't much farther now." It is also possible to shift the rest of the passage into the past perfect, to show relative tense: "And only after Rybnaia was behind her had she stopped Karka. . . . It wasn't far now."

When the present (or noncommittal) tense is sustained over more than one or two sentences, the distinction between narrated monologue and direct speech becomes less clear. The middle paragraph of 3.4*b*, translated literally into English (italicized version), sounds like the character's direct speech, rather than that of a narrator.[11] In Russian, however, there is every reason to assume it is a third-person narrator throughout, albeit one in close touch with Ananii Egorovich's thoughts. David Floyd makes the third-person narration explicit in English, which is almost essential, but he adds to it several markers of narrated monologue (the deictic "now" and the colloquialism "just kept on," for example), to soften the change. This example, which is but one of many in Russian prose, offers grounds for positing a narrative style that English simply does not possess. The fact that English must shift passages like this into the past emphasizes the quality of *narrated* monologue, whereas in Russian there is very little difference, grammatically speaking, between this and plain monologue.

Examples 3.3 and 3.4 illustrate the difference between Russian and English tenses. But it is wrong to infer an excessive rigidity to the English tense system. As in Russian, tense shifts are acceptable literary devices in English. Peter Rabinowitz points out just such a shift in Richard Wright's *Uncle Tom's Children*, for example, in which third-person, past-tense, standard English narration suddenly changes to a first-person, present-tense, Black-English voice. Rabinowitz goes on to discuss the range of stylistic possibilities that tense shifts offer: "It is not, of course, the case that a shift to the present necessarily indicates a shift from narrator to character. Sometimes it indicates a swing the opposite way, sometimes no shift at all. . . . The most we can say here is that tense shifts may be used in numerous ways, but that their presence alerts the reader to a possible change in source" (1987, 82). In other words, they play much the same role as in Russian, albeit with less frequency and less ease. In his translation of Solzhenitsyn's *One Day*, Willetts demonstrates the possibilities for tense shifts in English:

> The foreman shouted down to somebody. Another truck carrying cinder blocks had just pulled up. Not a sign of one for six months, then they come in droves. Work all out while they're bringing them. There'll be holdups later and you'll never get back into the swing of it. (102)

In this passage the first two sentences are past tense, the third is present, the fourth imperative, and the fifth future. The shifts suggest the thoughts of all present, narrator and characters alike, emphasizing their familiarity with the experience and the never-ending frustration of camp life.[12]

Impersonal Constructions

That the Russian language lends itself particularly well to impersonal expressions is clear even to the beginning student of the language. Vinogradov (1986, 384–85) enumerates eight lexical categories into which impersonal verbs tend to fall: being or becoming; natural phenomena and elemental phenomena; fate; internal physical sensations and physiological changes; sensations or feelings about external phenomena; psychological experiences; tendencies toward a goal; and involuntary actions. From this list it is clear that a great deal of literary drama can take place at an impersonal level. Many recent Soviet writers have taken advantage of the rich variety of such constructions to explore a kind of generalized narration, in which characters merge with their environment. Kathleen Parthé writes that village prose writers have a particular penchant for this style, "to emphasize a sense of accepted powerlessness." She adds, with a tone of despair, "Despite the fact that these constructions play such a central role in Village Prose, there is no natural way to translate them into English, and a whole level of meaning is unavoidably lost. The major difficulty in translating Village Prose is that a multilayered style is necessarily reduced to an almost undifferentiated one" (1986, 586). It is true that English often has no equivalents for particular Russian impersonal constructions, but it may not be necessary to give up entirely on translating this style. In the remainder of this section I will examine closely the stylistic effects of impersonal expressions in several passages and attempt to suggest ways in which English can convey at least some of their force.

Linguistically, the main advantages of Russian over English in the realm of impersonal constructions are that Russian omits personal pronouns in places where they would be required in English, and that it admits a neuter ending on reflexive or even transitive verbs which replaces the personal subject. Also, since the copula is omitted in the present tense, person need not be specified. A good example of the problems this causes is the title of Chekhov's story "Spat' khochetsia" (literally, something like "there is a desire to sleep"). This expression usually has the meaning, "I'm sleepy" or, as in this case, "*She feels sleepy.*" Two translators have dealt with this variously as "Let Me Sleep" and "Sleepy": the former introduces a definite narrative perspective, which does not accord well with the tone of the work, which drifts in and out of Var'ka's dreams, but always in the third person; the latter title retains the impersonal quality, but with a rather odd effect in English, conjuring up one of the seven dwarves, perhaps. To preserve the ambiguity of the original title, one might try an exclamation on the order of "Just Some Sleep!"

In narration, extended or even sporadic use of impersonal sentences can obscure the boundaries between narrator and character almost completely. For example, Rasputin uses this device in *Farewell to Matëra* to evoke an old woman's thoughts as she and her husband prepare to move off the island that has been their home for so long. Two passages from this work are given in example 3.5. The first of these passages is saturated with impersonals: *it fell, when to leave, better to do that.* A particular feature of Russian is the ability to assign a neuter subject to some transitive verbs, as in *pribilo* 'it washed [something] up' to indicate a passive or reflexive meaning with an active verb (in English, "[something] washed up" or "[something] was washed up"). There are other noncommittal constructions as well, such as *it makes no difference.* These are the character's thoughts, and except for the use of past tense the words give no clue as to whether they are also her speech or narrated from outside. The English translation reflects the old woman's thoughts, but by presenting them in the third person it erects a boundary between her and the narrator that is not present in the Russian. A possible solution would be,

(a) Уезжать пало на среду. Никакой, поди, разницы, когда уезжать, но верилось, почему-то, что лучше это сделать в середине недели, чтобы какой-то чудесной судьбой прибило когда-нибудь обратно, к этому же берегу.

(*Proshchanie*, 246–47).

It fell to leave on a Wednesday. [There is] no difference, perhaps, when one leaves, but it was believed, for some reason, that [it is] better to do it in the middle of the week, so that by some wonderful twist of fate [it] would wash [one] back up onto this same shore.

They were leaving on a Wednesday. It made no difference when *they* left, but *she* somehow felt that it was better in the middle of the week, so that by some miracle *they* would be brought back here, to the same shore. (Bouis, 57; emphasis added)

(b) А правда состоит в том, что надо переезжать, надо, хочешь не хочешь, устраивать жизнь там, а не искать, не допытываться, чем жили здесь. Уж если жили не зная, чем жили, зачем знать уезжая, оставляя после себя пустое место? Правда не в том, что чувствовать в работе, в песнях, в благостных слезах . . . — правда в том, чтобы стояли зароды.

(*Proshchanie*, 292)

But the truth is that it is necessary to move, it's necessary, whether you like it or not, to make a life over there, not to seek and try to understand how [we/you/they] lived here. For if [we/you/they] lived without knowing how, what's the point of knowing now, upon going away and leaving an empty space behind? The truth does not lie in what one feels while working, singing, or crying blessed tears . . . the truth lies in having the haystacks up.

And the truth was that *you* had to move, *you* had to willy-nilly start *your* life over there and not seek and try to figure out how *you* had lived here. If *they* had lived without knowing how *they* had lived, then why find out as *they* left, leaving nothing but a blank spot behind *them*? The truth wasn't in what *you* feel in the work, the songs, the thankful tears . . . —the truth was in taking care of the haystacks. (Bouis, 114–15; emphasis added)

Wednesday was leaving day. The timing wasn't that important, most likely, but for some reason midweek seemed the best time to go; that way, the waves of fortune just might wash back up here, onto this shore.

In 3.5*b* Rasputin again omits all personal subjects, except in the second-person expression *khochesh' ne khochesh'* 'like it or not'. There are several instances of the verb form zhili 'we/you/they lived', and noncommittal infinitives, with or without *nado* 'it is necessary.' Presumably because of the second-person phrase in the first sentence (which is, however, more of a set idiom than a real second-person construction), the translator resolves the other ambiguities by putting that whole sentence in the second person and then alternating third- and second-person narration in the subsequent sentences. The result is somewhat odd, but it suggests one way of retaining ambiguity in translating impersonal narration.

NARRATED MONOLOGUE—AN EXTENDED EXAMPLE

The distinction between Russian and English in impersonal constructions is fairly obvious, and commentators usually write it off as an insurmountable problem in translation. Each type of impersonal or noncommittal expression in Russian has a typical English translation, shifted "automatically" into a personal form. For example, infinitives without any complement (*nado pereezzhat', chto chuvstvovat', uezzhat' palo*—see example 3.5) tend to become second- or third-person expressions ("you have to move," "what you feel," "they were leaving"). In isolation, these changes do not seem too important. However, such phenomena rarely appear "in isolation" in prose fiction, and they may in fact be central to an author's style. It is worth looking at an extended example, in which a Russian author uses many of the evasive tactics discussed above to maintain an ambiguous narrative voice.

Example 3.6 is the opening scene in a story about a young collective farm pig breeder, who is torn between two impulses: first, her commitment to her life on the farm, epitomized by her elderly mother and the piglets she raises; and second, her desire for a happy married life. Here we see her common-law husband leaving for the city. We watch through Nastya's eyes as her life falls apart.

Nowhere in this passage does Tendriakov name the heroine or even refer to her with a pronoun. The sole grammatical reference to Nastya lies in a feminine singular ending on the verb *stoiala* '[she] stood' (translated by Falla as "She looked round her"). The effect of Tendriakov's omission of references to Nastya is to establish her as the passive center of the story, to show from the beginning just how completely she is trapped in the village. The other characters act, and they oppose her (even the mother *vstala naprotiv* 'stood up opposite [her]'). Not only does Nastya not act (the one verb that refers to her is the stative *stoiala*), she has no independent existence at all, except as a receptor. In Russian, the reference to "husband" and Keshka's speech leave no doubt that there is a woman in the scene whose perspective the narration reflects. There is, however, linguistic ambiguity as to whether this is first-person or third-person narration, since *muzh* 'husband', *mat'* 'mother', *slëzy* 'tears', *detstvo* 'childhood', etc., could all equally imply the modifier "her" or "my," and even *stoiala* could have a first-person feminine subject.[13]

In contrast, the translation refers directly to Nastya no fewer than eleven times (given in italics here). The heroine's name is introduced at the earliest possible moment (word two), and, what is more, she appears as the subject of five dynamic verbs (*she had shouted, she had implored, she had*

Ни крик в голос, ни слезы не помогли — Кешка Губин, муж недельный, собрал свой чемодан, влез в полушубок, косо напялил на голову шапку, кивнул на дверь:

— Ну? Не хошь?.. Тогда будь здорова. Сама себя раба бьет. В свином навозе тонуть не хочу, даже с тобою!

И дверь чмокнула, ударило Кешке по валенкам тугим морозным паром, — ушел.

Ни крик в голос, ни мольбы, ни слезы... Стояла посреди неприбранной избы, валялся на лавке клетчатый шерстяной шарф, забытый Кешкой.

С печи, шурша по-мышинному, сползла мать, встала напротив, сломанная пополам, зеленое лицо в сухих бескровных морщинах, в глазах — тоскливая накипь, знакомая с детства.

("Podenka," 356)

Neither shouting nor tears had helped—Keshka Gubin, husband of a week, had packed his bag, put on his coat, stuck his hat tilted on his head, and nodded at the door:

"Well? Not coming? . . . Then good luck to you. The slave is beating herself. I do not wish to drown in pig manure, even with you!"

And the door had smacked, a thick frosty mist had hit his felt boots,—he had gone.

Neither shouting, nor prayers, nor tears . . . She stood in the unkempt cottage, there lay on the shelf a checked wool scarf, forgotten by Keshka.

Down from the stove, rustling like a mouse, climbed mother, stood up opposite, broken in two, a green face with dry, bloodless wrinkles, in the eyes—a sad, bleary expression, familiar since childhood.

All *Nastya's* screaming, all *her* tears were of no avail. Keshka Gubin, *her* common-law husband, had already packed his bag; he now threw on a sheepskin coat, jammed his cap on sideways and said with a nod at the door:

"Well, if you won't come it's your own look-out—goodbye and good luck to you. I'm not going to spend the rest of my life wallowing in pig shit, even with you!"

The door clicked open, Keshka's leggings were enveloped in frosty vapour, and in a moment he had disappeared.

She had shouted at the top of *her* voice, *she* had implored him and finally *she* had burst out crying. Now *she* looked round *her* at the untidy room—a woolen scarf with a check pattern lay on a bench where Keshka had forgotten it.

With a rustle like the scurrying of mice, *Nastya's* mother climbed down from the stove on which she had been lying. She stood, bent in two, her sallow face seamed with dry wrinkles. Her eyes had the sad, bleary expression that *Nastya* remembered from childhood. (Falla, 161; emphasis added)

burst out crying, she looked round her, she remembered). In some cases Falla's decision to refer to Nastya directly is almost mandated by the difference between English and Russian possessive pronouns. In such cases, the translator into English automatically inserts a modifier for the implied referent: *her husband, her tears, her voice.* Linguistically, however, the issue of implied reference in this passage is quite complex, because the referent has never been mentioned. Since there is evidently some woman at the center of this scene, *muzh* is assumed to refer to *her* husband, *slëzy* to *her* tears, and *mat'* to *her* mother, but the way we know there is a woman present is precisely because there is a husband. And we don't even know *that* when the voice and tears are mentioned: they are essentially disembodied, on the one hand, and on the other, they are our first indication that there is *anyone* present at all. They refer forward, they cause us to start looking for someone to whom they might belong; the first person who appears is Keshka, the husband, and it takes some sophisticated (though unconscious for most readers) semantic deduction to figure out that the tears are not his. A similar dislocation occurs in the last sentence, about Nastya's mother. Since the old woman is clearly the center of focus in this sentence, the sallow face and bleary eyes are understood to be hers, but the final clause (literally: *familiar since childhood*) switches the implied referent back to (the still-unnamed) Nastya, for it refers to *her* childhood, not the mother's. The translator's automatic insertion of possessives does away, therefore, with all sorts of underlying tensions and confusions. It is the type of license that all translators must use sometimes, but one should differentiate between cases in which the original *lack* of a modifier is wholly unmotivated and cases, such as this, where a pattern is being established. In this passage, the result of Falla's overuse of this license is to turn an extensive structure of implied reference, with all the mystery and tension that entails, into a piece of straightforward narration, leaving nothing unsaid.

Indeed, the insertion of references to Nastya appears to be a symptom of a general desire on Falla's part to make the narration flow more smoothly than it does in the Russian. The narration in the original lacks elegance; it is choppy and filled with logical ellipsis, of which omission of possessive pronouns is but one example. The heroine is unconfident, anguished, frustrated, and the syntax reflects her state of mind. The Russian paragraphs are liberally punctuated with dashes, each implying a different type of connection between the two phrases it separates. ("—Keshka Gubin" means, roughly, "*all the same*, Keshka Gubin [left]"; "—ushel" means "*in short*, he left"; "v glazakh—tosklivaia nakip'" means "in the eyes *there was* a sorrowful expression.") There is an incomplete sentence in the fourth paragraph ("Not shouts, not prayers, not tears . . .") echoing the opening line. The subsequent sentence in the fourth paragraph is made up of two independent clauses, separated only by a comma, whose logical link is at best awkward. (Literally, it reads: "[She] was standing in the middle of the untidy hut, lying on a shelf was a checked wool scarf, forgotten by Keshka.") This draws a telling grammatical parallel between Nastya and the cast-off scarf, because both clauses open with similar verbs (past tense, imperfective, stative: *[she] was standing, [it] was lying*). The description of the mother is similarly awkward and impressionistic, since it is composed of an almost randomly arranged string of clauses, mostly independent, one broken, and with one dependent clause ("bent double") referring back two clauses earlier to "mother."

Although all these devices are common in Russian prose, they add up here to a strongly marked narrational style, representing the confused impressions of Nastya's own mind. None of the awkwardness of the passage is captured in the smooth translation, which does away with the dashes, clarifies and expands upon the sequence of tenses, and splits the final sentence into several more logical ones. The only markers of narrated monologue are very weak: the use of *now* and perhaps the dash in the fourth paragraph. My own translation, below, attempts to restore some of the ambiguities by making no reference to the heroine and by maintaining the odd sentence structures. In the last paragraph it was necessary to add possessives to refer to the mother (*her face, her eyes*), but *familiar* represents Nastya's unmediated viewpoint.

> *Nothing helped—not shouts, not tears. Keshka Gubin, husband of a week, packed his bag, slipped on his coat, shoved his cap on sideways, and nodded at the door:*
>
> *"Well? Sure you're not coming? Then good luck to you. Let the slave beat herself. I'm not about to drown in pig shit, not even with you!"*
>
> *And the door smacked, a thick frosty mist hit Keshka's felt boots—he was gone.*
>
> *Nothing—not shouts, not pleas, not tears.... And now there's just the mess in the hut all around, over there Keshka's checkered scarf lies forgotten, draped on a shelf.*
>
> *Down climbed mother from her bed on the Russian stove, rustling like a mouse, and stood opposite, bent double; dry, bloodless wrinkles covered her sallow face, and her eyes—her eyes had that old, familiar, sorrowful expression.*

NARRATED MONOLOGUE AS CULTURAL CATEGORY

Rabinowitz discusses the question of how readers determine just "who is speaking" at some length, pointing out the literary value of ambiguity on this score, and the importance of a cultural predisposition to it: "Indeed, even those authors, like Flaubert, who aim to muddle our thinking on this score can do so only because they assume we have certain procedures at hand that *can* be confused" (1987, 79). It is significant, however, that he chooses Flaubert, and not an English author, as his example. In fact, most of the examples he gives of narrative ambiguity are from Russian writers—Dostoevsky, Anton Chekhov, and Vladimir Nabokov—although he cites the passages in English. This forces us to ask whether Russian literature is not simply more hospitable to narrated monologue than English literature, language differences aside. Or, perhaps more to the point, whether the language differences are symptomatic of a broader cultural difference. Voloshinov's argument about the interdependence of syntactic structures and "stable social tendencies in the active reception of another's speech" (1929, 115) is relevant here. Societies, he claims, choose how to grammaticalize such devices as narrated monologue, selecting types of interaction and dramatic moments that are particularly significant to each society. Russian culture was based until relatively recently on oral traditions, which, on the one hand, allow for many voices without needing special grammatical features to distinguish them (different speakers, or different accents or intonations, will suffice), and which, on the other hand, condition the audience to accept a high degree of fluidity in the speaker's identity, to allow the storyteller to merge with many characters and speak with many voices in rapid succession.[14]

Pascal (1977, 26–27) claims that free indirect style depends upon a "bridge" (such as the use of past tense for narrated monologue) that emphasizes the presence of a controlling consciousness. This claim appears, in the translation context, to be especially anglocentric (even though he discusses Russian literature as well). He writes that "instead of experiencing the *style indirect libre* statement . . . as something qualitatively different from other forms of discourse, we normally experience it within a broader consciousness that implies distance between characters and the narrator (and reader)." He comments on the Magarshack translation of *The Idiot*, which backshifts narrated monologue from the present tense to the past, as in, "He had been friends with Rogozhin for a long time . . . —but did he know Rogozhin?" Pascal admits that Dostoevsky's use of the present tense ("but *does* he know Rogozhin?") enhances the reader's direct experience of what is going through Myshkin's mind. Nevertheless, he states, "Mr. Magarshack was quite right to turn them into the past tense, and thus to affirm clearly the nature of the passage as free indirect style" (130). Does this not imply, however, that the very "nature of free indirect style" is different in the two languages? After all, Dostoevsky does not seem to feel the need to "affirm clearly" the distance between narrator and character or the presence of a "broader consciousness." Pascal's analysis appears more normative than descriptive, and it creates a self-perpetuating circle: the style depends on distance, so distance must be created, even in translation.

Ann Banfield, in her influential book, *Unspeakable Sentences*, is even more dogmatic about the limited possibilities open to the writer of English: "[If] the represented E[xpression], unlike indirect but like direct speech, may introduce a new reference point for the present and future deictic adverbs, it may not, unlike direct speech, introduce a new reference point for the present tense. Indeed, except for the generic present, the represented E does not normally allow the present tense at all" (1982, 98). Thus the translator must decide whether to violate English usage and insist upon maintaining the immediacy of the Russian tense shifts, for example, or to fit the narration into standard English literary practice. One hesitates to introduce yet another term into the existing plethora, but something on the order of "narrated present" might capture the coexistence of a narrator and a character within an unattributed monologue in Russian. I believe that translators should at least explore alternatives that preserve some ambiguity of tense, and therefore of perspective, without discarding all the rules of English usage.

Willetts offers good examples of the possibilities in English for producing impersonal narration and ambiguous tense, and thus a more "Russian" type of narrated monologue, in his translation of *One Day*:

> Shukhov always got up at once. Not today, though. Hadn't felt right since the night before—had the shivers, and some sort of ache. And hadn't gotten really warm all night. In his sleep he kept fancying he was seriously ill, then feeling a bit better. Kept hoping morning would never come.
>
> But it arrived on time.
>
> Some hope of getting warm with a thick scab of ice on the windows, and white cobwebs of hoarfrost where the walls of the huge hut met the ceiling. (4)

After naming Shukhov in the initial sentence, the translator shifts to subjectless syntax: *Hadn't felt right, Kept hoping*. The effect is to go beyond a simple report of his viewpoint to more of an approximation of Shukhov's own internal voice (it is, after all, ambiguous whether the missing subject is *he* or *I*). In the last paragraph Willetts omits the main verb altogether, allowing him to avoid tense and person shifters and, again, to leave open the possibility that these are Shukhov's own words. Other English translations have "he" in every sentence in the first paragraph of this passage, and some indication of tense in the third: "Anyway, where *would* you get warm . . . " (Parker 18), and "Anyway, how *could* anyone get warm . . . " (Hayward-Hingley, 3).

Willetts also allows the narrative to shift explicitly into the present tense from time to time, when other translators maintain the English convention of past tense narrated monologue:

> Light work for the unfit, they call it, but just try getting the [slop bucket] out without spilling it! (Willetts, 5).

> A light job, that *was* considered, a job for the infirm, but just you try and carry out the muck without spilling any (Parker, 19).

> This *was* supposed to be light work for people on the sick list—but it *was* no joke carrying the thing out without spilling it! (Hayward-Hingley, 3).

English syntax may be more restrictive than Russian with respect to impersonal constructions and ambiguities of tense and person, but it often offers more latitude than translators, until recently, have been willing to take. It appears that the most important restriction has been not English grammar but English literary convention.

Historically, according to Voloshinov, Russian culture has been shaped by strong mystical influences; it places less emphasis on a rational, single perspective than does English or American mainstream culture. This peculiarity comes out especially vividly in recent Soviet literature, imparting both emotional power and naïveté. Rasputin virtually embodies the quasi-direct narrator of *Farewell to Matëra* in a mysterious, mystical animal, "a creature unlike any other. . . . No one ever saw it or met it, but it knew everyone and everything that happened from end to end and side to side of this isolated piece of land. . . . That was why it was Master: to see everything, know everything, and disturb nothing" (1978, 241–42; my translation). Formless and mobile, it goes in and out of the villagers' thoughts and expresses the island's own perspective, just as the narrative voice does. The fact that the reader cannot always tell "we" from "they" (or even from "you") does not signify mere linguistic ambiguity; it reflects the central themes of interconnectedness and collective consciousness.

Not surprisingly, when one looks for equivalent stylistic features in English literature, one finds them more often in regional literature and the literature of ethnic minorities (Richard Wright is Rabinowitz's main example; I would add other black American fiction [Toni Morrison, for example], Louise Erdrich's novels about American Indians, and André Brink's psychological explorations of South African life). This style is, perhaps, symptomatic of what Dale Peterson means by the "literature of the soul" that is common to Russians and African-Americans, "a culturally-constructed, dialogically shaped experiment in scripting what the world of literacy has yet to comprehend" (1992, 753). Among the more canonical English writers, especially the Victorians, the device is used mainly for irony. Otherwise, it is considered substandard, as becomes clear in the subtext of Banfield's book, *Unspeakable Sentences*. She analyzes many expressions of "free indirect style" in English, trying to establish a grammar of this style. Often she suggests a range of expressions, all variants of a literary text but with altered word order, tense, or person, in an effort to determine the boundaries of acceptability. However, her judgments are based upon a very restricted view of what is acceptable in English literature, thereby defeating the purpose of understanding the *literary* qualities of the device. Many times the expressions she dismisses as unacceptable are precisely the ones that would make good translations of Russian narrated monologue. For example, Banfield disallows exclamations from the subordinate clause of indirect speech. Thus, she claims, English permits the utterance,

"Yes, this is love," Constance sighed.

But not

Constance sighed that yes, that was love. (31)

It is true that the second instance violates certain rules of English grammar, but it is well within the purview of literary license to violate some of those rules. In fact, there are examples in English-language literary works of this very construction:

> Momma told him she imagined it had been a glorious affair, simply glorious, and she said Grandaddy Yount thought for a minute *and then responded that no, it had not been glorious exactly* but had seemed to him very much like musical wrestling. (Pearson 1985, 34–35; emphasis added)

The result is highly conversational and somewhat stylized, but no less "literary" for that.

The prevalent assumption that a work should fill the same niche in the target system (i.e., fit as well into the canon) as it does in the original system is, I believe, damaging precisely to such relative and communicative features as narrative voice. If we persist in believing that a reader should not be able to tell that she is reading a translation, then we devalue the translator's art and remove one of the main reasons to produce or read translations in the first place: the chance to glimpse another culture. When translators discuss the hardships they face, they often mention the difficulties of conveying cultural specifics (traditional clothing, for example, or forms of address) while not making the work sound too foreign in English. Perhaps it would be more fruitful to see the translated work as a challenge to canonical English literature, much like ethnic and regional works. Stylistic methods, such as *skaz* and narrated monologue, may, after all, be just as culturally significant as *borshch*, and therefore just as worthy of a certain degree of departure from "normal" English.

TRANSLATING THE "PENETRATED WORD"

Voices can intertwine in a narrative in many ways, in addition to narrated monologue. Bakhtin described Ivan Turgenev's prose as containing "character zones," in which speech peculiarities of a particular character would invade the narrator's diction when that character was central to a scene (see example 1.1). Bakhtin is also one of many who have observed a remarkable fluidity of voice in Dostoevsky's works, where words often take on a life of their own, reappearing significantly in the speech of various characters and in the narrator's discourse. Robin Feuer Miller (1981) sees the narrator of *The Idiot* as having many faces: observer, chronicler, cynic, unreliable witness, omniscient guide, and constant mirror of the inner thoughts of the characters. For Vinogradov (1976), this chameleon-like quality of Dostoevsky's prose allows him to express (in *The Double*) the viewpoint of a "poor person" from the inside rather than from above. For Bakhtin (1963), Dostoevsky's language gives equal weight to all viewpoints and allows him to create an entirely new type of novel.

All these scholars cite as examples repetitions of words or phrases in the discourse of various characters or the narrator. For the translator, this device should be relatively easy to reproduce. The evidence, however, shows otherwise. Translators seem to go out of their way to erase repetitions, as if they were unable to accept the equal weighting of different voices in the text. Vinogradov (1976, 128) notes that, in *The Double*, characteristic expressions from Golyadkin's vocabulary enter the narrator's voice, so that Golyadkin seems to speak from behind the narrator. As example 3.7 shows, this effect is not always retained in translation.

Vinogradov cites the passage in 3.7*a* to illustrate his assertion that "in 'indirect' speech Golyadkin's style remains unchanged, thereby becoming the author's responsibility" (1976, 128). Golyadkin's words permeate the narrative, resurfacing again and again. Garnett's translation of this passage produces the opposite effect, for here the quotation marks *separate* features of Golyadkin's vocabulary from those of the narrator.[15] For Garnett, the glance speaks in Golyadkin's words (many of which reappear two paragraphs later in his reported speech to the doctor, this time without quotation marks in English). For Vinogradov, the *narrator* speaks in Golyadkin's words, which is a very different matter. What is more, the grammar is normalized in the English version, neutralizing the evidence of Golyadkin's confused thought processes which the fragmentary Russian represents. Even the interruption *vo vsiakom sluchae* 'in any case' disappears in the English, making the sentence smoother and less personalized.

Example 3.7*b*, from later in the story, demonstrates how whole descriptive passages become set expressions describing Golyadkin's state of mind or the image he tries to project. The narrator again describes an air his hero assumes, using virtually identical words as in (*a*). Oddly, Garnett translates them differently this time: his appearance expresses *iasno* "plainly" in (*a*), "clearly" in (*b*) that he is *sam po sebe* "quite himself" in (*a*), "kept himself to himself" in (*b*) (the latter being the more accurate rendition of the meaning). Example (*c*) provides further evidence of the interpenetration of characters' and narrator's discourse in the original text, and of its loss in translation. Here a phrase that is later to appear in Klara Olsufievna's speech turns up first in the narration. The translator changes "worthlessness" to "immorality" and also alters the parts of speech (*notoriously, notorious*), so that the two phrases scarcely seem related in English.

A more dramatic illustration of phrases that take on lives of their own is seen in *The Brothers Karamazov* and discussed by Bakhtin in *Problems of Dostoevsky's Poetics*. Alesha Karamazov's speech often contains the revealed word, as in the chapter entitled "Not You! Not You!" (bk. 11, chap. 5; 14:40). Here Alesha assures Ivan that he does not believe that either Dmitry or Ivan killed their father, and that God has given him that message. For two pages he incants, *ne ty* 'not you' (nine times, plus the two in the title) and *ne on* 'not he' (three times), and Ivan repeats *ne ia* 'not I'. Whether Alesha is trying to (*a*) [Этот] взгляд вполне выражал независимость господина Голядкина, то есть говорил ясно, что господин Голядкин совсем ничего, что он сам по себе, как и все, и что его изба во всяком случае, с краю.

(*Dvoinik*, 115)

This glance entirely expressed Mr. Golyadkin's independence, that is, it said plainly that Mr. Golyadkin is perfectly all right, that he [is] on his own, like everyone else, and that he, in any case, minds his own business.

This glance, moreover, expressed to the full Mr. Golyadkin's independence—that is, to speak plainly, the fact that Mr. Golyadkin was "all right," that he was "quite himself, like everybody else," and that there was "nothing wrong in his upper storey." (Garnett, 483)

(*b*) Господин Голядкин тотчас, по всегдашнему обыкновению своему, поспешил принять вид совершенно особенный, — вид, ясно выражавший, что он, Голядкин, сам по себе, что он ничего, что дорога для всех довольно широкая, и что ведь он, Голядкин, никого не затрогивает...

(140)

Mr. Golyadkin immediately, as was his invariable custom, hastened to assume a most peculiar aspect, an aspect that expressed clearly that he, Golyadkin, [is] on his own, that he is all right, that the road is wide enough for all, and that after all he, Golyadkin, is not bothering anyone.

Mr. Golyadkin, as he invariably did, hastened to assume a quite peculiar air, an air that expressed clearly that he, Golyadkin, kept himself to himself, that he was "all right," that the road was wide enough for all, and that he, Golyadkin, was not interfering with anyone. (Garnett, 512)

(*c*) Narrator: «известный своею бесполезностью г. Голядкин-младший».
(204)

"Mr. Golyadkin the younger, known for his worthlessness."

"the notoriously worthless Mr. Golyadkin." (Garnett, 586)

Klara Olsufievna: «известный бесполезностью своего направления человек».
(207)

"a man known for the worthlessness of his tendencies."

"the slanderer . . . notorious for the immorality of his tendencies." (Garnett, 589)

---

convince himself or producing a mantra for his brother's troubled mind, the repetition is striking in the Russian. Curiously, most translators avoid reproducing it. Constance Garnett (570) and David Magarshack (706) have virtually identical versions of this exclamation by Alesha:

"But you didn't do it: you are mistaken: you are not the murderer. Do you hear? It was not you!"[16]

Presumably following English literary etiquette, they introduce syntactic and lexical variety in place of the repetitions.[17] The more recent versions seem less bound to stylistic scruples:

"But it was not you who killed him, you are mistaken, the murderer was not you, do you hear, it was not you!" (Pevear and Volokhonsky, 601–2)

"But it was not you who did it, you are wrong, the murderer is not you, do you hear, not you!" (McDuff, 693)

To compound the loss in the earlier translations, Ivan's rejoinder becomes "I know I didn't" (Garnett) and "I know myself it wasn't I" (Magarshack), instead of the more effective, if less grammatical, "I know very well it was not me" (Richard Pevear and Larissa Volokhonsky). (David McDuff's version is weaker: "I know that it was not.") Thus the older translations blunt the power of the passage, which crescendoes to Alesha's crucial, emphatic statement, "I give you this phrase for your whole life: *not you!*" Bakhtin cites from this chapter at length, calling it a "highly typical example of the penetrat[ed] word and its artistic role in dialogue. . . . Ivan's own secret words on someone else's lips evoke in him hatred and repulsion toward Alesha, and precisely because they have touched a sore spot they are indeed an answer to his question" (1984, 255).[18] (Unfortunately, the English translation of Bakhtin's book makes use of Garnett's version of the passage, and the force of the "penetrated word" is nearly lost.)

Crime and Punishment has a succinct, chilling example of the "penetrated word" and the way voices from dialogue merge and echo in Dostoevsky's narration (example 3.8). This is the fateful scene between Svidrigailov and Dunia Raskolnikova, in which she holds him at gunpoint to prevent him from raping her. He gives her several opportunities to shoot as he slowly approaches, and the tension builds as we all wait for her to reload after misfiring.

So many voices swarm in this passage that it is difficult to say who is talking and who is listening. The inner quotation in the first paragraph could belong to Dunia, or to Svidrigailov, or even to the reader. Because it echoes the phrase from the narration, *at two paces*, it suggests telepathy between narrator and characters. This impression reaches eerie proportions in the subsequent paragraphs, in which Svidrigailov's *brosila* 'she threw it away, gave it up' echoes the narrator's *otbrosila* 'she threw it aside'. Is Svidrigailov listening in on the narrator? Is he listening in on our thoughts? This is the moment at which the good character and the evil character peer into each other's souls and are caught up short. The reader, meanwhile, is so voyeuris-

Он стоял перед нею в двух шагах, ждал и смотрел на нее дикою решимостью, воспаленно-страстным, тяжелым взглядом. Дуня поняла, что он скорее умрет, чем отпустит ее. «И... и уж, конечно, она убъет его теперь, в двух шагах!»

Вдруг она отбросила револьвер.

— Бросила! — с удивлением проговорил Свидригайлов и глубоко перевел дух.

(Dostoevsky, *Prestuplenie i nakazanie*, bk. 6, chap. 5; 382)

He stood before her, at two paces, waiting and watching . . . Dunya understood that he would sooner die than let her go. "And...and of course she would kill him now, at two paces!"
Suddenly she threw the revolver away from her.
"Threw it away!" muttered Svidrigailov in amazement, taking a deep breath.

---

tically engaged in the story that she does not know herself what outcome to desire or where good and evil lie.

Most of the translations do not retain these internal echoes. Some simply substitute synonymous constructions, presumably to avoid repetitions and keep attention away from "the materiality of the signifier." Pevear and Volokhonsky have "two steps away" and then "from two paces" (496), and several other translators introduce similar variations. Garnett repeats "two paces" but entirely elides the other repetition:" Suddenly she flung away the revolver" and "'She's dropped it!'" (447). Jessie Coulson and McDuff go so far as to use entirely different meanings of *brosila*:

Suddenly she flung down the revolver.
"She has given up!" (Coulson, 477)

Suddenly she flung the revolver aside.
"She's given up the idea!" (McDuff, 571)

Pevear and Volokhonsky alter only the adverb, as is warranted by the difference between *otbrosila* and *brosila*. But their choice in the second instance of "threw it down" exaggerates the difference between the two:

Suddenly she threw the revolver aside.
"She threw it down!" (Pevear and Volokhonsky, 496)

Magarshack also comes close to retaining the echo, but he unaccountably alters the tense:

Suddenly she threw away the gun.
"Thrown it away!" (Magarshack, 508)

It is as if even those who are attentive to inner voices in the text find this instance of it too unsettling to reproduce. This becomes most clear in another version, by Sidney Monas, which preserves all the word repetitions, but only at a distance:

> All of a sudden she threw away the revolver.
> Svidrigailov said in surprise, "She threw it away!" (Monas, 478)

By shifting the narrative statement ("Svidrigailov said in surprise") so that it comes between the repeated phrases, Monas takes away their shock value and restores some sense of detachment to the narrator's role. In all cases, the translators have imposed a distance between the voices in this passage, keeping good and evil well apart from one another and the narrator above it all. Dostoevsky's text, it seems, produces a somatic response in its reader-translators that is so frightful that they cannot or will not pass it on.

Nils Erik Enkvist (1978, 182) describes such narrative devices as *erlebte Rede* and skaz as strategies for embedding one text in another (i.e., the narrator's text in the author's, or the character's text in the narrator's). Bakhtin goes a step further and speaks of skaz narration as a kind of "'nondirect speaking'—not *in* language but *through* language" (1981, 313). It seems to be a property of traditional translation to assert, even introduce, clear hierarchies among the voices in a text. The evidence of this chapter suggests that the translator is unwilling to take responsibility for the words of unreliable characters or unstable narrators (recall Vinogradov's comment that Golyadkin's words become "the author's responsibility" when they appear within the narration). My favorite example of this phenomenon is from an anonymous English translation of Victor Hugo's *Nôtre Dame de Paris*. The narrator is describing a brutal form of crowd control in fifteenth-century Paris, in which a stream of people joining the Feast of Fools parade is thrown into chaos.[19]

> C'ètait une bourrade d'un archer ou le cheval d'un sergent de la prévoté qui ruait pour rétablir l'ordre; admirable tradition que la prévoté a léguée à la connétablie, la connétablie à la maréchaussée, et la maréchaussée à nôtre gendarmerie de Paris. (13–14)

> This was occasioned by the thrust of some archer, or the horse of some one of the provost's sergeants prancing about to restore order—"which admirable expedient," observes our author, "the *prévoté* handed down to the *connétablie*, the *connétablie* to the *maréchaussée*, and the *maréchaussée* to our gendarmerie of Paris." (Everyman, 10)

Here and elsewhere in the work, the translator explicitly identifies "our author" with ironic language, encased in quotation marks for good measure.

Not being "*the* speaker," the translator is uncomfortable with simply stating the value judgments or repeating the narrational flourishes of the original in his or her own voice. To put it differently, the translator is claiming an independent voice (rather than analyzing and mimicking that of the author) and must, therefore, delineate the implied author's own intrusions. As a result, a new level of embedding is introduced, with the translator asserting a presence and a relationship to the author that are independent of the French text. (This is especially jarring in light of the fact that nowhere in the edition is the translator named, nor is there even any mention that it *is* a translation. A new voice seems to come out of the blue and enter the inner workings of the text.)

While this example exceeds the bounds of what we customarily call a "translation," it serves the purpose of bringing into the open a practice that may be hidden in more conventionally acceptable translations. At the very least, this translator/adaptor recognizes those places where the narrative voice is important in the work and admits his or her own helplessness to reproduce it. Often more unobtrusive translators will simply gloss over or eliminate these nuances, leaving the reader none the wiser. (The Modern Library translation, also unattributed, is as follows: "It was a dash made by an archer, or the horse of one of the provost's sergeants kicking and plunging to restore order—an admirable maneuver which the provosty bequeathed to the constabulary, the constabulary to the maréchaussée, and the maréchaussée to the present gendarmerie of Paris."[20] Note that this translator, while allowing the narrator's ironic "admirable" to stand on its own, has replaced the personal possessive *nôtre* with a pale time deictic, "the *present* gendarmerie of Paris.") In Bakhtinian terms, the first translator may be seen as exaggerating the multiplicity of voices in Hugo's novel, whereas the more traditional translator falls into the trap in which Bakhtin finds Dostoevsky critics, that of replacing "the interaction of several unmerged consciousnesses" with "an interrelationship of ideas, thoughts, and attitudes gravitating toward a single consciousness" (1984, 9).[21]

The evidence suggests that translators traditionally engage in rivalries not only with editors and authors but with the voices in the text, particularly with the voice of the narrator. They step in to impose standards of language propriety and even of moral propriety (keeping good and evil separate, as in the Dunia-Svidrigailov scene, or separating "truth" from "commentary," as in *Notre Dame*) upon the echoing refrains of the text. What we see in these instances is not reducible to questions of practicality, or of hegemony, or of subversive discourse. The translators are subtly altering all the power relations in and around the text—between character and narrator as well as between author and text or text and reader. Such a dynamic is not as significant, perhaps, in a work that maintains a single viewpoint throughout. Those works, however, that depend upon constant changes in perspective are vulnerable to the translator's insecurities. This is where recent translation theory can be of particular use. Ever since Walter Benjamin called for strict syntactic fidelity at the expense of intelligibility, the translator has, in theory, been free of responsibility for making the text meaningful or clear. More recently, Douglas Robinson has called for recognition of the translator as an emotional actor in the drama of translation. Robinson emphasizes our somatic response to language, the way a translator feels what solution works and what does not. The examples cited here, coupled with recent trends in narrative theory, suggest an expansion of this claim to include not just a somatic response to language but an emotional involvement with the voices in the text. The translator's authority has long been assumed to derive from a command of languages and an understanding of the original text and its culture. But authority is not so much asserted by the translator as given by the reader. It is in respecting the reader's ability to assume control of the text, to find its voices, to enter its blank spaces as well as its saturated ones, that the translator gains true authority.

POSTSCRIPT: THINGS LEFT UNSAID

The next chapter turns to some of the physically blank spaces in literary texts to observe their significance for the author-translator-narrator-reader axis. By way of transition, I offer an example (3.9) from a text in first-person narration. On the evidence of this passage, it seems that translators vary widely in their willingness to trust the narrator to communicate with the reader.

Dostoevsky's underground man reaches his most abject moment in this final scene with Liza. As a final parting insult, he "pays" her five rubles. The reader of the Russian original, left in the dark about what he has put in her hand, wonders if he has not perhaps redeemed himself. When on the next page the hero finds and identifies the "crumpled five-ruble note," it seems the ultimate degradation. It also represents a significant descent for the narrator: for once this man who has reveled in describing his baseness is unable to write the word for his worst sin, and that very fact seems to offer some redemption. Thus, when subsequently he does refer to the money it is in every way his lowest moment. Yet all these gradations of sin are lost in the earlier translations by Garnett and Ralph Matlaw (which in these passages differ only in punctuation). They blithely tell us he has put "money" in her hand well before he finds the banknote on his table and, in the Russian, admits the deed. These translators, it seems, do not trust their readers to interpret the ellipses, nor do they wish them to live in suspense for another page. Somewhat less condescending, but still wary of the reader's abilities, is the recent translation for the Norton Critical Edition, by Michael R. Katz. His version identifies the unstated item as "something" and shifts the ellipses so that they suggest a pause in the narration rather than an unspoken word. Jane Kentish avoids such condescension in her new translation of the work. By coupling her version to an introduction (by Malcolm Jones) that pays

(For these examples, closed-up ellipses are used in the English translations as well to indicate ellipses in the original.)

Я вдруг подбежал к ней, схватил ее руку, разжал ее, вложил... и потом опять зажал. . . .

Но я не хочу лгать и потому говорю прямо, что я разжал ей руку и положил в нее...

(176)

I suddenly ran over to her, grabbed her hand, pried it open, and stuck in...and then closed it up again.

But I do not wish to lie and therefore say straight out that I pried open her hand and put in...out of malice.

I ran up to her, seized her hand, opened it, thrust something in it and closed it again. . . .
But I don't want to lie, and so I will say straight out that I opened her hand and put the money in it. . . from spite. (Garnett, 137; Matlaw, 112)

Suddenly I ran up to her, grabbed her hand, opened it, put something in...and closed it again. . . .
But I don't want to lie; therefore I'll say straight out, that I opened her hand and placed something in it. . . out of spite. (Katz, 86)

I suddenly rushed up to her, grabbed her hand, unfolded it, put in...and then closed it again. . . .
But I do not want to lie so I'll tell you straight out that I unclasped her hand and placed in it...out of malice. (Kentish, 120)

homage to the subtleties of Dostoevsky's narrative voice, as well as to its importance in literary theory, Kentish (like Pevear and Volokhonsky, who treat this passage similarly in their 1993 version of this work)[22] raises her expectations of the reader to a level more in keeping with the ironic undercurrents of the tale.

Chapter Four

Translating the Written Text: Reanalyzing Form and Structure

> No iron can stab the heart with such force as a period put just at the right place.
>
> —Isaac Babel, "Guy de Maupassant"

MUCH OF THE DISCUSSION in the last two chapters has made use of aural metaphors in describing aspects of the text for which the translator must account. "Voice," "rhythm," "intonation," "polyphony," all imply that we *hear* the text and attempt to reproduce its *sounds* in translation. There is a danger in allowing this metaphor to take over our analysis, however, because we are considering the translation of written, not oral works, and the differences are profound. Maria Tymoszko (1991) describes translation in an oral culture as an approximate affair, a process of recasting a narrative to fit prevailing mores, with little regard for such notions as faithfulness or precision. Moreover, there is increasing agreement that certain elements of written texts, most notably punctuation, are fundamentally written devices with no analogues in oral speech. Some writers are particularly creative at manipulating the written language to produce effects that are simply not available orally, or that violate our ideas about how speech should "sound." Thus it is useful to attempt to account for the significance of form in written prose and its importance to the translator.

FORM AND MEANING

When you ask translators what they do with punctuation, you generally receive two answers. On the one hand, they say, different languages have different rules for punctuation, and in changing from one lexicon to another the translator must also change the syntax. On the other hand, punctuation is largely an intuitive matter, a translator must have a "feel" for it and must follow his or her instincts as to what "sounds" right. These two claims, which can be made by one and the same person, lead to an intriguing circularity: rules guide our behavior, but they derive from our own intuition. One way to reconcile this seeming paradox is to view punctuation as a web or net connecting the inner structure of a text with an external system that the reader understands intuitively—rather as the time signature of a musical piece produces visceral responses in its listeners while linking the piece to a larger cultural tradition.

Although everyone agrees that the sentence is a fundamental unit, perhaps *the* fundamental unit of writing, not to mention translating, sentences as such have received very little attention. Linguists love to parse sentences or, more recently, to look at their relationships to other sentences, but the sentence itself they take for granted. The question of what makes a sentence a sentence, what its boundaries mean, is rarely asked. Ron Silliman details the history of seemingly futile efforts to define a sentence in his essay "The New Sentence" (1989). Relegated, in Ferdinand de Saussure's system, to the level of *parole* rather than *langue*, but by its visual rather than oral nature alien to the very concept of *parole*, the sentence has fallen through the cracks of linguistic, literary, and philosophical inquiry. Punctuation has received even less attention, at least until the appearance of Geoffrey Nunberg's *Linguistics of Punctuation* in 1990. Both Nunberg and Silliman agree that sentences (and other units defined by punctuation) are fundamentally units of writing that have suffered neglect through their reanalysis as units of speech. Nunberg explains the prevalence of an ill-considered "transcriptional" approach to punctuation (that is, that punctuation transcribes oral prosodic features), as follows:

> [It] could mean that hearing readers tend to associate a kind of internal "acoustic image" with the presence of certain punctuation marks. This claim is surely right, in some sense; I suspect that it is what linguists have in mind when they endorse the transcriptional view of punctuation, and what writers are getting at when they say, for example, that the knowledge of how to use the comma depends in the end upon having "a good ear" or "a rhythmic sense." But whatever the psychological mechanism associated with such inner voices, it is not clear what explanatory purpose would be served by saying that punctuation "transcribes" them, particularly when, as with colons or parentheses, they have no actual correlates in ordinary speech. (1990, 15)

Thus he makes clear the circularity of our understanding of the rules of punctuation: it is right if it "sounds" right, it sounds right if it is right. He goes on to describe the grammar of well-formed texts as essentially a matter of "tacit knowledge" and properties "not accessible to casual reflection" (23). Yet he concludes his detailed study of certain observable rules of English punctuation by stating that punctuation is highly rule-guided; it is neither "neutral" nor independently coherent, but a localized and time-bound aspect of a living language (131). In other words, translators are correct in their seemingly conflicting intuitions: there are rules to punctuation, and we follow them by unconscious or tacit understanding rather than by conscious reflection.

These answers, then, are satisfactory when we speak of natural language, or natural written language. But what of stylized language? What of language that explicitly breaks the rules? What of written language that actively strives to be unlike ordinary speech or the voice in the reader's head? Here the complexity of our understanding of punctuation causes difficulties. If we are accustomed to following tacit rules in our writing, can we know when, let alone how, to break those rules if a work we are translating demands it? We seem to understand punctuation only through its behavior, and how it can be used only through how it *is* used. Therefore, by observing what translators do with punctuation we may learn not only what punctuation means (or does not mean) to them but also what stylistic effects it carries.

SENTENCE AS FOCUS: ALEKSANDR SOLZHENITSYN AND ANATOLII KIM

English translators regularly perform two types of transformations upon sentences and sentence boundaries in Russian prose. First, as we have seen in previous chapters, they show excessive devotion to the content of the sentence, retaining with care that information which forms the core content of the sentence, but often ignoring features that are external to the grammar of the sentence, such as pragmatic connectors, sentence parentheticals, modal particles, and idiosyncracies of punctuation. Second, they often exhibit insensitivity to sentence boundaries as such, arbitrarily cutting up long sentences or combining several short ones. This implies that syntax is internalized so subconsciously by the reader (and translator) that anything that falls outside its limits is lost to view, including the very features that shape it as a whole. It also implies a dichotomy between the translator-as-reader (who is extracting essential information from a sentence) and the translator-as-writer (who is exercising a perceived liberty with regard to punctuation).

One of the chief stumbling blocks to defining a sentence is the seemingly arbitrary way that sentence breaks can be assigned. The common definition of a sentence as a "minimum complete utterance" would seem to allow clauses separated by semicolons to qualify. Nils Erik Enkvist writes:

It is easy enough to recall styles in which the sentence division is unclear or ambiguous. If, for instance, a collector of folktales has recorded a text like

. . . and then the girl entered her grandmother's house and then she saw her grandmother in bed with a shawl around her head and then she went up to the old lady and then she said "Hello!" and then Grandmother sat up and then . . .

we may be hard put to decide whether *and then* marks the beginnings of new sentences, or whether the whole passage consists of one sentence made up of many clauses joined through parataxis and polysyndeton. (1971, 58–59)

Similarly, I. M. Schlesinger suggests that "from a linguistic point of view it is not clear whether a sentence always ends with the period mark; nor needs such a string of words always be the psychologically effective unit" (1968, 74 n. 5). These analyses, however, suffer from the confusion between written and oral speech outlined by Silliman. He distinguishes between an oral-type form (an "utterance"), such as Enkvist's example, and a written sentence. "The critical difference between the utterance and the sentence is that the utterance is indeterminate, a chain that can be more or less indefinitely extended. There is no sentence but a determinate sentence and this is fixed by the period" (Silliman 1989, 69).[1] While his pronouncement may seem somewhat arbitrary, it appears to be vindicated by Nunberg's assertion of a real hierarchy among punctuation marks and by the intuition of writers and readers. We do, after all, call a period but not a semicolon a "full stop," and many believe that semicolons point the reader forward to the next clause rather than marking closure.[2]

An intuitive definition of the effect of a period mark is that it signals the end of a complete thought. A more rigorous explanation, from the field of discourse analysis, is that the confines of a sentence enclose a topic (reference to old information) and a focus (what is being said about it). Maria Langleben explains the distinction between sentence clusters (separated by period marks) and compound sentences (with clauses typically separated by semicolons) as one of "communicative patterning." Within each sentence is a topic and a focus, but the focus in a simple sentence consists of a word or short phrase, while the focus of a compound sentence may be a whole clause.

> If a long succession of potentially independent sentences is represented by a conjoined cluster of sentences, then one should conclude that the intention of the author was to put a single accent on one of the conjoined sentences, and to leave in shade all the transitional constituents joining together a neutral topic with the accented focus. In this case a large amount of information is conveyed by only one focus, and the impression of concentration and close cohesion is sure to be evoked. (Langleben 1979, 252)

Thus long sentences can produce a very different effect than short ones: in Enkvist's example above, we might say the topic is "once upon a time" and the focus is the whole story, or even its telling. If, however, it were told in separate sentences, each episode would have a new topic and focus, and the overall emphasis would be more on the "realistic" depiction of events and less on the process of telling them.

Although they may not use the terminology of topic and focus, many critics have noted the importance of sentence boundaries in establishing "unity" of imagery or theme. D. E. Rozental' (1977, 25) points out that Lev Tolstoy used complex sentences because they are better than simple sentences at presenting an integral picture containing specific details. Langleben herself (1979, 252) offers several examples in which a single topic-focus combination is divided in translation, including a number from *Anna Karenina* and its translations.[3] Russian literature, in fact, should lend itself particularly well to a topic-focus analysis, since the corresponding idea of *tema-rema* 'theme-rheme' is codified within the Russian word order system and is therefore part of a Russian's tacit understanding of syntax. However, the disruption of topic-focus patterns occurs in translation into Russian as well. M. Stoliarov comments of Gustave Flaubert's complex sentences that they form "a picture . . . of a certain unified, though complex, whole, unfolding in time or space" (1939, 248–49). He and A. V. Fyodorov find that Russian translators tend to break up Flaubert's sentences, thereby "destroying . . . the unity of imagery" (Fyodorov 1968, 332). Lydia Polubichenko analyzes what she calls paragraph "topology" in *Alice in Wonderland*. She describes the phenomenon in terms very similar to those of the topic-focus model of sentences: "Carroll's overlong paragraphs make one think of a set of smaller pictures arranged together within a largish frame in such a way as to present them as one global whole. To disarrange the set would amount to a distortion of the general impression of globality; it would also lead to a distortion of the intention of the original supraphrasal unity" (1984, 201). Nevertheless, Polubichenko finds, *all* the Russian versions of the work split Carroll's long paragraphs into many parts.[4]

Thus researchers who look explicitly at sentence and paragraph breaks all seem to agree on a notion of unity or "globality" that is inherent within these syntactic units. This is true of scholars of widely different backgrounds in literature and linguistics. Yet translators appear to miss this feature of textual organization. Strong evidence of this is A. Tove's insistence that W. R. S. Ralston, in his Turgenev translation, "completely altered the structure of sentences and their division into paragraphs, making the latter significantly shorter. He also changed the chapter divisions. . . . Such textual subdivision significantly damages the impression left by this musical fragment, which is translated beautifully with respect to lexicon" (1966, 141). Curiously, Ralston himself declared in the Preface to *Liza*, "[I] have kept as closely as I possibly could to the original." This suggests that he did not recognize his structural changes as changes, which is, perhaps, our best clue to the difficulty of ascertaining the communicative force of syntactic breaks.[5]

A modern work that makes strong, consistent use of a syntactic pattern is Aleksandr Solzhenitsyn's *One Day in the Life of Ivan Denisovich*. Very early in the novella, Shukhov is lying in bed going over in his mind the various ways he could spend his "free" time to good effect in the morning (example 4.1). The Russian sentence is, admittedly, full of near breaks—dashes, colons, and

Шухов никогда не просыпал подъема, всегда вставал по нему — до развода было часа полтора времени своего, не казенного, и кто знает лагерную жизнь, всегда может подработать: шить кому-нибудь из старой подкладки чехол на рукавички; богатому бригаднику подать сухие валенки прямо на койку, чтоб ему босиком не топтаться вкруг кучи, не выбирать; или пробежать по каптеркам, где кому надо услужить, подмести или поднести что-нибудь; или идти в столовую собирать миски со столов и сносить их горками в посудомойку — тоже накормят, но там охотников много, отбою нет, а главное — если в миске что осталось, не удержишься, начнешь миски лизать.

(Solzhenitsyn, *Odin den'*, 9)

(*a*) Shukhov never overslept reveille. He always got up at once, for the next ninety minutes, until they assembled for work, belonged to him, not to the authorities, and any old-timer could always earn a bit—by sewing a pair of mittens for someone out of old sleeve lining; or bringing some rich loafer in the squad his dry valenki—right up to his bunk, so that he wouldn't have to stumble barefoot round the heap of boots looking for his own pair; or going the rounds of the warehouses, offering to be of service, sweeping up this or fetching that; or going to the mess hall to collect bowls from the tables and bring them stacked to the dishwashers—you're sure to be given something to eat there, though there were plenty of others at that game, more than plenty—and, what's worse, if you found a bowl with something left in it you could hardly resist licking it out. (Parker, 17–18)

(*b*) Shukhov never slept through reveille but always got up at once. That gave him about an hour and a half to himself before the morning roll call, a time when anyone who knew what was what in the camps could always scrounge a little something on the side. He could sew someone a cover for his mittens out of a piece of old lining. He could bring one of the big gang bosses his dry felt boots while he was still in his bunk, to save him the trouble of hanging around the pile of boots in his bare feet and trying to find his own. Or he could run around to one of the supply rooms where there might be a little job, sweeping or carrying something. Or he could go to the mess hall to pick up bowls from the tables and take piles of them to the dishwashers. That was another way of getting food, but there were always too many other people with the same idea. And the worst thing was that if there was something left in a bowl you started to lick it. You couldn't help it. (Hayward and Hingley, 1–2)

(*c*) Shukhov never overslept. He was always up at the call. That way he had an hour and a half all to himself before work parade—time for a man who knew his way around to earn a bit on the side. He could stitch covers for somebody's mittens from a piece of old lining. Take some rich foreman his felt boots while he was still in his bunk (save him hopping around barefoot, fishing them out of the heap after drying). Rush round the storerooms looking for odd jobs—sweeping up or running errands. Go to the mess to stack bowls and carry them to the washers-up. You'd get something to eat, but there were too many volunteers, swarms of them. And the worst of it was that if there was anything left in the bowl, you couldn't help licking it. (Willetts 3–4)

semicolons—but it is still a single sentence. As such, it presumably represents a single, complete thought: here, the complex machinations of Shukhov's mind as he thinks how best to use his free time. Like any skilled occupation, that of being an astute prisoner, or *zek*, requires that he keep all the possibilities in his mind at once, so that he can weigh their benefits and risks and act quickly. By throwing all the information into one sentence, Solzhenitsyn shows just how seasoned a *zek* Shukhov is. Ralph Parker's translation preserves Solzhenitsyn's compound sentence nearly intact. With his one structural alteration—setting apart the first clause as a separate sentence—he actually emphasizes the interdependent quality of the rest of the passage. Max Hayward and Ronald Hingley, on the contrary, and, more recently, H. T. Willetts, make nine sentences out of the original one. This gives the passage a slower, more ruminative quality than the Russian has, and it emphasizes the number and variety of choices rather than the jockeying among them. In addition, the pros and cons of the last option (getting something to eat, too much competition, licking out the bowls) receive separate treatment, as if they were explanations to the reader rather than part of Shukhov's decision-making process. Where Solzhenitsyn preserves a single, complex focus, that of figuring out how best to manage another day, Hayward and Hingley have introduced multiple new foci, one for each possibility open to Shukhov, plus separate ones for the practical and moral issues raised by the last choice.

It may seem unimportant to the work as a whole that such a shift in emphasis would occur in one passage. However, in this case it can be seen to have a subtle impact on the entire thematic structure of *One Day*. Because this is the first long explanatory paragraph, it sets a tone for the story as a whole. Moreover, the translators' interpretive pattern is repeated, in almost perfect mirror image, at the end of the novella. In the passage in example 4.1, Shukhov is lying in bed contemplating the day that lies ahead. Example 4.2 cites from very near the end of the novella. Here, Shukhov is back in bed at the end of the day, reviewing what he has done.

Solzhenitsyn's last long paragraph lists Shukhov's accomplishments for the day in one sentence (except for the final achievement: "And he hadn't succumbed to illness, he overcame it.") Hayward and Hingley (4.2*b*) again break up the long sentence, again into nine separate ones. In their version, each of Shukhov's memories has equal value with the last (which they render as simply, "And he'd gotten over that sickness," eliminating the word *peremogsia*, 'he overcame'). Willetts, too, makes nine sentences out of the original one (his version lacks the final sentence altogether). Once again, what was in Russian a single sentence about success—which in the camp is defined as survival—in the translation becomes nine sentences about individual successes. Solzhenitsyn's final, short sentence in this paragraph, about avoiding illness, carries a special weight: this is not some petty victory but the defeat of a deadly enemy. In Hayward and Hingley's translation it comes to seem the least important of the events of the day. Thus the original overriding theme about survival as an accomplishment in itself—reflected in the Russian title "One Day of Ivan Denisovich"—becomes in English a celebration of Shukhov's guile and hardiness, of one day among many. The Parker version, 4.2*a*, demonstrates how different the effect is when these achievements are all in one sentence. Each

Засыпал Шухов, вполне удоволенный. На дню у него выдалось сегодня много удач: в карцер не посадили, на Соцгородок бригаду не выгнали, в обед он закосил кашу, бригадир хорошо закрыл процентовку, стену Шухов клал весело, с ножевкой на шмоне не попался, подработал вечером у Цезаря и табачку купил. И не заболел, перемогся.

(Solzhenitsyn, *Odin den'*, 74)

(*a*) Shukhov went to sleep fully content. He'd had many strokes of luck that day: they hadn't put him in the cells; they hadn't sent his squad to the settlement; he'd swiped a bowl of kasha at dinner; the squad leader had fixed the rates well; he'd built a wall and enjoyed doing it; he'd smuggled that bit of hacksaw blade through; he'd earned a favor from Tsezar that evening; he'd bought that tobacco. And he hadn't fallen ill. He'd got over it. (Parker, 159)

(*b*) Shukhov went to sleep, and he was very happy. He'd had a lot of luck today. They hadn't put him in the cooler. The gang hadn't been chased out to work in the Socialist Community Development. He'd finagled an extra bowl of mush at noon. The boss had gotten them good rates for their work. He'd felt good making that wall. They hadn't found that piece of steel in the frisk. Caesar had paid him off in the evening. He'd bought some tobacco. And he'd gotten over that sickness. (Hayward and Hingley, 202–3)

(*c*) Shukhov felt pleased with life as he went to sleep. A lot of good things had happened that day. He hadn't been thrown in the hole. The gang hadn't been dragged off to Sotsgorodok. He'd swiped the extra gruel at dinnertime. The foreman had got a good rate for the job. He'd enjoyed working on the wall. He hadn't been caught with the blade at the search point. He'd earned a bit from Tsezar that evening. And he'd bought his tobacco. (Willetts, 181)

---

is such a small thing, especially from the point of view of those who are warm, well fed, and free, but altogether they account for the next comment: "The end of an unclouded day. Almost a happy one."

Even at the levels of paragraph and chapter structure the bias toward multiple foci surfaces in the Hayward-Hingley translation. The original runs as a single connected narrative, with just two breaks (blank lines) right near the end. These set off the concluding comments, first Shukhov's evaluation of the day, as he drops off to sleep, and then the omniscient narrator's summary of Shukhov's whole prison sentence:

> Just one of the 3,653 days of his sentence, from bell to bell.
> The extra three were for leap years. (Willetts trans., 182)

This structure creates a topic-focus relationship at the textual level similar to that at the sentence level. The day may consist of a series of events, setbacks, and accomplishments, but it is important as a *whole day*; the main achievement is that Shukhov survives this day, with his spirits intact, so he can go on to survive the whole term. At another level, if we see the emphasis on packing the events of the day into one sentence as an indication of how trivial each is but how they add up to a whole, this ending reminds us that even the whole day is trivial within the vast stretch of Shukhov's sentence, which puts the entire book in horrific perspective. Curiously, Hayward and Hingley set up a different pattern altogether: they insert breaks at frequent intervals in the narrative, marking episodes, shifts of narrative voice, or changes in location, and they leave out the two breaks at the end for the summary. Just as they diffuse the focus of the summary sentences, these translators subtly alter the main theme of the text as a whole, again highlighting the individual moments of the day instead of the integral quality that Solzhenitsyn gives it.

The examples from Solzhenistyn's novella may be cases of unconscious use of textual patterns, driven by the writer's empathy for the subject and unswerving devotion to his moral message. The works of Anatolii Kim suggest a more intentional manipulation of sentence boundaries to serve literary ends. Kim writes mystical-realist novels in which people communicate with one another across generations, young men speak to their yet-to-be-born grandchildren and the grandchildren respond to their long-dead grandfathers. Time and space are fluid in his writing, a quality that is mirrored in individual sentences. Between one period and the next the narrative may range over long expanses of time, endure several digressions, and shift viewpoint more than once.

The sentence in example 4.3a comes from the novel *Otets-les* (*Father-Forest*, 1989), which has not yet appeared in English. This sentence begins with Nikolai Turaev observing the construction of a well on his property before the turn of the century and ends with his son Stepan returning to the same.well half a century later. In the interim, the well has been constructed, served its purpose, and then crumbled away and become once again nothing but a hole in the ground with water glistening in its depths. The translator's natural inclination would be to split such a sentence up into more manageable units with clear subjects, but this would thwart the thematic effect, in which the well (and, in the novel's context, the forest) is the focal point around which the ephemeral human lives revolve.

Example 4.3b, from a 1985 short story, shows how radically Kim transgresses the traditional unities of a sentence even when the sentence is relatively short. This sentence has two "I"s, one male and one female, and their two perspectives clash dramatically across a single semicolon. The translator has chosen to shift the whole sentence into third-person narration, and to use quotation marks to break it up rather than to maintain the fluidity of perspective. The result is that a detached narrating perspective overarches the two speakers' viewpoints and neutralizes the quality of floating consciousness, of multiple layers of communication. This is a graphic example of the conflict between our tacit inclination to use punctuation to make a work "sound" right and some writers' deliberate flouting of punctuation rules to thematic effect.

There are many examples of translations that adhere scrupulously, or

(a) Тураев Николай стоит, заложив руки за спину, и смотрит, как мужики из Княжей копают колодец: двое оборванцев склоняются над ямой, вытягивая бадью с землею, затем подают в этой же бадье заготовленные колоды для сруба; шахта вырыта уже довольно глубокая, а воды все нет, и это беспокоит барина — вдруг ее не будет совсем; но вода все же появляется, и она блестит далеко внизу, помаргивая там, в сырой глубине земли — комья земли сыплются вниз из-под ног Тураева Степана, сына Николая, он нагнулся над краем давно заброшенного колодца в тот день, когда пришел с войны на лесную поляну своего детства, еле живой дотащился до той мерцавшей в его гибельной памяти опушки леса, где он впервые в жизни нашел огромный белый гриб, совсем недалеко от колодца, что предстал теперь его взору без верхней надземной клетки сруба — просто квадратная яма вровень с землей, заглянув куда он угадал в глубине блеск недосягаемой воды.

(*Otets-les*, 15–16)

Nikolai Turaev stands with his hands behind his back and watches the muzhiks from Kniazhia dig the well: a pair of ragged men stoop over the pit and drag out tubfuls of dirt, then use the same tub to transfer prepared blocks for the walls; the pit is already quite deep but no water is to be seen, which disturbs the landowner—what if there's no water there at all; but the water does appear, glistening far below, down in the damp depths of the earth—clods of dirt slip away under his feet as Stepan Turaev, Nikolai's son, bends over the edge of the long-disused well on the day of his return from the war to the woodland glade of his childhood, dragging himself barely alive to this woodside that flickers in his fatal memory, this spot where he found his first giant white mushroom, right near the well, which now appears before him without its upper structure but only as a square pit even with the ground, peering into which he could make out deep below the sparkle of unattainable water.

(b) Я думала, говорю ему, что уже давно умерла для тебя; совершенно верно, ответил я, так и было, но ведь случается, что воскресают из мертвых...

("Prikliucheniia m. n. s.," 1985, 76)

I say to him I thought as far as you were concerned I'd died a long time ago; you're absolutely right I answered her, that used to be the case but people do, after all, get resurrected . . .

She said "I thought that as far as you were concerned, I'd died a long time ago"; "you're absolutely right," he answered, "that used to be the case, but after all, people do rise from the dead. . . ."[8]

at least very closely, to the sentence pattern of the original. David Magarshack is careful to preserve exaggerated structural effects, such as Nikolai Gogol's seemingly interminable sentences in *Dead Souls*. (See, for example, the opening paragraph of his chap. 6.) Constance Garnett, on the other hand, is generally faithful to sentence and paragraph boundaries *except* when they are strongly marked. (She breaks the longest sentence in the same paragraph from Gogol's novel into two, and the chapter of *The Brothers Karamazov* entitled "Elders" [bk. 1, chap. 5], which consists in Russian of seven very lengthy paragraphs, she splits into sixteen, giving each substory and each direct quotation its own.) Of the two, Garnett's is a less defensible posture from the point of view of style. It is precisely the exaggerated or unusual effects that one should work to preserve. Stoliarov, for example, discusses the importance of the architectonics of the paragraph: "Does the translator," he asks, "have the right to decrease or (more important, in the practical sense) increase the number of sentences in a paragraph, by combining or breaking up the original ones?" (1939, 248). He answers that it depends upon the writer: for those, like Flaubert or Marcel Proust, who were very careful about architectonics, this element must be retained in translation; Emile Zola, on the other hand, didn't seem to pay this issue much attention, and so in his works it is less important.

As we have seen many times in the translation examples above (most notably 4.1), translators take the liberty of changing sentence boundaries as a prerogative of their craft. Many would explain the changes they make by saying that English somehow lends itself to shorter sentences and paragraphs, either because of its more analytic nature or by convention. This does not account, however, for the fact that translators also *combine* sentences and paragraphs, or for the fact that Russian translators regularly break up English sentences. Polubichenko (1984, 203) chooses a one-sentence paragraph from *Alice in Wonderland* that becomes two paragraphs and eight sentences in the hands of one translator, four paragraphs and seven sentences for another. Furthermore, different translators may go in opposite directions in their treatment of sentence or paragraph length. Hayward and Hingley merge the final nine paragraphs in *One Day* into five, and Parker divides them into eleven.

A different explanation for translators' cavalier attitudes toward syntactic boundaries might lie in what Shoshana Blum-Kulka calls the "explicitation hypothesis" (1986, 19). Under this hypothesis, translators tend to make their texts more redundant than the originals, as a result of the necessary process of interpretation they perform. Paragraphs with shorter sentences tend to contain more redundancies (the same subject may need to be repeated in each sentence, for example) and are usually easier to read (see Schlesinger 1968, 72–73). Within the topic-focus model, the shortening of syntactic units in translation implies that translators try to introduce as little new information at each stage as possible, so that the connection between topic and focus is always optimally explicit. They thus stay in control of the narrative as it develops, rather than allowing unwieldy syntax to weave global or circular connections around the main thread of the story. The danger with this method comes when circularity or interconnectedness or the grasp of the whole *are* the themes of the story, as in Kim's and Solzhenitsyn's works.

It is not only sentences that reveal the importance of punctuation. Some writers concern themselves with the printed page as a visual object, not just a medium for conveying a verbal work, and for these artists punctuation is important in its own right. Preoccupation with punctuation, almost as an illustrational tool, marks the works of Abram Tertz. Tertz almost always writes about writing, and his narrators can be profoundly self-conscious about their sentences and punctuation. He once experimented with writing about prison life using prose heavy with square brackets as a means of depicting the walls of the cell.[7] The short story "Graphomaniacs," about writers and their obsession with the printed page, contains this excursus on the book-as-object: "It was a brilliant forgery. . . . I turned the leaves from cover to cover and even smelled the paper. Without any concealment I expressed my delight to the author. I especially liked the commas, so tiny and exact—in a word, completely genuine commas" (Hingley trans., 193). Commas are usually the last thing we notice in a text; the narrator is turning upside down traditional notions about the value of writing—especially in the context of Soviet censorship, where "language as material" must supersede the "materiality of language." Example 4.4a from *Kroshka tsores* (*Little Jinx*, 1980) depicts the physical strain of writing late into the night. The fictional Sinyavsky's trembling and leg cramps (or "pins and needles") have their best expression not in his awkward words but in the dots on the paper. (Here, too, the translation does not fully capture this effect.)

Little Jinx is a novella about a stutterer named Andrei Sinyavsky who receives the gift of speech from a good fairy. But he finds that his control of his tongue's movement is limited to individual words; he can follow none of the rules of connected speech—grammatical, social, or political. His declamations are studded with incorrect usage, mixed metaphors and impolitic blurtings that jeopardize the safety of all around him. One element runs throughout his inelegant grandiloquence and seems, always, to represent the place where he is most comfortable, a kind of graphic representation of home. That is the ellipsis marker that concludes virtually every paragraph and many sentences in between. It is as if the old familiar (and safer) stuttering of his early childhood has become a punctuation mark. (One of the novella's sources is an E. T. A. Hoffmann story about a repugnant little man known as "Klein Zaches." A fairy has blessed him so that the virtues of others will be attributed to him. He speaks in garbled expletives and ellipses [marked by dashes in the original German], which give his listeners the opportunity to interpolate any wonderful meaning they choose. The ellipsis here is thus the locus of wishes and mistaken perceptions.[8] For Tertz/Sinyavsky, ellipses are also pregnant with politically dangerous innuendo.) At the end of the story Sinyavsky's five dead brothers reappear, talking about him and his mysterious father in partial phrases, then meaningless syllables, (*a*) [Н]у ладно — нервы! Сколько можно все время, непередаваемо, дрожать?.. Заснул бы с удовольствием, да ногу сводит...

(*Kroshka Tsores*, 71)

[Look], it's only nerves! How long can a person tremble like this, inexpressibly? . . . I'd have gone to sleep with pleasure, except that my legs kept cramping . . . (Joseph and May, 53)

(*b*) ...... В тюрьму его...... Ну умер, так и умер...... Одно беспокой..... Выродок.... Нет, вы знаете, в нем что-то бы.... Нам-то ку..... За мир во всем ми..... Да здра.....До сле..... Как прия...... Ну бросила и бро..... Так быва...... Кто бы мо..... Вы ду...... Пи..... Рэ........ Ля............ Си.................. До.........

(*Kroshka Tsores*, 109–10)

   "... him in jail.... So he died, plain died.... Just one big nuis—. Black sheep.... But, you know, there was something about him. So what if... For peace on the entire ear—.... Long live.... Until nex—.... How nic—... Well, she dumped him and—... That happ—... Who would have... ? You don't sup... 'P'... Re... La... Ti... Do... " (Joseph and May, 80)

(*c*) Жизнь это, вообще, ожидание написанного...

(*Spokoinoi nochi*, 437)

Life is what you do while waiting to write . . . (Lourie, 358)

---

which finally just dissolve into a stream of dots (example 4.4*b*; again, the translation is unfortunately rather less "dotty" than the original). This punctuation seems not only to convey but to depict their confusion, and to foreshadow the way they themselves dissolve into marks on the paper ("Only five brothers, like five fingers blackened on my hand as I wrapped up my work on the ream of pages written throughout the night...." [80]).

   The ellipsis can signify an unspecified continuation, a pause, something that is left out or cannot be included. Throughout Tertz's fiction about writers and writing it serves as an emblem of insecurity, fear, and censorship. It seems to contain a secret, to refer the reader to something outside the work but also to return him or her to the printed page. As such, it represents all of Little Jinx's conflicting attitudes toward writing: its privacy, its publicness, its necessity, its danger, and its self-referentiality. "Graphomaniacs" begins with an ellipsis, suggesting that it is merely part of the greater current of written pages, flowing through history. Perhaps the ultimate expression of the ellipsis as the return to within the world of writing is in an aphorism near the end of Tertz's autobiographical novel *Goodnight!* (example 4.4*c*; literally: *Life is, in general, the expectation of the written...*). The dots here turn the writing in on itself, for they represent something yet to be written; the ellipsis, within the logic of this sentence, appears to be the picture of life itself.

Even when a writer's punctuation is visually striking, the translator's temptation is to impose greater normalcy on it. For the most part it is exceedingly difficult to assess the importance of punctuation in translation, because it is one of the most conventional—and therefore both deeply culture-specific and often unconscious—aspects of written prose. It is probably safe to say that a writer who uses punctuation in a striking or unusual way does so for a reason. This is the argument put forward by Eugene Bristow in his introduction to his edition of Anton Chekhov's plays, which contains the following caveat:

> . . . the Russian conventions of punctuation have been rather consistently followed. This is especially true in instances pertaining to Chekhov's notorious suspensions (...) that are liberally deployed. Although some translators like Ronald Hingley have omitted all those dots—he has noted that when the dots have been retained, "there are occasions when the page of a translated text appears to be suffering from a severe attack of measles"—I believe that these Chekhovian dots have both point and purpose and are significantly related to both structure and character, as well as to language and thought. Ronald Hingley may see "measles," but I see impressionism, almost pointillism. (1977, xxxi)

This is a clear case of a clash of conventions, resolved in opposite ways by the two translators. For one, the printed page should not call attention to itself, and so ordinary English usage is followed. For the other, the original is sufficiently exceptional to merit an unusual treatment in translation. This may seem a trivial matter, especially in the case of a dramatic script, which is intended not for reading but for performance. However, punctuation is especially vulnerable to the stylistic prejudices of translators, precisely because it is so conventionalized. Thus, translators may elide unusual punctuation in order make a work read more easily, but at the expense of stylistic nuances. Conversely, they may insert new overtones, as Ivan Turgenev did in his Russian translation of Flaubert. Stoliarov points out one passage in which Turgenev has inserted seven ellipsis markers and two exclamation points, none of which are present in the original. Stoliarov (1939, 252) derides this use of "lyrical 'fading out'" (*liricheskaia "zamiraiushchaia" kontsovka*), which imparts a "lyric-dramatic" tone to Flaubert's emphatically objective and "impassive" one.

Other punctuation marks than the ellipsis also contribute to special stylistic effects. In our discussion of colloquial narration in chapter 2 we saw many instances of dashes and other breaks in the flow of the writing that suggested oral speech patterns. The dash can carry many meanings, and it appears to be important in establishing a rhythm in prose. The Russian narration of *One Day* is peppered with dashes, sometimes signifying a clarification or an example, sometimes just a pause, sometimes covering for something left unsaid.

Там, верное дело, месяц погреться негде будет — ни конурки. И костра не разведешь — чем топить? Вкалывай на совесть — одно спасение.

(10)

> You could bet your life that for a month there'd be no place where you could get warm—not even a hole in the ground. And you couldn't make a fire—what could you use for fuel? So your only hope was to work like hell. (Hayward and Hingley, 4)

> There wouldn't be a warm corner for a whole month. Not even a doghouse. And fires were out of the question. There was nothing to build them with. Let your work warm you up, that was your only salvation. (Parker, 19)

> You could count on a month with nowhere to go for a warm, not so much as a dog kennel. You wouldn't even be able to light a fire out in the open—where would the fuel come from? Your only hope would be to dig, dig, dig, for all you were worth. (Willetts, 5)

In example 4.5 each sentence in the Russian paragraph follows the same rhythm, with a descriptive (or prescriptive) introduction, a dash, and a two-word conclusion. The visual repetitions create a somewhat different effect from the more intangible "intonational" effects cited in example 2.12, as if the passage represented a poem on the value of work. Willetts makes no attempt to preserve the rhythm, but both the Hayward and Hingley and the Parker translations acknowledge its stylistic importance: the former repeats the punctuation, the latter replaces the dashes with sentence breaks. However, both exempt the final sentence from the pattern, as if they were uncomfortable with the singsong regularity. In doing so, they also lose some of the sense of pounding frustration, and of weariness, of how obvious and how tiresome this piece of wisdom is.

All these readings of sentence and paragraph meaning appear to tend toward similar metaphors: unity, globality, and cohesion within the confines of the punctuation (within a sentence or a paragraph) and visual metaphors of "architectonics" and "topology" to describe texts as a whole. These are consistent with Nunberg's and Silliman's claims about punctuation as a visual effect, and they point toward a new way of describing the physical text. Let us consider punctuation marks, especially parenthetical commas, dashes, parentheses, periods, and paragraph breaks (these being the ones that *enclose* segments of the text), as boundary lines within the written text. If we can describe what happens at those boundaries, we can make some progress toward understanding the text as a communicative act, and therefore toward mapping the translator's role within its communicative framework.

One thing a sentence surely does is break up the narrative into manageable pieces, both for the reader and for the translator. There is no conclusive proof that readers always pay attention to sentence boundaries in making sense of a piece of writing. The reader's eye does not necessarily scan for period markers, but rather focuses on certain spots on a page and scans the writing in their vicinity (Schlesinger 1968, 27–28).[9] There is, however, experimental evidence for the sentence as the "unit of decoding," with the reader processing entire sentences at once. Thus longer sentences are more difficult to process, since the reader must keep the early parts of the sentence in mind ("partially decoded or else retained in the memory as undecoded symbols") until all the information, the "message as a whole," is received.[10]

Thus, Kim's description of the well in 4.3 does not just present two distinct perspectives on the well, it also conveys a greater "message as a whole." It closely juxtaposes the two perspectives and draws the reader little by little into the characters' realm of confused time and space. English readers are familiar with this process of gradual decoding in the long, complex sentences characteristic of William Faulkner's style. An effective illustration of the impact that explicitation of complex syntax can have on communicative dynamics is seen in back-translating Faulkner from Russian, as in example 4.6.

Rita Rait-Kovaleva, a highly gifted and respected translator, maintains many of the lexical nuances, the length of the sentence and even its punctuation, but with a few subtle insertions she breaks Faulkner's complex whole into smaller, grammatically complete units. A portion of the sentence is translated back into English here to demonstrate this normalizing effect. Parsing Faulkner's sentence, the principal statement, which runs with many breaks through the whole long sentence, is something like: "[the] trip had been [an] interference with and interruption of the solution to their problems: the watching, which had been his one need. . . . " In the translation this becomes four independent clauses: "the first time it was a confusion, a stupid interruption"; "each trip interfered with the solution to his problem [delo]"; "[they] should have waited, left him in peace"; "all those months he had had one need—to wait." The English reader feels a kind of grammatical imperative, an urgency about getting to the end of this sentence because its inner logic is so fractured. In Russian this urgency abates as we are allowed to process each segment of the sentence separately. The English sentence draws the reader through the murky realm of emotions, forcing the reader to decode it as a whole, while the Russian version presents it as discrete thoughts that are far less of a challenge.

For many translators, the implication of this decoding idea is that they should produce shorter, more manageable sentences. After all, they are decoding a foreign language for the reader, why not decode the style, too? Schlesinger's readability studies offer an interesting counterargument. He finds no significant decline in comprehension as sentences become more complex. He hypothesizes that readers handle complex sentences and nested constructions well, precisely because they rise to the challenge: "It may well be that reading rate and comprehension scores are not affected by the degree of nesting, because the reader makes up for the greater difficulty of the sentence by investing more effort" (1968, 107). Thus, a simplified work

Because he hadn't had time to listen. In fact, that whole first trip, handcuffed to the deputy, from his jail cell to the courtroom, had been a senseless, a really outrageously foolish interference with and interruption, and each subsequent daily manacled trip and transference, of the solution to both their problems—his and the damned law's both—if they had only waited and let him alone: the watching, his dirty hands gripping among the grimed interstices of the barred window above the street, which had been his one, his imperious need during the long months between his incarceration and the opening of the Court. (Faulkner's original, *The Mansion*, 3)

Так что слушать ему было некогда. В сущности, и в тот первый раз, когда его повели в наручниках из камеры в зал суда, это была бессмысленная, возмутительная нелепость, глупое вмешательство, лишняя помеха, да и каждый раз это хождение в суд под конвоем только мешало правильно решить дело — его дело, да и дело этих проклятых судей, — надо было выждать, оставить его в покое: *все эти долгие месяцы под арестом и судом у него была одна-единственная, самая насущная потребность — ждать, стиснув грязными пальцами ржавые прутья тюремной решетки, выходившей на улицу.*

(Rait-Kovaleva, 8; emphasis added)

. . . all these long months between the arrest and the trial he had had one sole, most essential need—to wait, clenching in his dirty fingers the rusty bars of the jail window looking out on the street. (My translation of the italicized Russian)

will produce less astute readers, and its stylistic impact will diminish further as a result. We could generalize this statement to apply to other stylistic devices as well—consider the Underground Man's unspoken sin in example 3.9: when the translator expects the reader to read between the dots, the reader surely does so.

Another thing the sentence does is organize the reader's active participation in the work. Caryl Emerson comments, "In dialogic writing, ideas grow out of contexts; the shape of a sentence governs the shape of the response. A translator is first of all and foremost a good reader, and must be sensitive to that shape" (1983, 32). The question of what a "good reader" does with a sentence is, however, quite complex, and as Schlesinger suggests, the same reader can become better or worse, depending on the difficulty of the sentence. For Wolfgang Iser (1980*a*), a good reader preserves a "wandering viewpoint": blanks between sentences, paragraphs, and chapters serve as invitations to the reader to make projections, fill in the blanks, or seek equivalences. A good translator, then, would offer future readers the same wealth of opportunities.[11]

By its topic-focus construction, the sentence may prompt the reader to follow a certain temporal flow. This is the argument put forward by Iser and by Stanley Fish, both of whom emphasize the "developing responses of the reader in relation to the words as they succeed one another in time" (Fish 1980, 73).[12] Within this process, Fish finds the reader to be constantly projecting "syntactical and/or lexical probabilities" and then noting whether or not they occur (74). Iser takes this idea still further: "The activity of reading can be characterized as a sort of kaleidoscope of perspectives, preintentions, recollections. Every sentence contains a preview of the next and forms a kind of viewfinder for what is to come; and this in turn changes the 'preview' and so becomes a 'viewfinder' for what has been read" (1980b, 54). Thus, one gets a picture of a reader leaping from sentence break to sentence break, reevaluating and refocusing with each jump. Through the practice of explicitation, translators do much of the jumping for the reader, rendering the new reading process far less active.

What these various theories about sentences have in common is a willingness to see the boundaries between sentences as not just a blank spot, not just "the 27th letter of the alphabet" (Silliman 1989, 92), but a locus of great activity. Much as the space between neighborhoods or nationalities is often the scene of greatest dispute and violence, and the space between languages is the site of greatest change, so do linguistic boundary markers locate much of the interaction between narrator, author, reader, and translator. Consider the passage from Yurii Trifonov's *Another Life* in example 4.7. Here the punctuation describes not topic-focus or "global" concerns but a mental tension that draws the reader into the character's state of mind. The short sentences reflect the heroine's aggravation with her difficult husband; this is the spasmodic rumination of a tired and angry mind.

In the Michael Glenny translation, the reasoning is more logical, more connected. The "whim" is relegated to a weak, merely explanatory spot in a long sentence, rather than taking clear, indignant emphasis. The comment on insomnia, too, seems more like an explanation than a complaint. Thus, normalization of the punctuation interferes with the emotionality of the passage and with its ability to resonate with the reader's own emotional rhythms.

In chapters 2 and 3 we saw that interjections could shift attention from character to narrator or vice versa. The role of commas or other delineating punctuation in this is clear: they can establish boundaries within which a shift can take place. At the period marker or paragraph break, the world outside the text (author, reader, translator) may also come into play. Sentence and paragraph length are known to be characteristic of particular writers. Ernest Hemingway's short sentences are considered a sign of sureness and authority in his works. (And, in turn, his writing gives authority to the sentence. Silliman comments, "Hemingway strives for an art of the sentence as the novel's determining language-unit" [1989, 14].) The longer, complex sentences of Faulkner or Joyce direct the reader's attention from statements to words, to subtle flows within the characters' minds or among words and languages. Thus we could conclude that the area within the sentence itself is the domain of language and character, while the space after the period mark

А иногда он проснется ночью без всякого подпития — просто так, неизвестно отчего. Это уже было вовсе блажью. Ведь не старик он. Бессонница бывает у стариков.

("Drugaia zhizn'," 220)

And sometimes he would wake up in the night even if he hadn't been drinking—just like that, for no apparent reason. That was pure caprice. He wasn't some old man, after all. Insomnia is for old men.

Sometimes he would wake up at night when he hadn't been drinking at all—just like that, for no apparent reason other than mere whim. It wasn't as if he were old; insomnia is something old men suffer from. (Glenny, 12)

(between sentences) belongs to the author.[13] Gertrude Stein explains and demonstrates this notion in her essay "Sentences": "A sentence is an interval in which there is finally forward and back. A sentence is an interval during which if there is a difficulty they will do away with it. A sentence is a part of the way when they wish to be secure. A sentence is their politeness in asking for a cessation. And when it happens they will look up" (1973, 132). The sentence becomes a world of its own, traversable in either direction, a microcosm within which problems are solved, security is partially guaranteed, truce is declared. And at the end, "they will look up" and see the world around, the world of the author. This is not very different from Emerson's comment (1983, 30) about the importance of maintaining the "distinction between inner and outer in a sentence" in translating Bakhtin's prose. The breaks in narration are where the reader and writer become equals, the copossessors of the text.

Paragraph breaks, it seems, serve functions similar to those between sentences, with the addition of some possible implication of turn-taking if there is more than one voice in the text. Voloshinov makes the similarity explicit: "The paragraph is something like a vitiated dialogue worked into the body of a monologic utterance. Behind the device of partitioning speech into units, which are termed paragraphs in their written form, lie orientation toward listener or reader and calculation of the latter's possible reactions."[14] Silliman, too, says that a prose poem that divides paragraphs at each sentence break "brings the reader's attention back time and again to the voice of the narrator" (1989, 83). Thus the translator's assertion of a prerogative for altering sentence and paragraph boundaries seems to be part of a larger struggle for ownership of the text. By imposing a more even rhythm, a more ordinary flow of sentences, translators reduce the temptation to "look up." The moment when we meet the author's sharp gaze is now softened by the more diffuse light of translation syntax.

This is especially true when the writing is self-consciously about writing, as is the case in Tertz's "Graphomaniacs" (example 4.8). In Russian, the

Было жарко и душно. Пушкинский бульвар иссыхал. В воздухе чувствовалось дыхание приближающейся грозы. Мне это понравилось. Надо запомнить, использовать: «В воздухе чувствовалось дыхание приближающейся грозы». Этой фразой я завершу роман «В поисках радости». Непременно вставлю, хоть прямо в гранки. . .

(Tertz, "Grafomani," 7)

It was hot and stuffy. Pushkin Boulevard was sweltering. In the air was the breath of an approaching thunderstorm. I liked that. Must make a note of it and use it: "In the air was the breath of an approaching thunderstorm." I'll end my novel The Search for Happiness *with this phrase. I'll put it in no matter what, even directly in the proofs.*

It was hot and stuffy. Pushkin Boulevard was sweltering, and the breath of an approaching thunderstorm could be sensed in the air. The phrase appealed to me. I must memorize it and use it: "the breath of an approaching thunderstorm could be sensed in the air." With this phrase I would end my novel *In Search of Joy.* I would make a point of inserting it, if necessary in proof. (Hingley, 171)

---

initial short sentences seem authoritative, suggesting a realistic scene, with a logical author-narrator leading the reader along the landscape. Suddenly it becomes clear, however, that the narrator is describing his words, not his experience: "I liked that. Must make a note of it and use it." At first we think he "liked" the sense of the impending storm, but it becomes clear that he just liked his phrasing about it. The translation reduces this effect in two ways. The sentence in question is combined with the one before it, so that it loses its telegraphic authority—both as description and as literary fact. Then the indefinite reference from the fourth sentence backwards ("I liked that"), which seems at first to refer to the scene and to situate the narrator on Pushkin Boulevard, becomes in the translation an unambiguous reference to the writing ("The phrase appealed to me"), easing our confusion about where the writer is and where the sentences are taking us.

Thus, sentence boundaries are where we take our bearings, fit each new piece into the logical (or otherwise) construction of the whole. Iser (1980*b*, 55) describes the sentence as setting expectations that must be fulfilled. The frustration of these expectations, he claims, is one of the foundations of literature. Tertz illustrates this idea at many levels: what frustrates the reader's expectations is literature itself. (The published translation, by this reasoning, offers a frustration of the frustration, sapping away the most literary feature of the passage.)

When we "look up" at the end of a sentence, we look where the author has instructed us to look. Kim would have us look at the mystical force that unites generations and continents. Tertz would have us look at the printed page, training our eyes in the Gestalt technique of seeing both the sense of the words and their shape. Solzhenitsyn would have us see the naked truth about the camps. In each case we are, of course, looking into the authorial personae of these writers: Kim the interleaver, Sinyavsky/Tertz the three-dimensional/two-dimensional pair, Solzhenitsyn the champion of truth. One difficulty the translators face is that their readers may know less about the writers and their personae than would readers of the originals, so these moments of recognition may fail. Mere fidelity to punctuation will not necessarily tell the reader where to look, as the Faulkner example demonstrates. But if translators will allow their readers the space to explore, rather than cleaning up the boundary areas, building bridges across them, or sweeping them away altogether, they might find their readers rising to the challenge.

Teaching Literature in Translation

> The truth of the doctrine of cultural . . . relativism is that we
> can never apprehend another people's or another period's
> imagination neatly, as though it were our own. The falsity of
> it is that we can therefore never genuinely apprehend it at
> all. We can apprehend it well enough, at least as well as we
> apprehend anything else not properly ours; but we do so not
> by looking *behind* the interfering glosses that connect us to
> it but *through* them. Professor Trilling's nervousness about
> the epistemological complacency of traditional humanism is
> not misplaced. The exactest reply to it is James Merrill's
> wrenching observation that life is translation, and we are all
> lost in it.
>
> —Clifford Geertz, "Found in Translation"

THE DANGER OF TEACHING Russian literature in
translation "straight," as though the translations were transparent windows
onto the originals, is that the course will be merely *about* Russian literature,
or, more likely, about Russian cultural history. The political climate of suspi-
cion or assimilative zeal that has characterized relations between the English-speaking world and Russia has often made literature into a source of
information rather than of pleasure or challenge. Simultaneously, translators
have responded to various aesthetic demands, and perhaps their own insecurities, by converting open-ended, dialogic play into completed wholes, dis-
placing ebullient or unreliable narrators, imposing a single perspective on
the narration, and smoothing out the visual product. The reward of looking
through translations, observing their "interfering glosses," is that the literature becomes not about but *of* Russia, and of our culture at the same time.
True, there are aspects of any important work that will not be translatable or
even explainable in our different cultural and linguistic vocabulary. Genuine
failure of translation is beyond description.[1] But the issues described in this

book are not failures in that sense; they are divergences among conceptions of literature rather than among languages, and as such they provide some of the best opportunities for explaining Russian literature to those who cannot read the originals.

The most obvious pattern on the translation glass is that of *cultural prejudice*. American literature, for example, prides itself on clarity and forcefulness and is not above imposing such values on translations. Moreover, English speakers have particular expectations of translations: that they will be accessible, easy on the eye, even seemingly transparent. (In fact, translation reception in general may invert the usual understanding of literary style. For original works, style is what makes them original and unlike other works; for translations, what is important is their similarities to the norm.) It may seem fruitless, or needlessly antagonistic, to explain this to a classful of students. But in certain contexts it may also be the key to important insights. Imagine explaining Russian formalism to students exposed only to translations. They may grasp the outlines of the phenomenon, but its energetic core will probably elude them, and not only because they are unlikely to find in their translations the specific linguistic features the formalists discuss. Point out to students not the specific but the general translation effect, however, show them this tendency on the part of translators (and others responsible for processing literature for consumption) to highlight content at the expense of form, and students might also be able to see the source of the theoretical movement in Russian literature's special attitude to form. Banfield (1982, 10), for example, comments that the formalists may have been the first to pay close attention to narrational devices because of the "curiously retarded historical appearance of the Russian narrative" (which she ascribes to the longevity of its oral culture). Our culture has so long taken written narration for granted that our translators are virtually blind to its self-consciousness in Russian.

Also etched on the glass of translation are the (question) marks of *authority*. Most modern theories of literature try to account in some way for the reader's role in processing or even generating the text. Roland Barthes may have gone too far in declaring the death of the author, but his distinction between "readerly" and "writerly" texts is valuable. The former, for Barthes, is like many of the translations discussed here: "committed to the closure system of the West, produced according to the goals of this system, devoted to the law of the Signified."[2] The reader receives it passively, unable to enter into its creation. Opposed to this is the "writerly" text, which invites the reader to participate in its creation. If the translator has usurped the role of reader in this schema, the text is closed to students' participation in it. But even a closed text *plus* a "writerly" account of the original could have the opposite effect: by seeing how the translator has taken charge of the text, students might discover that they, too, have that power. Furthermore, since translators make their deliberate alterations in anticipation of readers' evaluations,[3] readers who are cognizant of these alterations may also become aware of the creative significance of their manner of reading literature. In questioning why the translator expected them to want this or that change, they might also begin to wonder what the original author had done for the reader's benefit. Thus, the question of ownership of the words would become a challenge rather than an abstraction, which in turn might brighten their understanding of such concepts as dialogism, national literatures, and translatability.

Related to the question of authority is the notion of *truth* in literature. When translators choose the readerly path, they err, for Barthes and his school, in the direction of *vraisemblance*, or "literature's attempt to legitimize itself as the expression of the real or the natural."[4] The ideas of "the real and the natural" do not accommodate what Lawrence Venuti (1992) calls the "opacity" or materiality of language. A realistic or natural translation, it seems, is one that makes the translator invisible, as realism makes the narrator or the frame invisible. Peter Brooks describes the process of transference in psychoanalysis in similar terms: the analyst tries to reconstruct the analysand's experience in a more persuasive form, at times not re-creating an old but creating a "new truth" that by its very presentation is so convincing that it becomes the analysand's memory of the event. "Such is no doubt the conviction sought by any storyteller, as also by the reader when he attempts to retransmit his experience of a text: when he becomes a critic, for instance, and tries to convince his listeners or readers that his construction of the text *must be* right" (1986, 61). Constance Garnett, for one, had this gift of convincing her readers that she "must be right"; far from questioning her translations, they accepted her word *as* Turgenev, *as* Chekhov, *as* Russian prose. But for much of Russian literature, the truth is in the telling rather than in the story, it is in those moments of defamiliarization, of mistrust of the narrator, of disjunction. One could give students the Pevear and Volokhonsky translations of Dostoevsky to demonstrate his penchant for prevarication and noncommittal narration; it might be more powerful still to give them a page of Garnett's trustworthy, conscientious "truth" for comparison.

Ultimately, the reason to teach or study a national literature in translation is to enlarge our understanding of culture in general and of our own culture in particular. To the extent that a foreign literature fits neatly into our conception of the literary, it raises the question, Why? which points our gaze to the external circumstances that might allow two such different societies to find similar means of expressing their burning issues. To the extent that a foreign literature does not fit neatly, it directs our gaze inward, to the features we take for granted in literature, to our very notion of what literature is. If we can use translations as *both*—surrogates for the originals, and keys to their inaccessible qualities—then we can hope to enlarge our comprehension of literature as both inner and outer, the confluence of centrifugal and centripetal forces.

Translations of Russian literature are not simply stand-ins for their originals. They themselves form a body of literature, subject to its own historical and political constraints, observing its own rules of syntax and communication. They act upon Russian literature at all its boundary lines: at those between cultural periods, between readers and writers, between characters and narrators, between one sentence and the next. These boundaries, like the walls of an organic cell or the xylem of a tree, are the foci of activity, the places where literature lives and breathes. Classical models of perfection have kept attention focused on the flaws, the necessary imperfections of translations. But recently the margins have come to be seen as more privileged, vibrant locales, and translation's natural place at the margins—shaping them, connecting them, tending to them—makes it particularly intriguing. A description of a literature that includes a description of its translations can be a powerful tool for explaining both individual works and cultures and the very idea of literature itself.

Fact vs. Fiction: Two Translations of Bulgakov's
Master i Margarita

Mikhail Bulgakov, *Master i Margarita*, in his *Romany* (Leningrad: Khudozh-estvennaia literatura, 1973), 423–812.

———. *The Master and Margarita*, trans. Mirra Ginsburg (New York: Grove Press, 1967).

———. *The Master and Margarita*, trans. Michael Glenny (New York: Harper & Row, 1967).

As with many potential best-sellers, Mikhail Bulgakov's *The Master and Margarita* came out in English very quickly after its Russian publication. Mirra Ginsburg's translation appeared within months after the novel came out in the journal *Moskva* in 1966–67. Unfortunately for the hasty translator, there soon came a revelation that this was an abridged version, lacking some 23,000 words. A fuller version, obtained abroad, inspired a second translation, by Michael Glenny, which also appeared in 1967.[1] This would seem to be suffi-cient reason to dismiss the Ginsburg translation (which has unaccountably never been updated) in favor of the more complete version. However, the Glenny translation has omissions of its own, compared with the somewhat more authoritative version published in Moscow in 1973. These include some segments also missing from the Ginsburg translation, and some other seg-ments that Ginsburg did use, but they also reveal a more important pattern of stylistic and syntactic shifts that make the Ginsburg translation, in the end, the more valuable of the two, especially when used with a few supplements.[2]

One of the major themes of Bulgakov's novel is the value of narrative for creating reality. Fiction and fact, historical novel and worldly action inter-twine in this work in miraculous ways. The most convincing narrative in the work is the Master's own novel about Pontius Pilate. Woland mesmerizes the two "literary gentlemen," Berlioz and Bezdomny, by recounting the first seg-ment; then Bezdomny dreams the second part; and finally Margarita reads the conclusion (or nearly) from the Master's manuscript, miraculously risen from its own ashes. Thus, the story has an existence of its own, and it is so convincing as to support Woland's claim that he actually witnessed its events (459–60). Furthermore, its "real" conclusion (when the Master frees Pilate) then coincides with that of Bulgakov's novel (except for the epilogue), taking it to a new dimension in relation to the "real" world (real, that is, within the confines of Bulgakov's novel).

The Pilate story first appears as Woland's method of proving the existence of Jesus Christ. Jesus had unexpectedly come to life in an antireligious poem by Bezdomny, and Berlioz was attempting to explain his folly when the mysterious foreigner arrived. Thus, the life-giving power of literature is twice affirmed in the novel's opening pages: once in the poet's unintentional inspiration, once in Woland's spellbinding story. That the story does not coincide with the accounts in the Gospels is yet one more proof: canon and law, like paper money, are fictions that take meaning from social contracts—which may be broken at any time by the hypocritical or avaricious—while a powerful story is a living force.

In the Moscow portions of the novel, the theme of fiction and fact recurs at almost every turn. As ruble notes turn into foreign currency or into worthless scraps of paper, as people find themselves suddenly in distant cities or in other impossible situations, accepted truths keep breaking down. Woland, Koroviev, and Begemot repeatedly test the value of contracts, identity cards, and documents, which for bureaucratic Moscow have become the ultimate truths. When asked for documents certifying him as a member of the writers' union, Koroviev answers, "Really, this is ludicrous, after all . . . It's not documents that prove someone is a writer, but the things he writes!" (chap. 28, 769).

The Moscow events are impossible in themselves and also impossibly told, with breaks in time and space, with intrusions and digressions by the narrator, with dizzying shifts in point of view, register, and tone, so that it is often hard to tell who is speaking. When Woland tells his story of Jesus and Pilate, he suddenly loses his accent and all trace of colloquialism and jargon and shifts into an apparently unmediated depiction of events: not realism, even, but *reality*. Before and after, however, we are constantly reminded that the Moscow story is an artificial narrative, constructed of language. Throughout there are shameless puns and plays on the word devil (*chërt*), on slang that invokes the devil, and on other references to unearthly powers. Narrator and characters quote one another freely: one narrative digression about a "vision from hell" ends, "Oh gods, my gods—give me poison, poison!" (chap. 5, 477), which is a citation from Pilate's thoughts as he feels a migraine coming on (chap. 2, 441). Elsewhere, Woland uses Berlioz's own words against him ("'Really, you of all people should know that not one thing that is written in the Gospels ever really happened . . . ' [said the professor], . . . and Berlioz was caught up short, because he had said precisely the same thing to Bezdomny [earlier]" [chap. 3, 459]). Many other characters fall afoul of their oaths, exaggerations, or promises when the devil's entourage makes them tell the truth. The emphasis on words for their own sake is clearest in the Master's claim that before he finished the novel he knew "that its last words would be: *the fifth Procurator of Judea, the horseman Pontius Pilate*" (chap. 13, 554). When the novel-within-the-novel concludes (chap. 26, 746), it does indeed end with a slight variation on these words. This is not really the end of the Master's novel, however; he still must set Pilate free, so the entire novel again concludes with the predicted phrase (chap. 32, 799), and, for good measure, so does the epilogue (again, with a slight variation, 812).[3] (The middle of these repetitions is missing from the Ginsburg version, since the ending was heavily cut in the *Moskva* version.)

Both translations maintain the broad outlines of this conflict between fact and fiction, as it is often the meat of the novel. However, at more subtle levels of narration the Glenny translation, in particular, lacks some important stylistic qualities that strengthen the fact/fiction dichotomy. Foremost among the stylistic devices of the text is the strong shift in style between the Pilate story and the rest of the narrative. While the Moscow story is told in rambling style, full of digressions, statements of opinion, and direct address to the reader, the Pilate story features longer, complete sentences with a clear point of view, many foreign words that lend authenticity to the scenes, and a great deal of descriptive language with few of the colloquialisms or substandard terms of the main body of the narrative.[4] Both translators maintain this shift in style, although Glenny has a tendency to shorten sentences in the Pilate sections and to normalize the language and syntax of the rest of the work so as to diminish their difference, while Ginsburg's English is occasionally too awkward to convey the effortlessness the Master's style seems to possess.

It is in the more unbridled narration of the Moscow story that the two translations diverge most strongly. Here, the narrative is peppered with strong colloquialisms, parentheticals, and modal particles that call its veracity into question. Both translations make some effort to maintain the colloquial turns of phrase:

Но кот отмочил штуку почище номера с чужими часами.
(chap. 12, 536)
But the tom pulled an even neater trick. (Ginsburg, 136)
But the cat put the watch trick in the shade. (Glenny, 119)

«Где это он так наловчился говорить по-русски, вот что интересно!»
(chap. 1, 429)
"I'd like to know where he picked up his Russian." (Ginsburg, 9)
"What I'd like to know is, where did he manage to pick up such good Russian?" (Glenny, 9)

However, when the narrative shifts are less a matter of register and more a case of intrusion by the narrator, the shortcomings of the Glenny version become obvious. Note, for example, this passage about the fateful apartment No. 50:

Объяснимся: Степа Лиходеев, директор театра Варьете, очнулся утром у себя в той самой квартире, которую он занимал пополам с *покойным* Берлиозом, в большом шестиэтажном доме, покоем расположенном на Садовой улице.

Надо сказать, что квартира эта — № 50 — давно уже пользовалась *если не плохой, то, во всяком случае,* странной репутацией. *Еще* два года назад владелицей ее была вдова ювилера де Фужере...

И вот два года тому назад начались в квартире необъяснимые происшествия: из этой квартиры люди начали бесследно исчезать.
(chap. 7, 491; emphasis added)

Stepa Likhodeyev, manager of the Variety Theater, had waked up that morning in the apartment that he shared with Berlioz in a big six-story block of apartments on Sadovaya Street. This apartment—No. 50—had a strange reputation. Two years before, it had been owned by the widow of a jeweler called de Fougère. . . .

Odd things began happening in that apartment—people started to vanish from it without a trace. (Glenny, 74)

Here, all the emphasized phrases are omitted in the English, with the result that the narrator's intrusive presence, and with it the qualities of rumor and general bewilderment, disappear.[5] Other examples of such omissions are legion.

Надо заметить, что редактор был человеком начитанным . . .
(chap. 1, 425)
It must be added that the editor was a well-read man . . . (Ginsburg, 5)
The editor was a well-read man . . . (Glenny, 5)

Но позвольте спросить, каким образом?
(chap. 4, 464)
"But how, if you will allow me to ask?" (Ginsburg, 51)
"But how on earth could he?" (Glenny, 46)

Но довольно, ты отвлекаешься, читатель! За мной!
(chap. 5, 474)
But enough, you are digressing, reader! Follow me! . . . (Ginsburg, 63)
But I digress, reader. (Glenny, 55)

The first two are cases of obvious omission. The third is an odd twist on the

Russian, in which the original satire on the narrator-reader relationship becomes a simple apology. Moreover, Glenny renders the title of chapter 6, "Shizofreniia, kak i bylo skazano" ("Schizophrenia, as has already been said"), simply as "Schizophrenia." The overall result of these omissions is to make the narration seem more authoritative than it is in Russian, to add a veneer of "realism" to the fantastic events, which takes the reader's attention away from the telling, and especially from the words.

Bulgakov, on the other hand, is constantly luring us away from pictures and into words. To this end he substitutes the logic of figurative or expressive language for the logic of daily life. And it is here, especially, that Glenny puts up almost invisible barriers to understanding the pervasiveness of Bulgakov's theme. As Ivan Bezdommny falls asleep in the asylum,

...Он заснул, и последнее, что он слышал наяву, было предрассветное щебетание птиц в лесу. Но они вскоре умолкли, и ему стало сниться, что солнце уже снижалось над Лысой Горой, и была эта гора оцеплена двойным оцеплением...
(chap. 15, 587)

The last two phrases are, of course, the beginning of the next chapter of the Pilate story. Glenny translates them as follows:

As he fell asleep the last thing he heard was the dawn chorus of birds in the wood. But they were soon silent again, and he began dreaming that the sun had already set over Mount Golgotha and that the hill was ringed by a double cordon . . . (168)

But in the Russian, Ivan does not dream *that* the hill is ringed, it *is* ringed. This phrase does not describe a dream, it leads into the Pilate novel, and its words must be (*are*) exactly the words of the novel, not a paraphrase of them. What starts as indirect discourse (to dream *that*) becomes direct citation. Similarly, the description of the musical and culinary uproar at a Griboyedov dinner ends:

...Словом, ад.
И было в полночь видение в аду.
(chap. 5, 477)

In short, hell.
And at midnight there was a vision in hell. (Ginsburg, 66)

In short, hell.
At midnight there appeared a vision in this hell. (Glenny, 58)

The Russian, like Ginsburg's English version, extends the metaphor so that the figurative hell becomes the "real" (and unique) hell. Glenny, however, particularizes it to "this" hell, diminishing the power of the word as well as the subsequent description of the headwaiter as a diabolical pirate. In effect, Glenny resists internal citation, turning instead to indirect speech that obscures the diabolical power of words in Bulgakov's work.

Bulgakov plays with the ability of language to build up worlds and then destroy them with a logical fallacy or a violation of ordinary rules of communication. Glenny appears to be uncomfortable with such lapses and often introduces subtle corrections. For example, Ivan blurts out to Woland,

«Взять бы этого Канта, да за такие доказательства года на три в Соловки!»
(chap. 1, 429)

"That Kant ought to be sent to Solovki for three years for such arguments!" (Ginsburg, 10)

"Kant ought to have been arrested and given three years in Solovki asylum for that 'proof' of his!" (Glenny, 9)

Note how the historical discontinuity of Ivan's suggestion is smoothed over by Glenny's use of the past tense ("ought to have been"). Ivan still seems overly zealous in his version, but not utterly ignorant of intellectual history, as he appears in the Russian. By making Ivan's outburst conform to historical logic, Glenny does away with the very defiance of human logic upon which Woland's world is constructed.

Bulgakov's narrator is also not above introducing humorous non sequiturs that call further attention to the disjunction between words and their meaning.[6] Perhaps the best example of this irreverence for logic comes in chapter 18:

Все смешалось в доме Облонских, как справедливо выразился знаменитый писатель Лев Толстой. Именно так и сказал бы он в данном случае. Да! Все смешалось в глазах у Поплавского. Длинная искра пронеслась у него перед глазами... (ch. 18, 617).
(chap. 18, 617)

"Everything became jumbled in the Oblonsky household," in the apt words of the famous writer Lev Tolstoy. And these are the words he would have used in the present instance as well. Yes. Everything became jumbled in Poplavsky's eyes. A long spark flashed across his vision . . . (Ginsburg, 216)

"Everything was in a mess in the Oblonskys' house," as Leo Tolstoy so truly put it, a remark which applied exactly to the present situation. Everything was in a mess for Poplavsky. A long sliver of light flashed in front of him . . . (Glenny, 198–99)

The opening phrase is a citation from the second paragraph of *Anna Karenina*. In the first place, the phrase is rather commonplace to merit such exalted literary citation, but in addition, the narrator then uses it in a different, more literal sense (things blurred in Poplavsky's eyes), thus obviating any need for the literary reference and creating an absurd confusion. Between the lines is another phrase, that everything is jumbled in the narrator's mind—literary texts, random phrases, the events he is recounting. The Glenny translation does its best (or worst!) to correct this confusion by retaining the figurative sense of Tolstoy's phrase in reference to Poplavsky ("everything was in a mess *for Poplavsky*"), and by releasing Tolstoy from any implied complicity in this chaos ("a remark which applied exactly," instead of "that is exactly what he [Tolstoy] would have said"). In addition to losing the actual sense of the Russian, that things are swimming before Poplavsky's eyes, Glenny loses the *non*sense of the Russian, and this is a greater loss in the grand scheme of Bulgakov's novel.

There is, at times, a system to Bulgakov's narrator's violations of literary etiquette. In speech act theory, H. Paul Grice (1975) has described rules of implicature that demand that, if a sentence refers to previous information, then the speaker must believe that information to be true. Bulgakov's narrator holds no such prejudices, however, routinely undermining the reader's faith in his authority and in our understanding of language.

Следовало бы, пожалуй, спросить Ивана Николаевича, почему он полагает, что профессор именно на Москве-реке, а не где-нибудь в другом месте. Да горе в том, что спросить-то было некому.
(chap. 4, 469)

One might, perhaps, ask Ivan Nikolayevich why he assumed that the professor would be precisely near the Moskva River and not anywhere else. But the trouble is that there was no one to ask this. (Ginsburg, 56)

Somebody should of course have asked Ivan Nikolayich why he imagined the professor would be on the Moscow River of all places, but unfortunately there was no one to ask him. (Glenny, 50)

The first sentence (in Russian) explains what question should have been asked, but the second perversely denies all possibility of asking a question. Glenny gets around this violation of communicative propriety by rephrasing the opening sentence to allow for the possibility that there might not be an interlocutor available (by using the indefinite "somebody"). His version makes sense, but sense is decidedly not the point here.

We find a similar lapse in the explanation of the name of Griboyedov House:

Дом назывался «Домом Грибоедова» на том основании, что будто бы некогда им владела тетка писателя — Александра Сергеевича Грибоедова. Ну владела или не владела — мы точно не знаем. Помнится даже, что, кажется, никакой тетки-домвладелицы у Грибоедова не было...
(chap. 5, 471)

The building was called Griboyedov House, since it was said to have belonged at one time to an aunt of the writer Alexandre Sergeyevich Griboyedov. Whether it did or did not belong to her we do not know. But if we remember rightly, it seems to us that Griboyedov had never had any such home-owning aunt. (Ginsburg, 59)

The house was called Griboyedov House because it might once have belonged to an aunt of the famous playwright Alexander Sergeyevich Griboyedov. Nobody really knows for sure whether she really owned it or not. People even say that Griboyedov never had an aunt who owned any such property. (Glenny, 52)

In all three cases, the reference to "her" in the second sentence implies the existence of an aunt (*vladela ili ne vladela*, whether it did or did not belong to her," "whether she really owned it"), which the third sentence negates. In the first two versions, it is the narrator who both introduces the aunt and denies her existence, while in Glenny's formulation the negation comes from what "people even say," rather than from what the narrator remembers. This allows a logical explanation: the narrator asserts her existence, and "people" deny it—nothing commits the narrator to disbelieving his own assertion. Thus, Glenny consistently thwarts the narrator's attempts to manipulate our instincts about truth and falsehood, possibility and impossibility.

In Glenny's defense, the version of the text he used appears to have downplayed the narrator's role as well. Some of the outright textual omissions in Glenny's version (which Fiene says "may actually correspond to omissions in the typescript used by Glenny" [349]) serve this same unconscious project of demystifying the narrator. At the end of chapter 12 the narrator cites the words of a song he imagines he hears, then adds, "Or, perhaps, these were not the words at all. Perhaps there were others to the same tune, all of them highly scandalous. But this isn't really the point" (Ginsburg, 147). By omitting this passage, the Glenny version spares the narrator an embarrassing moment. In chapter 1 there is another important omission, from the point of view of narrative, when Woland first appears:

Afterward, when—frankly speaking—it was already too late, various official institutions filed reports describing this man. A comparison of these reports can only cause astonishment. Thus, the first says that the man was short, had gold teeth, and limped on the right foot. The second, that the man was of enormous height, had platinum crowns, and limped on the left foot. The third states laconically that the man had no special distinguishing characteristics. We must discard all these reports as quite useless.

To begin with, the man described did not limp on either foot, and was neither short nor enormous in height, but simply tall. As for his teeth, he had platinum crowns on the left side of his mouth, and gold ones on the right . . . (Ginsburg, 6–7)

Afterward, when it was frankly too late, various persons collected their data and issued descriptions of this man. As to his teeth, he had platinum crowns on the left side and gold ones on the right . . . (Glenny, 6)

In the longer version, the narrator takes some glee in reporting eyewitness accounts and debunking them, thus suggesting a special "truth" that belongs only to the narrator. Once again, official documents are devalued in comparison to "real" storytelling. The shorter version has the opposite effect, indicating that these official accounts are our source for Woland's "real" appearance, and that the narrator, too, gets his information from them.

The Ginsburg translation, as is evident from the examples above, keeps quite close to the syntax of the original and carefully preserves the narrator's interventions. One wishes that she could have had Glenny's flair for English, and, of course, that her version were more complete. Nevertheless, I would recommend her translation to anyone interested in the themes of writing and reality in this novel, in its plays on words and logic, or simply in its humor.

(As this is going to press, another translation of Bulgakov's novel is being promised for publication by Ardis. We can hope that it will be not only complete but also attentive to the various gradations of "truth" and "reality" in the original.)

Observing the Grotesque: Two Classics of
Formalist Criticism and English Translations

ONE OF THE MAJOR contributions of Russian Formalist criticism lay in its close attention to the mechanics of literary style. Among the Formalist "classics" are two attempts to identify the elements of the grotesque: Boris Eikhenbaum's study "How Gogol's 'Overcoat' Was Made" (1919), and V. V. Vinogradov's discussion of Dostoevsky's *Double* in "Toward a Morphology of the Natural Style." Both locate the sources of comic and grotesque effects in patterns of language use and style shifts. For Eikhenbaum, Gogol created "aural patterns" and a "sound-speech" that lifted his story from the banal to the poignantly grotesque. Vinogradov was more interested in semantic patterns and repetitions as literary devices than in "sound." In both cases, the critics' close attention to the words of these important texts pose special problems for English speakers interested in Formalism. It is worth considering whether the nuances the Russian critics distinguish are observable in the existing English translations of the literary works they discuss.

(A) Boris Eikhenbaum, "Kak sdelana 'Shinel'" Gogolia," in vol. 3 of *Poetika: Sborniki po teorii poeticheskogo iazyka*, 151–65 (Petrograd: Gos. tipografiia Leshtukov per., 1919).

In this essay, which introduces the notions of prose "intonation" and "sound gestures," Eikhenbaum discusses Nikolai Gogol's narrative language in great detail. The first device he singles out is that of punning or double entendre, which is always difficult for translators to capture. In this case, however, the final version of Gogol's story (unlike the drafts, which had more shameless plays on words) uses a subtler form of pun (*kalambur*) that does often carry over into English. This is the repeated use of one word with different idiomatic meanings, or of a word in one meaning followed by the antonym of a second meaning. The result is to call subtle attention to the words themselves and the shiftiness of semantics.

(*a*) Тогда только замечал он, что он не на середине строки, а скорее на середине улицы.
(Gogol, 145; Eikhenbaum, 162)[1]

(*b*) ...Какая именно и в чем состояла должность *значительного лица*, это осталось до сих пор неизвестным. Нужно знать, что *одно значительное лицо* недавно сделался значительным лицом, а до того времени он был незначительным лицом.
(Gogol, 164; Eikhenbaum, 163)

(*c*) ...которые не дают никому советов, ни от кого не берут их сами.
(Gogol, 147; Eikhenbaum, 156)

(*d*) Таким образом и произошел Акакий Акакиевич.
(Gogol, 142; Eikhenbaum, 161)

In (*a*) Gogol uses the phrase "to be in the middle of" in both an abstract sense (a line of print) and a physical, geographical sense (a street). This, obviously, poses no difficulty to the translators, who come up with the following contrasts to "middle of the street:" "middle of his writing" (Garnett, 7),[2] "middle of a line" (Magarshack, 238), and "middle of a sentence" (Wilks, 76). Similarly, the opposition in (*b*) between the emphasized "title" of Important Person and its deemphasized opposite, an unimportant person, is captured by Garnett (26), who creates a "Person of Consequence" out of a person of no consequence, and Wilks (96: "this Important Person," "an *unimportant* person"). Magarshack (260) contrasts a "Very Important Person" to "quite an unimportant person," which might have been more effective as "a very unimportant person," in order to preserve not just the strict meaning but also the reference to language and titles as a source of power.

The contrast in (*c*) is slightly trickier, although English has corresponding idioms, "to give advice" and "to take advice," with the same tension between the surface antonymy of the verbs (give/take) and the slightly different contrast in meaning between the idioms (offer/accept). Wilks (77) and Magarshack (240) both preserve this subtle *kalambur* ("who give advice to no one, nor take it from anyone"; "who give no counsel to any man, nor take it from anyone, either"). Garnett, characteristically, chooses to emphasize the semantic opposition without calling attention to the wordplay of the "give/take" contrast: "even those who neither give counsel to others nor accept it themselves" (8). The contrast between "give" and "accept," though it is accurate as to the semantic opposition, produces no verbal resonance for the English speaker.

Eikhenbaum singles out (d) as an example of the play with narrative form, the use of a "business-like" expression in a personal setting. Moreover, it plays with several senses of the term *proizoshel*, which implies origins or provenance, production, and general occurrence. All three are applicable to this description of Akaky's birth and naming, and the appropriate translation would be "Thus Akaky Akakievich came to be," or even "Thus occurred Akaky Akakievich." All three translators avoid this unusual usage, however, preferring to single out the *naming* as the central meaning of the sentence:

This was how he came to be Akaky Akakyevitch. (Garnett, 4)

It was in this way that he came to be called Akaky. (Magarshack, 235)

And that was how he became Akaky Akakievich. (Wilks, 73)

In all cases, one layer of meaning (the reference to Akaky's birth as well as his naming) is lost, as is any foregrounding of the language for its own sake.

Wordplay is only a symptom of the more general stylization that Eikhenbaum identifies in Gogol's story, a tendency to use language in such a way that it "never creates the impression of ordinary [*bytovoi*] speech" (158). This is the secret of Gogol's mastery of the grotesque, claims Eikhenbaum, who finds its sources not only in puns but in such devices as abrupt shifts among stylistic registers within the narrative, and in what he calls "articulatory mimicry" or "sound gestures." The latter are the most difficult to pin down (in fact, Vinogradov later took Eikhenbaum to task for introducing such subjective, "aural" criteria into his discussion of written works).[3] In the case of Gogol, concrete examples of the deliberate use of awkward or odd-sounding turns of phrase are readily found, however. "The Overcoat" is full of repetitions of meaningless or redundant morphemes and the obvious abuse of the semantic content of words in favor of their rhythmic weight or inherent clumsiness.

The clearest example of this is the description of Akaky Akakievich in the second paragraph of "The Overcoat."

Итак, в *одном департаменте* служил *один чиновник*, чиновник нельзя сказать чтобы очень замечательный, низенького роста, несколько рябоват, несколько рыжеват, несколько даже на вид подслеповат, с небольшой лысиной на лбу, с морщинами по обеим сторонам щек и цветом лица что называется геморроидальным.
(Gogol, 141; Eikhenbaum, 157)

And so in a certain department *worked* a certain civil servant, *a civil servant who could not be called the least bit remarkable, a civil servant of shortish height, somewhat pock-markedish, somewhat reddish-haired, some-*

what—even to the naked eye—nearish-sighted, with a small bald spot over his forehead, with wrinkles on both sides of his cheeks, and with that coloring known as hemorrhoidal.

Noting that this final version is markedly more convoluted and grotesque than earlier drafts of the same passage, Eikhenbaum (157) calls it not a "description" but a "reproduction" of Akaky's physiognomy. As he puts it, the passage follows not usual semantic laws but "the principle of sound-semantics." It begins with a series of noncommittal nonstatements (*nel'zia skazat' chtoby . . .*) and redundant use of words and morphemes denoting unremarkableness (*-en'kii; ovat; neskol'ko*).[4] Eikhenbaum claims that these accumulated effects "sound grandiose and fantastic, beyond any relationship to their meaning" (157). Moreover, he believes, they form a crescendo which builds to "that drumroll of a word, almost deprived of logical sense, but nevertheless with an unusually strong articulatory expressiveness,—'hemorrhoidal' [*gemoroidal'nym*]."

The major translations of this story all, in one way or another, neutralize the effect Eikhenbaum describes.

> And so, in a certain department there was a government clerk; a clerk of whom it cannot be said that he was very remarkable; he was short, somewhat pockmarked, with rather reddish hair and rather dim, bleary eyes, with a small bald patch on the top of his head, with wrinkles on both sides of his cheeks and the sort of complexion which is usually associated with hemorrhoids. (Garnett, 3)

> And so *in a certain department* there served *a certain Civil Servant*, a Civil Servant who cannot by any stretch of the imagination be described as in any way remarkable. He was in fact a somewhat short, somewhat pockmarked, somewhat red-haired man, who looked rather short-sighted and was slightly bald on the top of his head, with wrinkles on both cheeks, and a rather sallow complexion. (Magarshack, 233–34)

> In a certain department, then, there worked *a certain civil servant*. On no account could he be said to have a memorable appearance; he was shortish, rather pockmarked, with reddish hair, and also had weak eyesight, or so it seemed. He had a small bald patch in front and both cheeks were wrinkled. His complexion was the sort you find in those who suffer from piles . . . (Wilks, 71)

Garnett retains a form of the final, monstrous word, but she has so diluted the earlier repetitions and elaborated the meaning of *gemoroidal'nym* that it loses some of its visual or "aural" power as a triumphantly unprepossessing conclusion to the description—the last word in Akaky's unremarkableness. Magarshack retains more of the crescendo effect ("somewhat . . . somewhat . . . somewhat"), but he and Wilks lose the climax altogether by seeking simple synonyms for Gogol's concluding word-monster. All three clearly err on the side of making *sense* of what Eikhenbaum identifies as an inherently non-sensical, grotesque phrase.

The translators do a better job with some other rhythmic features Eikhenbaum notes in the story. For example, the famous "humanitarian" passage ("'Leave me alone! Why are you insulting me?'. . . " [Gogol, 143–44]) is marked by "a mounting tension in the intonation, with a solemn, pathetic quality" (Eikhenbaum, 161) brought on, in part, by repetitions of initial *i*. The translators, by and large, retain the pragmatic connectors in this passage:

> *And* long afterwards, at moments of the greatest gaiety, the figure of the humble little clerk with a bald patch on his head rose before him . . . *And* the poor young man hid his face in his hands, *and* many times afterward in his life he shuddered, seeing how much inhumanity there is in man. . . . (Garnett, 6; see also Magarshack, 236, Wilks, 74; emphasis added)

The most difficult narrative device to capture in translation may be shifts in stylistic register, because different languages have different registers and different ways of signaling the changes between them. Nevertheless, some of the incongruities Eikhenbaum locates in Gogol's narrative are possible to convey in translation. He notes, for example, the long passage describing the various after-hours activities of Petersburg clerks (Gogol, 146–47; Eikhenbaum, 157–58), in which the overarching "declamatory pathos" is interrupted by "low" words and phrases, producing a comic effect. All three translators reproduce the pathos, but the interruptions they treat in different ways. Eikhenbaum (158) singles out such phrases as *shliapenok, smazlivoi devushke, prikhlebyvaia chai iz stakanov s kopeechnymi sukhariami* as humorously out of place. These are translated variously as:

> women's hats; some attractive girl; sipping tea out of glasses to the accompaniment of farthing rusks (Garnett, 8)

> some silly women's hats; some pretty girl; sipping tea from glasses and nibbling a penny biscuit (Magarshack, 239)

> cheap little hats; a pretty girl; sipping tea from glasses and nibbling little biscuits (Wilks, 76–77)

Garnett, once again, can be seen to smooth over stylistic incongruities, replacing all three phrases with ones that are neutral or even elevated ("to the accompaniment of"). Magarshack and Wilks both show more sensitivity to register here, as elsewhere.

The other major example of register shifts that Eikhenbaum cites is in the description of Akaky's death (Gogol, 168–69; Eikhenbaum, 164). His passing is narrated simply, then complicated by a banal and bureaucratic list of his possessions (buttons, socks, paper). Then the narrator leaps into a melo-dramatic epitaph ("And Petersburg was left without Akaky Akakievich . . . "). Since the choice of images is somewhat independent of register here (but-tons and death do not mix in any language), the translators have no difficulty retaining the incongruities. One curious idiosyncracy, however, is in their treatment of paragraphing in this passage. Garnett, following Gogol's lead, lumps all the components of this odd obituary into one paragraph (31). Mag-arshack decides that the death itself should occupy the place of honor at the end of a paragraph, thus separating it from the buttons:

> At length poor Akaky Akakyevich gave up the ghost.
>
> Neither his room nor his belongings were put under seal because, in the first place, he had no heirs, and in the second there was precious little inheritance he left behind, comprising as it did all in all a bundle of quills, a quire of white Gov-ernment paper, three pairs of socks, a few buttons that had come off his trousers, and the *capote* with which the reader has already made his acquaintance. (265)

Wilks keeps death and buttons in one paragraph, but then introduces a full line break to separate the epitaph, or at least its most melodramatic part:

> Akaky Akakievich was carted away and buried. And St. Petersburg carried on with-out its Akaky Akakievich just as though he had never even existed.
>
> So vanished and disappeared forever a human being whom no one ever thought of protecting, who was dear to no one, in whom no one was the least inter-ested . . . (102)

In this case Garnett's lack of a strong feel for register seems to have kept her more true to Gogol's jumbled narrative style, while the other two translators were so cognizant of the shifts that they treated them as separate narrative moments and lost some of the grotesque quality Eikhenbaum values so highly.

(B) V. V. Vinogradov, "K morfologii natural'nogo stilia. Opyt lingvistichesko-go analiza peterburgskoi poemy 'Dvoinik'" (1921–22), in *Poetika russkoi lit-eratury*, 101–40 (Moscow: Nauka, 1976).

Vinogradov, as was noted earlier, took exception to Eikhenbaum's tendency to treat written words as "aural" production. Instead of observing an author's "intonation," which he considered a subjective category, Vinogradov collect-ed more concrete empirical evidence about literary devices. These included register shifts, repetitions of words and phrases, patterned transformations of verb forms, oxymorons, chains of verbs and adverbs that increase in inten-sity, and other visible language play.

While some critics felt that Fyodor Dostoevsky's style in *The Double* was excessively wordy and repetitious,[5] Vinogradov finds in this affectation something thematically important, a quality of "unmediated observation" and "careful description of all actions, of all the hero's forms of motor expression, in chronological order, without regard for repetitiveness" (110). As such, he claims, Dostoevsky's style here represents the next stage of development of the "Gogolian School." Thus, for example, he singles out devices that convey the paranoia or confusion of Golyadkin's thoughts and distinguish the "heavy tempo" of his mental processes from the "convulsive dynamics of the action" (116).

Because these effects are less subjective than some highlighted by Eikhenbaum, they also often fare better in translation. All the major translators, for example, capture Dostoevsky's grotesquely saturated use of detail. The most obvious repetitions, especially those that are contiguous, also hold up in translation. During Golyadkin's first visit to the Rutenshpits, he looks at the doctor

с беспокойством, с большим беспокойством, с крайним беспокойством. . . (117)[6]

All the translators reviewed here preserve this odd crescendo, in which "the tension of emotions and actions seems to grow before the reader's eyes" (Vinogradov, 115). The exception is Bird, whose choice demonstrates by omission how illuminating Vinogradov's analysis of the style here is. Compare Jessie Coulson's and George Bird's renderings of the passage:

> Although Mr Golyadkin had said all this with the utmost possible distinctness and clarity, confidently, weighing his words and calculating their probable effect, nevertheless it was now with anxiety, with great anxiety, with the utmost anxiety, that he gazed at Christian Ivanovich. (Coulson, 138)[7]

> But though Mr. Golyadkin had spoken throughout with the utmost clarity, precision and assurance, weighing his words and relying on those calculated to produce the best effect, he was now looking at the doctor with ever-growing uneasiness. (Bird, 28)

In Coulson's version, as in the Russian, the obvious subjectivity of the repetition leads the reader to reevaluate the whole sentence as reflecting Golyadkin's confused point of view, so that the "clarity" and "precision" of his speech are also called into question. Bird's version, which can only be explained by a desire for literary "clarity," locates the viewpoint in a more reasonable, well-ordered mind and prompts us to accept the earlier assertion of Golyadkin's "clarity" at face value. In any case, we lose in Bird's version "the 'strange' atmosphere of constantly changing actions and events, surrounded by a mist of enigmatic indefiniteness" (Vinogradov, 115).

Vinogradov observes a frequent tendency on the part of the exaggeratedly "business-like" narrator to enumerate Golyadkin's actions at length. Translators do reproduce the resulting sequences, but they often alter the subtle, ironic clues that call attention to this as a bureaucratic stylization in Russian. Vinogradov notes, for example, a tendency to pepper these series with the word *finally* (*nakonets*) as an "ironic play on the [reader's expectations] in a lengthy enumeration" (107 n. 12). This effect is often muted by translators, who either leave out some instances of *finally* or vary them with *at last, lastly,* or *at length.*

Наконец, он почувствовал, что на него надевают шинель, что ему нахлобучили на глаза шляпу; что, *наконец,* он почувствовал себя в сенях, в темноте и на холоде, *наконец,* и на лестнице. *Наконец,* он споткнулся. . . (137; emphasis added, here and below)

At last he was aware that they were putting on his greatcoat, that his hat was thrust over his eyes; *finally* he felt that he was in the entry on the stairs in the dark and cold. *At last* he stumbled . . . (Garnett, 508–9)

Finally he felt his overcoat being put on him and his hat being pulled down over his eyes; then he felt himself in the passage, in the dark and the cold, and *lastly* on the stairs. *At length* he stumbled . . . (Coulson, 164)

At last he felt that his overcoat was being put on him, that his hat had been clapped down over his eyes, that *finally* he found himself in the entranceway, in the darkness and in the cold, and *at last* on the stairway. *Finally,* he tripped . . . (Harden, 46)

He felt himself being put into his overcoat, and his hat being rammed down over his eyes. He became aware of the cold dark landing and the stairs. *Finally* he tripped . . . (Bird, 70)

Here (except, again, in Bird's strongly "normalized" version, which eliminates the repetitions), the translators retain at least three of Dostoevsky's four repetitions of *nakonets,* but they vary the phrasing enough to mute the absurdly officious quality of the passage.

Another repetition that is too awkward for most translators is Dostoevsky's narrator's "constant indications of a preceding basic action . . . through repetition of the corresponding verb construction . . . in a new syntactic whole" (Vinogradov, 109). In other words, Dostoevsky describes actions and then repeats whole verb phrases in the past gerundive form as a way of leading into the next action. The result is to create an exaggeratedly plodding logic and enhance the contrast between Golyadkin's circular thought processes and his headlong actions.

(a) Голядкин... выпрыгнул из постели.... Выпрыгнув из постели, он. . .
(109)

(b) Господин Голядкин остановился перед квартирою... Остановившись, . приготовился дернуть за шнурок... Приготовившись дернуть за шнурок.. он немедленно и довольно кстати рассудил. . .
(114)

(c) Господин Голядкин успокоил, наконец, вполне всю свою совесть.. Успокоив теперь вполне свою совесть. . .
(145)

The example in (a) is representative of many similar repetitions throughout the work. The translators treat it as follows:

But a minute later he leapt out of bed . . . From his bed he . . . (Garnett, 477)

he leapt from his bed with one bound . . . As soon as he had sprung out of bed he . . . (Coulson, 127)

But a moment later he leapt out of bed in a single bound . . . Upon jumping out of bed, he . . . (Harden, 4)

he bounded out of bed, and ran to a small round mirror (Bird, 12)

Coulson and Harden retain some of the pattern of verb forms, but they alter the verbs (leapt-sprung, leapt-jumping). Garnett retains the logical connection but imposes a more elegant style, eliminating the second verb. Bird, as we have come to expect, speeds up the whole process and does away with the entire effect.

In (b), Dostoevsky offers a more elaborate example of this device. Here the narrator creates a logical chain that is not only grammatically excessive (after all, any competent reader could do without all the explicit logical connections) but comically overexact. "Having prepared to pull the bell-rope" is a tautology, since he in fact *has not done* anything.

Mr. Golyadkin . . . stopped before flat number five . . . Stopping at the door, our hero made haste to assume an air of propriety . . . and prepared to pull the bell. As he was about to do so he promptly and rather appropriately reflected . . . (Garnett, 482)

Mr Golyadkin . . . stopped at the door of number five . . . Coming to a halt, our hero hastily tried to give his countenance a suitably detached but not unamiable air, and prepared to give a tug at the bell-pull. Having taken hold of the bell-pull, he hastily decided, just in time . . . (Coulson, 133)

Mr. Golyadkin . . . stopped before Apartment No. 5 . . . Standing there, our hero hastened to plant a presentable, unconcerned expression . . . and got ready to tug the bell-pull. Once ready to give a tug to the bell-pull, he immediately and quite appropriately reasoned . . . (Harden, 10)

Mr. Golyadkin . . . stopped outside Flat No. 5 . . . Standing before the door, our hero lost no time in assuming a countenance of due ease, . . . and prepared to pull the bell. Thus poised, he came to an immediate and rather opportune decision . . . (Bird, 21)

Only Harden, who is generally extremely conscientious about repetitions, preserves the ludicrously drawn-out preparations to ring the bell. Otherwise, all the translators dilute this passage's saturated deliberation, through synonyms (*he stopped . . . coming to a halt, he prepared to give a tug . . . having taken hold*), elimination of the sequence "past tense-past gerund" (*he stopped . . . standing there*), or simple rephrasings of the second component (*as he was about to do so, thus poised*). None of them, including Harden, attempts to preserve the comical sequence, *he stopped . . . having stopped, he prepared to pull . . . having prepared to pull*. Again, the narration loses some of its self-consciousness. By way of contrast, (*c*) is an example of a more explicit use of this device which shows that translators can reproduce it when it is very obvious. Even Bird is conscientious here: "and so salving his conscience completely. And so, his conscience salved, he picked up his pipe . . ." (Bird, 86).

Finally, Vinogradov identifies another important pattern of repetitions in the story. These are phrases that resound throughout the narration and the dialogue, muddying the boundaries between the two. As Vinogradov states, "Since Golyadkin says the same things not only with his voice but with his . . . gaze, appearance, gestures, and movements, it is clear that almost all the descriptions (significantly indicating Mr. Golyadkin's 'constant custom') are peppered with unattributed citations from his speech" (128). Golyadkin, for example, announces to the doctor that he is *kak i vse* ("just like everybody else"), a phrase his gaze has already announced, his appearance will later convey, and the narrator will use for him. Another common expression is that Golyadkin is *nichego*, variously translated as "quite all right," "fine," "has nothing to worry about," and so on. (Unfortunately, English has no equivalent that conveys the literal meaning of the term, that he is "nothing.") The translators, by and large, maintain these repetitions, although Garnett and Bird are particularly prone to alter the phrasing or introduce variations. (Garnett alternates "like everybody else" and "like every one else"; Bird has "he had nothing to worry about" and "he was quite all right.") Most significantly, Garnett tends to place these statements in quotation marks, marking them as quotations *from* Golyadkin's voice, rather than allowing his "gaze" or his "appearance" to have voices too:

He subsided into silence. He made up his mind that it was better to keep quiet, not to open his lips, and to show that he was "all right," that he was "like every one else," and that his position, as far as he could see, was quite a proper one. (Garnett, 506)

By taking the words out of the narrator's mouth and attributing them to Golyadkin, Garnett does away with an important fluidity among the voices of the text. It should be noted that one of the important revisions Avrahm Yarmolinsky worked on her version was to remove these quotation marks.[8]

A crucial device noted by Vinogradov relies on phrases that turn up in the narration or the dialogue of one character, only to echo later in someone else's words—someone who could not have heard the first instance of the phrase. Thus (as we saw in example 3.7), Klara Olsufievna's letter characterizes the false Golyadkin as

«известный бесполезностью своего направления человек»
(207),

while a few pages earlier the narrator had used a similar expression,

«известный своей бесполезностью господин Голядкин-младший»
(204).

The translators treat the echo in different ways. Harden and, surprisingly, Bird preserve the similarities; the former, for example, has "a man notorious for his worthless tendencies" (159–60) and "Mr. Golyadkin Junior, notorious for his worthlessness." Coulson makes them unrecognizable: "That wicked intriguer, whose evil tendencies are so well known" (257), and "the notoriously worthless Mr. Golyadkin junior" (254). (Again, Garnett's original version was also fairly far from the mark: "the slanderer . . . notorious for the immorality of his tendencies" [589] and "the notoriously worthless Mr. Golyadkin" [586]; but Yarmolinsky's revision brings the two closer: "the slanderer . . . notorious for the uselessness of his tendency" [144] and "the notoriously useless Mr. Golyadkin" [140].) This might seem a trivial alteration, but Harden shows that it can have a real bearing on interpretation of the work: "I have tried to translate recurring words and expressions identically each time they appear so that the reader will become aware of Mr. Golyadkin Senior's style of thought and speech. In this way it becomes clear, I believe, that Mr. Golyadkin has to be the author of the letter from Klara Olsufyevna, as it is couched in terms that he constantly uses" (xxxiii).

Thus, the translators' general tendency to smooth over repetitions appears here, more than anywhere, as a *psychological* normalization of the work, a muting of the paranoid delusions, of the extreme self-consciousness, of the sheer confusion of the hero. Bird's translation goes farthest in this direction; in trying to convey a clear picture of the events of the story he loses the true portrait of Golyadkin's psyche that Dostoevsky was painting (the introduction to Bird's translation, by Mark Spilka, even commends Bird for adding "force and clarity" to Dostoevsky's language).[9] Other translators clearly have more concern for the formal aspects of the work, and this concern can be shown to have increased over time, perhaps in response to formalist ideas. Thus Harden's scholarly approach is the most faithful to the repetitions, and Yarmolinsky's revision of Garnett's version brings out this device as well. By contrast, Garnett's original, and Bird's and Coulson's renderings, seem to follow the goal of making the work more clear or elegant in English. For teaching purposes, then, Harden's version would probably be most illustrative of Vinogradov's ideas, and Bird's the most interesting for demonstrating by default their true stylistic importance.

Notes

INTRODUCTION

1. For a discussion of translators' problems in achieving cultural and economic recognition, see Venuti 1986, 180–81.

2. The terms "author in the text" and "reader in the text" seem preferable here to "implied author" and "implied reader," coined by Wayne Booth and Wolfgang Iser, respectively. My concern is less with actual or potential readers than with the various ways the reader and author may be encoded within the text and, above all, with the way the translator alters the codes. Unfortunately, these are unwieldy terms. I have actually used, simply, "author" and "reader," with the hope that the context will make clear what aspect of those concepts I mean. More complex is the term "narrator," which I use in a broader sense than many theorists. Much of my discussion revolves around the illusion of a speaking voice created within third-person narration; there is no first-person narrator in these texts, and no individual identified with that role. Instead, there is a storytelling voice that is distinct from omniscient, "voiceless" narration. In *The Rhetoric of Fiction*, Booth discusses at length a whole taxonomy of authorial and narrative voices. His discussion, however, is particularly applicable to fiction in English; a vital part of my argument is that Russia has qualitatively different narrational traditions that require special attention to voice on the part of translators. Wayne C. Booth, *The Rhetoric of Fiction* (Chicago: University of Chicago Press, 1961); Wolfgang Iser, *The Implied Reader* (Baltimore: Johns Hopkins University Press, 1974).

3. Vladimir Nabokov, "Translator's Introduction," to Aleksandr Pushkin, *Eugene Onegin*, 1st rev., vol. 1 (Princeton, N.J.: Princeton University Press, 1975), 10. This is a good example of what Theo Hermans calls the "creative genius" problem: "If the literary artist is viewed as a uniquely gifted creative genius endowed with profound insight and a mastery of his native language, the work he produces will naturally come to be regarded as exalted,

untouchable, inimitable, hallowed." On the other hand, he continues, it is conventionally assumed that the work of the translator is "not only second-hand, but also generally second-rate" (1985, 7–8).

4. Niranjana's book contains a lengthy essay on the abandonment of historicity in the writings of Walter Benjamin, Jacques Derrida, and Paul de Man. One contributor to Venuti 1992, John Johnston, explicitly reformulates Walter Benjamin's argument about literalism as a matter of "territoriality."

CHAPTER 1: TRANSLATION CULTURE

1. The Everyman's Library label is found on a great many translations, from various languages, with no translator mentioned anywhere in them. Other publishers are more scrupulous, but the majority still hide the translator's name, leaving it off the book jacket and out of *Books in Print* and other reference guides (see Venuti 1986, 180).

2. *Foreign Quarterly Review* 21 (April 1838): 33.

3. From *Westminster Review* 36 (July 1841): 43.

4. *British Quarterly Review* 21 (January 1855): 130; qtd. in Gettmann 1941, 14.

5. Carl Schurz, "Glossy Polish Hides Savage Vigor" (1900), in Anschel 1974, 190–93.

6. Such stereotypes were strongly and widely held: "Until we [Britain] became indirectly Russia's ally early in this century, the prevailing image of Russia was that of a cruel aristocracy governing a vast horde of barbaric peasants (they were called 'Scythian hordes' in 1854 just as the Germans were called Huns in the 1914–1918 war!)." Kingsley Martin, *The Triumph of Lord Palmerston* (London: Hutchinson, 1963), 21.

7. To give the translator his or her due, there is a disclaimer in the introduction to the effect that the Russian language presents "almost insurmountable" problems to the foreigner, "but if it were possible for him to [master it] perfectly, he would discover an extraordinary copiousness, a delicacy, and beauty of expression that would indeed surprise him." *Sketches of Russian Life in the Caucasus*, 7.

8. This text is mentioned with horror by more than one critic. See G. Phelps 1958, 431–32, C. Proffer 1964, and Nabokov 1944, 62–63.

9. By an anonymous reviewer in *Saturday Review*, 29 March 1862, 361–62; qtd. in Davie 1990, 273–74.

10. *Proceedings of the Anglo-Russian Literary Society* 17 (London: Imperial Institute, 1897). See also Gettman 1941 and Orel 1977 on the availability of Russian works in England in the late nineteenth century.

11. Gettmann (1941, 37) counts sixteen American translations of Turgenev works, including six books, between 1868 and 1873; the corresponding

figures for Britain were five or six translations, including three books. See also E. M. de Vogüé (1887).

12. M. M. Kovalevskii, in *Ivan Turgenev v vospominaniiakh sovremmenikov* 2:142; qtd. in Alekseev 1989, 253.

13. From an obituary for Turgenev written by James for the *Atlantic Monthly*, 26 April 1877; repr. in James 1984, 1006–34. Davie (1990, 271) notes that James commended Turgenev to William Dean Howells, who proceded to proselytize for the Russian author in America.

14. "Ivan Turgénieff," *North American Review*, April 1874; repr. in James 1984, 968.

15. Alekseev writes, "Even before her Russian poems first apppeared in print, Karolina Pavlova, one of the most talented Russian translators, produced equally perfect translations of Schiller into French, of Pushkin and Iazykov into German, and of Pushkin, Iazykov, Viazemskii, and Baratynskii into French" (1989, 272).

16. The French, however, were themselves not above producing mutilated versions of Russian works. C. Proffer writes of Ernest Charrière's 1859 translation of *Dead Souls*, "[He] called the chapters 'songs' and affixed chapter titles such as *Le fou et le sage dans les steppes*. The fragments of Part Two were added, and the work was 'completed' with a French translation of a continuation of *Dead Souls* written by a Ukrainian named Vaščenko-Zaxarčenko. A truly Gogolian fate!" (1964, 420).

17. This haphazard exposure to the Russian language did not always benefit literature. Turgenev once noted a terrible version of *Eugene Onegin*, in English rhymed verse, "by some retired colonel, an incredibly—astonishingly—decrepit man, and an equally astonishing blockhead" (Alekseev 1944, 133).

18. H. B. Wells (1932) estimated that millions of Russians had come to the United States between 1890 and 1910.

19. James, "Ivan Turgénieff," *North American Review*, April 1874; repr. in James 1984, 974.

20. "Count Lyof Tolstoi," *Contemporary Review* 94 (1908): 272; qtd. in Orel 1954, 465.

21. From *Thus to Revisit* (1921), as qtd. in G. Phelps 1956, 52–53.

22. From "Ivan Turgénieff," *Library of the World's Best Literature*, ed. C. D. Warner (New York: R. S. Pearl & J. A. Hill, 1896); repr. in James 1984, 1029–30.

23. From "Ivan Turgénieff," *North American Review*, April 1874; repr. in James 1984, 974 and 982. See also G. Phelps 1956, 71.

24. "Ivan Turgénieff," *Atlantic Monthly*, January 1884; repr. in James 1984, 1007.

25. A more usual, and more literal, translation is *A Nest of Gentlefolk* or *A Nest of the Gentry*. Ralston was not acting willfully in changing the title; he had Turgenev's personal approval for the new name. Turgenev commented,

"I find the title 'Liza' to be very apt, the more so as the name '*Dvorianskoe gnezdo*' is not quite right [*ne sovsem tochnoe*] and was chosen not by me but by my publisher." Letter to W. Ralston, 8 December 1868 (Tove 1966, 138). In any event, it was a more appropriate choice than another translator's *A Nest of Hereditary Legislators*. The latter volume, whose cover claims not that it is translated but that it is "done into English," has a foreword that brazenly extols the "simplicity and naturalism of the language of Turgueni-eff," in spite of the translator's own wooden prose. *A Nest of Hereditary Legislators*, trans. Frantz Davidovitch Davis (London: Simpkin, Marshall, Hamilton, Kent, n.d.), v.

26. "Mr. Turguenief's *Liza*," *Spectator*, 23 October 1869, 1242; Galagan 1966, 144.

27. *The Novels and Stories of Ivan Turgenieff*, trans. Isabel Hapgood, 16 vols. (New York: Charles Scribner's Sons, 1903–4).

28. *The Nation*, 4 February 1904, 94; qtd. in Moser 1988, 434.

29. A. Bennett, "Ivan Turgenev" (1899), in *The Author's Craft and Other Critical Writings of Arnold Bennett*, ed. Samuel Hynes (Lincoln: University of Nebraska Press, 1968), 102.

30. That Conrad did not love Russia is clear from his Author's Note (1920) to *Under Western Eyes*, in which he comments that for him to portray Russians objectively required "detachment from all passions, prejudice and even from personal memories." He virtually apologizes for treating his protagonist sympathetically, calling the other characters "apes of a sinister jungle" and lamenting "the sanguinary futility of the crimes and the sacrifices seething in that amorphous mass." J. Conrad, *Under Western Eyes* (London: Thomas Nelson & Sons, 1956), viii–ix.

31. Clarence Decker writes that in 1886 "The *Spectator*, for example, was deeply impressed with a French translation of *Crime and Punishment*, although it doubted seriously that the novel would ever be popular in England" (1937, 547).

32. The Anglo-Russian Literary Society was formed in 1893 and soon succeeded in establishing at Oxford the first British professorship of Russian. The *Proceedings of the ARLS* were published three times a year and covered many topics in Russian culture, as well as questions of Russian language training.

33. According to Hemmings (1950, 39), de Vogüé's "astonishment" may have been disingenuous. The viscount, he suggests, was "tempering his own more favorable opinion of Dostoevsky in order to suit the conservative tastes of readers of the *Revue des Deux Mondes*." Hemmings cites evidence from de Vogüé's correspondence to support this claim.

34. De Vogüé calls for similar "overhauling" and "recasting" of Dostoevsky's works to make them more approachable in French. Hemmings responds, also with regard to French practices, "Those who made such suggestions failed to foresee that the 'recasting and overhauling' was almost

bound to be entrusted to men who, without the slightest inkling of Dosto-evsky's intentions, would cut and trim the original works with a view to pan-dering to the thirst for sensationalism of the widest possible circle of readers" (1950, 17). Thus, while English translators worked to tame these works, French translators appear to have made them more racy.

35. The enmity between Dostoevsky and Turgenev was well known, resulting, for example, in Dostoevsky's scathing caricature of the other writer as Karmazinov in his novel *Besy*.

36. *Letters of Robert Louis Stevenson*, vol. 2 (New York: Charles Scrib-ner's Sons, 1911), 323. Parts of this passage are also cited in Knowlton 1916, 450, and G. Phelps 1956, 165.

37. John Lomas, writing for *Macmillan's* (January 1887, 187–98), does admit that, of the four major novelists, Dostoevsky "has the most interest and importance for English readers," but he dismisses all his works after *Crime and Punishment* as excessively polemical.

38. G. Phelps (1956, 157), citing George Saintsbury and various unnamed critics for American and British journals.

39. "Bibliographical Notes," *Academy* 60 (2 March 1901): 180. G. Phelps writes,

> In American literary circles indeed there was something approaching a "Rus-sian craze," and the number of translations during this period rose even more steeply than in England: by 1889 there were, for example, twenty-seven edi-tions of Tolstoy's novels and tales, representing sixteen different titles, and twenty-one separate translations; and according to the *Westminster Review* for September 1888 "rival translations" of his books were "competing for sale in Boston as they competed in Paris." (1956, 39)

40. G. K. Chesterton commented in 1912, "We know not what to do with this small and noisy moralist who is inhabiting one corner of a great and good man." "Sympathy and Tolstoy," in *Sympathy and Tolstoy* (London: Arthur L. Humphreys, 1912), 13.

41. *Literary World* (Boston), 23 July 1887, 233; Davie 1990, 271.

42. Orel 1977, 4. The process was not perfectly smooth. Davie (1990) describes the difficulties of getting "The Kreutzer Sonata" into English, over the pruderies of translators and publishers alike.

43. "A Russian Novel: The Difference between Russian and That Anglo-Saxon Fiction Which Only Succeeds in Being Stupidly Indiscreet," *New York Times Book Review*, 30 June 1912, 389.

44. Lawrence Irving's adaptation replaced the pawnbroker with an evil landlord who makes unwelcome advances to Sonia, an innocent maiden. Raskolnikov is a student revolutionary who kills the landlord to protect Sonia's honor. The German literary historian Walter Neuschäffer (1935, 6) indicates that the changes were made to suit the English public, and that

they did succeed in bringing Dostoevsky's name into the public eye.

45. Such comments would serve as confirmation for Davie's later hypothesis (1990, 277) that, appearing in English when they did, Tolstoy and Dostoevsky were subject to a Freudian backlash. In a 1928 essay, Rebecca West describes fearing for her safety when reading Dostoevsky, in terms that ring distinctly of Freud:

> Now when one picks oneself up after the wind of Dostoevsky's ecstasy has blown over one and counts the spoons there are never any missing. The ecstasy has been an authentic translation of the senses, which by sympathy has translated one also to an intenser life. It has not been a chloroform mask clapped over one's face while a thief who loves to filch from men what little they have of truth goes through one's habitation. The only case one has against Dostoevsky is that he does not invest his work with the suave form that would count the spoons for us as he went along, that would convince us from the beginning that here is one of the white company that use the mind for righteous purposes. (1976, 146)

46. Letter of 27 May 1912, qtd. in Muchnic 1938–39, 73.

47. Letter to Catherine Carswell, 27 November 1916, in *The Collected Letters of D. H. Lawrence*, vol. 1, ed. Harry T. Moore (New York: Viking Press, 1962), 488.

48. Winifred Smith 1916, 103. Her claim is illuminating; Goncharov was the first author Garnett translated, in 1894, and Lermontov's *Hero of Our Time* had appeared before as well, but by 1916 they were once more unknown.

49. "The Renaissance of Interest in Russian Literature," *Current Opinion* 58 (March 1915): 198.

50. The use of wartime translations as propaganda appears, as well, in a version by Hogarth of Ivan Shmelev's *It Was*. Semion Rapoport writes, "The [author], needless to say, treats the enemy with the same impartiality as he does other partners of the War, but where he uses simply the word 'German' his translator, in the best style of the year 1914, uses 'German horde,' and thus lends an impress to the novel altogether out of keeping with its whole tone" (1928, 506).

51. Mirsky 1979, 300. It should be noted that Mirsky wrote in the *London Outlook* of the "distilled poison" of Chekhov's writing, calling him a "superior artist" (qtd. in "Is the Art of Chekhov a Distilled Poison?" *Current Opinion* 71 [October 1921]: 505–7.)

52. "Chekhov 25 Years Later," *Nation*, 3 July 1929, 5.

53. Her husband, Edward Garnett, was a respected writer, critic, and scholar, and her son became a writer as well. The family friends were a Who's Who of British literary society: D. H. Lawrence, Joseph Conrad, and John Galsworthy were among their regular visitors and correspondents.

54. Letter to R. Rubenstein, qtd. in Rubenstein 1974, 361.

55. *Times Literary Supplement*, 30 April 1954, 277.

56. Woolf wrote,

Of all those who feasted upon Tolstoi, Dostoevsky, and Tchekov during the past twenty years, not more than one or two perhaps have been able to read them in Russian. Our estimate of their qualities has been formed by critics who have never read a word of Russian, . . . who have had to depend, blindly and implicitly, upon the work of translators.

What we are saying amounts to this, then, that we have judged a whole literature stripped of its style. (1925*b*, 244)

57. The translator wrote at the time, "This is perhaps the first time in the history of the last few decades that a Russian book, inspired by Russian life, written in Russia and in the Russian language, should see its first light not in Russia but abroad, and not in the language in which it was originally written, but translated into a foreign tongue." Gregory Zilboorg, foreword to E. Zamiatin, *We* (1924), trans. Zilboorg (New York: Dutton, 1952), xiii.

58. "Teaching of Russian in the United States," *School Life* 40 (March 1958): 79–80.

59. Struve defends this trend as follows: "If at present many of the published studies in the field of Soviet literature tend to be politically and socially oriented, the blame for this should fall on Soviet literature itself: its destinies are too closely interwoven with politics, and it is almost impossible to study it *qua* pure literature" (1964, 143).

60. For a lengthy discussion of the American "school" of translating (or lack thereof), in comparison to the Soviet Union's strong promotion of this field, see Lauren G. Leighton's *Two Worlds, One Art* (1991).

61. David Magarshack's translation finds a middle ground, keeping the euphemism "goodness" and eliminating some of the narrator's interjections, but generally giving more of a sense of confusion: "But Ivan got himself into such a position that Smerdyakov began, goodness only knows why, to consider himself in some sort of league with him. He always spoke in a tone of voice that suggested that the two of them had some secret understanding about something. . . . " (313).

62. Richard Lourie, "Raskolnikov Says the Darnedest Things," *New York Times Book Review*, 26 April 1992, 24.

CHAPTER 2: NARRATOR AND TRANSLATOR

1. The *Random House Dictionary of the English Language*, 2d ed. (New York, 1987), gives as its current definition of philology "the study of literary texts and of written records, the establishment of their authenticity and their original form, and the determination of their meaning." The obsolete

definition is "the love of learning and literature." In S. I. Ozhegov's Russian dictionary *filologiia* is defined as "the set of disciplines that study the culture of a people, as expressed in its language and works of literature." Ozhegov, *Slovar' russkogo iazyka*, 11th ed. (Moscow: Russkii iazyk, 1975).

2. Leighton (1991) compares the Soviet and American "schools" of translation in detail. Among other differences, he notes that Russian translators pay far greater attention to theory than their American counterparts. Leighton writes, "It is not appropriate to use the word *formalism* in reference to the Soviet school. The word carries too much ideological baggage and is blamed as the cause of literalist and scientific adventurism. But setting aside terminology, it might be possible to suggest that the deep respect in the Soviet school for textual analysis constitutes a faith in objective-text value. It is not possible to find in Soviet translation discussion any denigration of primacy of text." 1991, 239.

3. Lev Trotsky, *Problems of Life* (London: Methuen, 1924); qtd. in Robin 1992, 166.

4. Maurice Thompson noted with dismay the prevalence of "dialect literature" in American fiction of the late nineteenth century. *Literary World*, 23 July 1887, 233.

5. Robin (1992, 174–76) describes the trajectory of socialist realism as the opposite of Shklovsky's ideas on defamiliarization, of "art as technique."

6. G. Medynskii, "Mar'ia," *Zvezda* 1949, 3:3–31, 4:3–41, 5:3–72, 6:21–85. E. Dorosh, "Mar'ia ili Mariia Karpovna?" *Zvezda* 1 (1950): 179–187.

7. From "On Language" ("O iazyke"), one of a series of lectures on the writer's art given by Zamiatin in 1920–21 at the Dom Isskustv in Petrograd. Most of this lecture is published in *Novyi zhurnal* 77 (1964): 97–113. This citation, however, does not appear in that redaction; it is from an unpublished version of the lectures in Green Library archives, Stanford University, p. 11.

8. From a speech on "Contemporary World Literature and the Tasks of Proletarian Art," at the first Congress of Soviet Writers, *Pervyj vsesoiuznyj s"ezd sovetskikh pisatelei: Stenograficheskii otchet* (Moscow: Khudozhestvennaia literatura, 1934), 316.

9. Valentin Ovechkin, "Raionnye budni," *Novyi mir*, September 1952.

10. See C. Proffer 1984, xvii.

11. A thorough explanation of the phenomenon of deixis is given in Stephen C. Levinson, *Pragmatics* (Cambridge: Cambridge University Press, 1983), chap. 2.

12. There are other inaccuracies, mostly relating to the reinterpretation of this passage as a description of a single event, especially the odd substitution of the definite "—it wasn't lying exactly right—" for the hypothetical *esli ne tak* 'if it's not right'. Also, in the final sentence, Parker misreads *on* 'he, it' as referring to the mortar, rather than the brick, and so leaves out *skhvachen* 'grabbed, set.'

13. Peter Rabinowitz stresses the importance of beginnings and endings of literary works to the reader's understanding of the theme. He comments that "our attention during the act of reading will, in part, be concentrated on what we have found in these positions, and our sense of the text's meaning will be influenced by our assumption that the author expected us to end up with an interpretation that could account more fully for these details than for details elsewhere" (1987, 59). Therefore, it is legitimate to pay special attention, even to an unstressed, semantically nearly empty, opening conjunction.

14. Valentin Rasputin makes the rural cachet of the terms explicit in this comment from the mouth of a young villager in *Poslednii srok:*

> "He said you shouldn't call them 'babas,' that it's insulting somehow. But why should that be insulting? Why am I not insulted to be called a muzhik? It's even the other way around—call me a *muzhchina* and I feel upset somehow, insulted, as if I can't make it as a muzhik, as if I'm not cut out for the work or the home life. But a muzhik is what I am—what more do I need? It's the same with a baba. What's so insulting about that? Take old Anna, for instance. She's lived her whole life as a baba and never been insulted by anyone. Just let anybody else try to be a better baba. Nobody, not one soul, would say a word against her; nobody has the right." (1970, 235–36; my translation)

15. Compare the colloquial narrators of Fyodor Abramov and Rasputin to that of Fyodor Panferov, whom Gorky took so much to task in the 1930s for his use of *skaz.*

> И в эту годину жители Широкого Буерака ждали ее, весну. Они каждое утро поднимались с одной и той же мыслью, шли за околицу, щупали там пахоту и пристально всматривались в даль полей. Над полями висело серое, тупое и вязкое, как вата, небо. Временами оно разрывалось, тогда по нему начинали метаться непричесанные тучи, посыпая землю мелким, колючим дождем.

Panferov, *Bruski*, in *Sobranie sochinenii v shesti tomakh*, vol. 1 (Moscow: Gosudarstvennoe izdatel'stvo khudozhestvennoi literatury, 1959), 7. Compared to Abramov's narration in *Two Winters*, this is standard literary Russian, except for the archaic *godina*; the sentence structure is mostly literary (note the participles and gerund in the last sentence), without ellipses and with every pronoun in place. Thus we can see how much broader the realm of acceptable styles had become in the intervening three decades.

16. A good description of the *oral* colloquial language is given by A. N. Vasil'eva (1976, chap. 3). She singles out as important its emphasis on the communicative and concrete, its unmediated quality, its strong emotional component and use of extralingual signs (gestures, etc.), the relatively low density of

content, with each sentence expressing a single idea, the tendency toward modal/imperative constructions, use of ellipses and incomplete sentence structures, and the presence of elements from various linguistic registers.

17. The terminology here is confusing, because the word *prostorechie* is variably defined. The encyclopedia calls it "an organic part of the literary language but simultaneously existing outside its boundaries" (s. v. "*Russkii iazyk*"). Vasil'eva divides the concept in two, the first being "vulgarisms used for emotional effect. These," she explains, "are included in the concept of literary language." On the other hand, "there exist vulgarisms of a semidialectal nature, which lie outside the framework of the literary language" (1976, 86, n. 1). The distinction between these and *razgovornye* 'colloquial' words is not always clear.

18. On two randomly chosen pages (382–83) of S. I. Ozhegov, *Slovar' russkogo iazyka* (1975 ed.), there are thirty-six words or phrases marked "*razg.*" (colloquial) and eight "*prost.*" (low, vulgar). Another was listed as "colloquial-ironic," and two as "colloquial-jesting." On the other side of the spectrum, there was one marked "high," two "bookish," two "archaic," and six "specialized." The *Great Soviet Encyclopedia* also clearly distinguishes colloquial elements from the "neutral," written language (s.v. "*Russkii iazyk*").

19. *Shorter Oxford English Dictionary* (1977 ed.), ix. On two randomly chosen pages (728–29, "Farther–Fat") there are at least two expressions that I would identify as strongly marked colloquialisms ("fast women" and "to play fast and loose with") which are not singled out in any way in the dictionary.

20. Titunik writes of (first-person) skaz: "Zoščenko's skaz addresser is not a point of view but *the* authority. . . . [It] is, of course, in the longer works that play on authorial authority achieves consummate expression" (1971, 93).

21. In vol. 1, chap. 5, the narrator describes Chichikov's first impressions of Sobakevich's house:

. . . дом вроде тех, как у нас строят для военных поселений и немецких колонистов.
(Gogol 1951, 93)

In the Norton edition of the Reavey translation this appears as "the sort of house that is usually built in Russia for military settlers or German colonists" (95). Magarshack's version is very similar: "the sort of house that is built in Russia for military settlements or German colonists" (102). (I am grateful to Therese Malhame for this observation.)

22. See the discussion of this phenomenon in the translation of Victor Hugo's *Nôtre dame* in chap. 3.

23. "Most frequently . . . translation from one language into another substitutes messages in one language not for separate code units but for entire messages in some other language. Such a translation is a reported

speech: the translator recodes and transmits a message received from another source" (Jakobson 1987, 430).

24. See, e.g., Parthé 1992, chap. 3.

25. Benjamin 1968*b*, 72. See esp. Joseph Graham 1985, which contains Jacques Derrida's famous essay, "Des Tours de Babel," and Venuti 1992.

26. See Richard Lourie, "Raskolnikov Says the Darnedest Things," *New York Times Book Review*, 26 April 1992, 24.

CHAPTER 3: NARRATED MONOLOGUE: TRANSLATING A SHIFTING VIEWPOINT

1. Some scholars seem to use the various terms interchangeably, while others distinguish between them. B. A. Uspenskii (1970, 49), following V. N. Voloshinov, restricts the term *nesobstvenno-priamaia rech'* to expressions like,

Трактирщик сказал, что не дам вам есть, пока не заплатите за прежнее («Ревизор»).

Literally: The innkeeper said that I won't give you anything to eat until you pay for what you've had already. ("The Inspector-General")

This both includes a verb of speaking and does not shift out of the first person, so it is another phenomenon entirely from narrated monologue as Dorrit Cohn defines it. Uspenskii admits to using a narrow definition, "to denote an intermediate phenomenon between direct and indirect speech, that is, one that can be changed (with greater or lesser accuracy) into either direct or indirect speech by the use of particular operations" (1970, 51). His term "interior monologue" is closer to Cohn's idea, embracing situations "when the thoughts and feelings of a character are given, and moreover a text typical of that character is divined [*ugadyvaetsia*], but given in the third person." M. M. Bakhtin and T. G. Vinokur, on the other hand, use *nesobstvenno-priamaia rech'* for this device. To further complicate matters, Cohn (1966, 109) distinguishes "interior monologue" from "narrated monologue" in that the former uses the first person and, in English, present tense.

2. For a detailed discussion of the phenomenon from a Soviet perspective, see L. Sokolova 1968. A brief survey of the discussion is given in Hughes 1977, chap. 8.

3. J. E. Lorck, *Die "erlebte Rede": Eine sprachliche Untersuchung* (Heidelberg: Carl Winters Universitätsbuchhandlung, 1921). English-language scholarship has been much slower to observe and comment on the device. Notes Cohn, "Scholars writing in English, at any rate, tend to dismiss the concept of *erlebte Rede* as an equivalent of stream of consciousness, or

they regard it as a superfluous category" (1966, 100–101). She singles out René Wellek and Austin Warren, who, she says, "regard *erlebte Rede, le style indirect libre,* and *le monologue intérieur* as variants of a technical device of the 'objective novel,' for which the English phrase 'stream of consciousness . . . is the loose, inclusive correspondent.'" Wellek and Warren, *Theory of Literature* (New York: Harcourt, Brace, 1949), 233; qtd. in Cohn (1966, 101 n. 10). Ann Banfield (1982) makes an extensive study of the grammar of what she calls "represented speech and thought" which addresses this lack to some degree; however, precisely because she limits herself to examples from English and French, her generalizations about an overarching grammar of the style are specious, depending as they do upon the peculiarities of tense shifts in these languages.

4. Banfield objects to this idea that narrated monologue effaces the role of the author. She writes, "It is only a false impression that sentences of non-reflective consciousness somehow show the author's ordering hand more than those of reported thought. This is because reflection can have a linguistic realization, but, since non-reflective states cannot, their style must necessarily be other than what the character would have himself said" (1982, 212). However, her assertion that "non-reflective states cannot . . . have a linguistic realization" is hotly disputed. I, for one (and there are many others), am not convinced by her division of literary works into objective and subjective sentences, not allowing for both at once.

5. Sokolova (1968) goes on to say, however, that the device is no longer necessary in Soviet literature of the 1960s, since such boundaries have been erased by social development, and so it is used only for didactic purposes or to hide the author's voice, not as a goal in itself.

6. Uspenskii (1970, 29) points out another feature of Russian (and not of English) that is valuable in this regard, that of free word order. He compares the expressions

Voshla Natasha, ego zhena (a case of ordinary narration by an uninvolved narrator),

Voshla Natasha (internal monologue, spoken by someone who knows her),

Natasha voshla (Natasha's own viewpoint, perhaps).

He writes, "The syntactical organization of the third sentence is such that it cannot correspond either to the hero's perspective or to that of an abstract, external [*postoronnii*] observer; most likely the point of view used here belongs to Natasha herself." English has much less leeway with word order, and so cannot achieve such subtleties in this way.

7. K. S. Aksakov, "*O russkikh glagolakh,*" in *Polnoe sobranie sochinenii,* vol. 2, part 1 (Moscow, 1875), 414; qtd. in Vinogradov 1986, 442.

8. As examples Vinogradov (1986, 442) cites, "Vsiakii den' prokhodil u

nas odnoobrazno: ia *podoidu* k ego dveri, stuknu raza dva, on *otvorit"* (future used in past tense meaning), and "On ne mnogo teriaet chasov na razgovory, kazhdoe utro on *skazhet* mne: zdravstvui, i poshel k sebe zanimat'sia" (future form in present tense meaning).

9. Vinogradov (1986, citing N. P. Nekrasov, *O znachenii form russkogo glagola*, St. Petersburg, 1865), 133.

10. One of his examples, from Turgenev, is: "Ia bylo strusil, a Matrena-to *kak udarit* vozhzhami, da *kak pomchitsia* priamo na vozok." "In this case," Vinogradov notes, "the speaker is as if transported into the past moment, 'without, however, forgetting that he is there in imagination only'" (1986, 470–71). The example is from Turgenev, "Petr Petrovich Karataev," and the final quotation is from L. P. Razmusen, "O glagol'nykh vremenakh i ob otnoshenii ikh k vidam v russkom, nemetskom, i frantsuzskom iazykakh." *Zhurnal ministerstva narodnogo prosveshcheniia* 6 (1891): 388.

11. Banfield (1982, 78) indicates that, if such represented thoughts in the present tense are introduced by a verb of communication or thinking, they automatically become direct speech, as with the example *He thought, women are always like that.*

12. The editors of the *Grammar of Contemporary English* (Quirk et al. 1972, 787) indicate that backshifting is not required in English when "the validity of the statement reported holds for the present time as much as for the time of utterance." Their example is, *Socrates said that nothing can harm a good man.*

13. Note example 3.2c, from the same work, in which the implied possessives are best read as "your" but translated as "her."

14. See, e.g., the discussion of oral and literary conventions in Rachel May, "Powers of Speech: Speech Acts in the Russian *Primary Chronicle*," in *Dialogue and Critical Discourse*, ed. Michael Macovski (Oxford: Oxford University Press, forthcoming). Scholes and Kellogg maintain that ironic distance between author and narrator is possible only in written narrative, while "traditional, oral narrative consists rhetorically of a teller, his story, and an implied audience" (1966, 53).

15. The original passage hammers repeatedly at the idea of Golyadkin's aloofness, while Constance Garnett changes the meaning of several relevant phrases: "sam po sebe" ("on his own two feet," "by himself") she gives as "quite himself," suggesting health rather than independence; "ego izba s kraiu" she also changes into an expression of mental health ("nothing wrong in his upper storey"), rather than detachment (the full expression, "moia izba c kraiu; ia nichego ne znaiu" is something like "Don't ask me, I live at the end of the block"). A better translation might be, *"This glance gave full expression to Mister Golyadkin's independence, that is, it plainly said that Mr. Golyadkin was quite alright, that he stood on his own two feet, just like anyone else, and that in any case he 'kept his curtains closed.'"*

Vinogradov (1976, 128) chooses this passage as an example of internal echoing in the work, showing how these same expressions of Golyadkin's come up later in the narration:

Господин Голядкин тотчас . . . поспешил принять вид совершенно особенный, вид, ясно выражавший, что он, Голядкин, сам по себе, что он ничего, . . . и что ведь он, Голядкин, сам никого не затрагивает. (Dostoevsky, *Dvoinik*, 252)

Oddly, Garnett renders one of the repeated phrases differently (this time she comes somewhat closer to the original meaning): " . . . that he, Golyadkin, *kept himself to himself,* that he was 'all right,' . . . " (512).

16. This is the Garnett version. David Magarshack has, "But you did not do it. You are mistaken. You are not the murderer. Do you hear? It is not you!" (706).

17. Lawrence Venuti includes among the strategies for achieving fluency and transparency in translation that of avoiding "pronounced rhythmic regularity or sound repetitions—any textual effect, any play of the signifier, which calls attention to the materiality of language, to words as words" (1992, 4). See also Venuti 1986 for a more detailed discussion of this idea.

18. In her 1984 translation of Bakhtin's book, Caryl Emerson renders *proniknovennoe slovo* as "penetrative word," a phrase she now acknowledges to be inaccurate and would change in the next edition. I use her preferred term, "penetrated word," here.

19. The English version given here is from Victor Hugo, *Notre-Dame de Paris* (London: Dent, Everyman's Library, 1964), 5. The original copyright is given as 1910. This translation was also used in an undated edition put out by T. Nelson & Sons.

20. Victor Hugo, *The Hunchback of Notre Dame* (New York: Modern Library, n.d.), 6–7. No translator is named.

21. It would be interesting to study this (all too prevalent) attitude toward translation in light of Peter Brooks's discussion of the role of the psychoanalyst in reconstructing a narrative: "The work of the analyst must in large measure be a recomposition of the narrative discourse to give a better representation of the patient's story, to reorder its events, to foreground its dominant themes, to understand the force of desire that speaks in and through it" (1986, 53).

22. Their version is,

I suddenly ran to her, seized her hand, opened it, put . . . and closed it again.
But I don't want to lie, so I'll say directly that I opened her hand and put . . . in it out of malice. (Pevear and Volokhonsky, 126)

CHAPTER 4: TRANSLATING THE WRITTEN TEXT: REANALYZING FORM AND STRUCTURE

1. Others agree with this delimitation, although their arguments are muddy. Schlesinger comments, in his study of readability, "It is reasonable to assume that the reader pauses habitually on reading [the period] at the end of a sentence, because it marks, in most cases, the end of a meaningful unit" (1968, 74–75). Again, "meaningful unit" is as much a matter for subjective debate as Enkvist's question about dividing the story. Langleben looks at the question from the point of view of the text as a whole and writes, "Final intonation and a full-stop as its written substitute are responsible for isolation of all kinds of sentence from a textual continuum" (1979, 248). This is less ambiguous, but preserves the oral/written confusion in its premise. Also see Langleben for a discussion of the hierarchy Text—Sentence cluster—Non-simple sentence—Simple sentence, and the role of punctuation in pragmatic effect.

2. Dillon (1978, 38) distinguishes the period from the semicolon on the basis of "degree of separation," for example.

3. Langleben cites an example from J. Carmichael's translation of *Anna Karenina*, where one long sentence is bisected, causing "the destruction of the original communicative pattern" (1979, 252). As she explains, the translation loses the smooth transition from topic to accented focus, splitting the original unitary focus into a topic and a focus and introducing an entirely new second focus.

4. Polubichenko, however, opens a can of worms with her argument about the "intention of the original supraphrasal unity" (1984, 201). Her own evidence shows that paragraphs lie outside our conscious understanding of prose. Even if literary theory would allow us to consider the "intentions" of the author, the very fact that translators alter paragraph boundaries at will suggests that writers in general lack coherent rules or intentions in creating their paragraphs in the first place.

5. It does not help that many of the scholarly investigations of the phenomenon are vague and impressionistic. For example, Tove's assertion (1966, 141) that Ralston's paragraphing "severely damages the impression" lacks rigor and tells us little about the true significance of the change.

6. Nancy Downey, "The Adventures of a J. R. A.," unpublished translation, Brown University, 1989.

7. Personal communication, March 1992.

8. In a scene in the E. T. A. Hoffmann story, as translated from the Russian, a gentleman picks Zaches up and kisses him, at which Zaches has a tantrum and "squeals":

"Let me go...Let me go...That hurts...Ouch!...Ouch!...I'll scratch out your eyes...I'll bite off half your nose!"

"No," exclaimed the professor, setting him down on the sofa, "No, my dear friend, enough of your excessive modesty!"

In German, Zaches's speech is:

»Laß mich los—laß mich los—es tut mir weh—weh—weh—ich kratz' dir die Augen aus—ich beiß' dir die Nase entzwei!«

E. T. A. Hoffmann, *Dichtungen und Schriften, sowie Briefe und Tagebücher*, vol. 3 (Weimar: Erich Lichtenstein, 1924), 167.

9. Dillon analyzes some particularly difficult examples and concludes that readers are not always bound by consciousness of sentence structure, even to the extent of trying to make sense of a particular sentence. On reading Wordsworth and Faulkner, he writes, "There is one fairly reliable clue that one is not reading for sentences: upon reaching a period, one asks himself 'what did the sentence say?' and cannot exactly answer" (1978, 131). The tension he describes, however, is not one of indifference to the sentence-as-such but of heightened awareness of it, as a barrier to normal comprehension. Were he to be asked about translation policy, I suspect that Dillon would acknowledge that this very opacity should be retained, and that would involve close attention to sentence boundaries, punctuation, and the like.

10. Schlesinger (1968, 74), citing W. L. Wonderly, "Some Factors of Meaningfulness in Reading Matter for Inexperienced Readers," in *A William Cameron Townshend en el XXV Aniversario del I.L.V.* (n.d.), and G. R. Clare, *The Measurement of Readability* (Ames: Iowa State University Press, 1963).

11. See, e.g., the discussion of "gap-sentence links" in I. R. Galperin, *Stylistics* (Moscow, 1971), 231–33.

12. See also Wolfgang Iser's comment that "if we are to grasp the unseen structure that regulates but does not formulate the connection or even the meaning, we must bear in mind the various forms in which the textual segments are presented to the reader's viewpoint in the reading process" (1980*a*, 112).

13. Langleben, in her study of "communicative stress" in the sentence, states that "the patterning of all the supersentential units, including a text, consists in exploiting the modulations of resilient boundaries of constituent sentences to produce subtle stylistic nuances inherent in the personal manner of a writer" (1979, 253). Victor Streeter's study of co-occurrence of similar sentence types indicates that repetitions of sentence types are not random but characteristic of a writer's style. Streeter concludes, "It is unreasonable to believe a priori that writers produce well-formed linguistic units in a random fashion, uninfluenced by thought and language just expressed" (1973, 116).

14. Voloshinov 1929, 111; see also Silliman 1989, 76–77.

CONCLUSION: TEACHING LITERATURE IN TRANSLATION

1. Andrew Benjamin, paraphrasing Donald Davidson's "On the Very Idea of a Conceptual Scheme" (1984), says, "There can be no 'intelligible' account of either partial or complete 'failure' of translation." Benjamin, *Translation and the Nature of Philosophy* (London and New York: Routledge, 1989), 61.

2. Roland Barthes, *S/Z*, Richard Miller (New York: Hill & Wang, 1974), 7–8.

3. Jiří Levý writes, "Translators, as a rule, adopt a pessimistic strategy, they are anxious to accept those solutions only whose 'value'—even in the case of the most unfavourable reactions of their readers—does not fall under a certain minimum limit admissible by their linguistic or aesthetic standards." After enumerating the probabilities of certain solutions, he concludes, "Without making any numerical computations, translators in fact intuitively make guesses concerning the possibilities of the different evaluations by readers." "Translation as a Decision Process," in *To Honor Roman Jakobson*, vol. 2, *Janua Linguarum* series major 31–33 (The Hague and Paris: Mouton, 1967), 1180–81.

4. Jean Franco, "History and Literature: Remapping the Boundaries," *Literature and Society in Imperial Russia, 1800–1914*, ed. W. M. Todd III (Stanford, Calif.: Stanford University Press, 1978), 22.

APPENDIX 1: FACT VS. FICTION: TWO TRANSLATIONS OF BULGAKOV'S *MASTER I MARGARITA*

1. A complete discussion of the textual history of the novel, the sources of the various manuscripts and of the translations, and the discrepancies between them all is found in Fiene 1981.

2. Fiene indicates that "Ginsburg's translation . . . is generally much more faithful to the original than Glenny's" (1981, 351). But he also writes, "It would be ideal if Glenny would do the revised translation," based on the complete Soviet text (349). The evidence I will present in this paper suggests otherwise.

The omissions from Ginsburg's version are listed by Fiene in great detail, too much detail to be useful to the teacher wishing to provide a supplement to her translation. I would recommend that the teacher make available to the class the following substantial omissions:

Chap. 7, on disappearances in the apartment (491–93);
Chap. 13, the introduction to Aloysius Magarych (560–62; most of this is also missing from Glenny's version);
Chap. 15, Nikanor Ivanovich's dream (578–87);
Chap. 28, Koroviev and Begemot in the Torgsin Store (762–67);

Chap. 29, Koroviev and Begemot tell their story about the Griboyedov fire (777–78);

Chap. 30, Margarita tells the Master of her bargain with the devil (780–83);

Chap. 31, Begemot's farewell whistle (792–93);

Chap. 32, Woland explains Koroviev's change (795), and parts of the final two paragraphs, where the Master is freed (799);

Epilogue, on the fates of Nikanor Ivanovich and Aloysius Magarych (806–7).

3. Fiene (1981, 351–53) reviews the various interpretations of the last six words of the Master's novel. He shows that only the end of the last chapter (chap. 32) coincides exactly with the phrase the Master claimed would be his conclusion and suggests that only this larger novel is truly coterminus with the Master's.

4. Vida Taranovski Johnson describes the distinction well. The Pilate sections are "phraseologically marked by long, complex sentences with numerous participial clauses, inverted word order, and exotic, defamiliarizing names and epithets. . . . [Their] objective, transparent, 'elegant' narrator is also completely dissociated from the subjective, chatty, even coarse narrator who opens the main story" (1981, 274–75).

5. As Johnson points out, the narrator's "constant clarifying remarks . . . "expose him as the storyteller, the filter through which all events and characters are refracted. He establishes an explicit relationship, one of complicity with the reader by addressing him . . . and by occasionally using the first person plural. . . . However, the reader discovers almost immediately that although this narrator is accurate in his description of events, he is unreliable in his interpretation" (1981, 278).

6. Johnson calls non sequiturs the source of "much of the humor in the novel" (1981, 280).

APPENDIX 2: OBSERVING THE GROTESQUE: TWO CLASSICS OF FORMALIST CRITICISM AND ENGLISH TRANSLATIONS

1. Russian quotations are from "Shinel'," (Gogol, 1938).

2. The Garnett translation cited here is the 1963 Anchor-Doubleday edition.

3. Vinogradov, 1966, 25. This essay was originally given as a report to the annual open meeting of the Department of Verbal Arts, 29 November 1925.

4. See example 2.1b for a discussion of the repetitions and their treatment in translation.

5. See, e.g., the comments of Dostoevsky's contemporaries cited by Evelyn Harden in her introduction to her translation of *The Double*. L. V.

Brant wrote in *The Northern Bee* (28 February 1846), "There is no end to the wordiness—heavyhanded, annoying, irksome, to the repetitions, to the circumlocutions for one and the same thought, for one and the same words which the author has come to like so much" (qtd. in Harden's intro., p. x).

6. Russian quotations are from Dostoevsky 1972b.

7. Garnett renders the phrase in question as, "with anxiety, with great anxiety, with extreme anxiety" (486); Harden has "with uneasiness, with great uneasiness, with extreme uneasiness" (16).

8. The revised version is "He subsided into silence. He made up his mind to keep quiet, not to open his mouth, to show that he was quite all right, that he was like everyone else, and that his situation, as far as he could see, was quite a proper one." *Three Short Novels of Dostoevsky*, Constance Garnett, rev. and ed. Avrahm Yarmolinsky (Garden City, N.Y.: Anchor-Doubleday, 1960), 39.

9. This introduction adds its own layer of confusion to the work. Mark Spilka complains of Dostoevsky's "prolix and repetitious" style, then adds, "George Bird . . . finds only praise for Dostoevsky's technique, which certainly gains force and clarity from his deft translation. He fails to see, however, that a new idea calls for new means of expression, and that Dostoevsky had merely improvised to meet this end" (6). As I understand this argument, Spilka is accusing Bird of being too faithful to Dostoevsky's style, at the same time that he commends him for adding "force and clarity." Perhaps, however, it was Bird's modifications that made it seem to Spilka that there was no "new means of expression" here.

References

Abramov, Fyodor. 1954. "Liudi kolkhoznoi derevni v poslevoennoi proze." *Novyi mir*, 4:210–31.

———. 1982*a*. *Dve zimy i tri leta*. 1968. In vol. 1 of *Sobranie sochinenii v trekh tomakh*, 279–574. Leningrad: Khudozhestvennaia literatura.

Two Winters and Three Summers. Translated by Jacqueline Edwards and Mitchell Schneider. Orlando: Harcourt, 1984.

Two Winters and Three Summers. Translated by D. B. Powers and Doris C. Powers. Ann Arbor: Ardis, 1984.

———. 1982*b*. "*Oleshina izba*." In vol. 3 of *Sobranie sochinenii v trekh tomakh*, 410-26. Leningrad: Khudozhestvennaia literatura.

"Olesha's Cabin." Translated by Paul Gorgen. In *The Barsukov Triangle, The Two-Toned Blond, and Other Stories*, edited by Carl Proffer and Ellendea Proffer, 129–45. Ann Arbor: Ardis, 1984.

———. 1991. "Vokrug da okolo." 1963. In vol. 3 of *Sobranie sochinenii v shesti tomakh*, 193–238. Leningrad: Khudozhestvennaia literatura.

The Dodgers. Translated by David Floyd. London: Flegon, 1963.

Aitmatov, Chingiz. 1980. *I dol'she veka dlitsia den'*. *Novyi mir* 11:3–185.

The Day Lasts More than a Hundred Years. Translated by John French. Bloomington: Indiana University Press, 1983.

Alekseev, M. P. 1944. "Angliiskii iazyk v Rossii i russkii iazyk v Anglii." *Uchenye zapiski Leningradskogo gosudarstvennogo universiteta*, Seriia Filologicheskikh nauk 9, no. 72, 77–137.

———. 1964. "William Ralston and Russian Writers of the Later Nineteenth Century." *Oxford Slavonic Papers* 11:83–93.

———. 1989. *Russkaia literatura i ee mirovoe znachenie*. Edited by B. N. Baksakov and N. S. Nikitina. Leningrad: Nauka.

Anschel, Eugene, ed. 1974. *The American Image of Russia, 1775–1917*. New York: Ungar.

Arndt, Walter. 1960. "'Modal Particles' in Russian and German." *Word* 16:323-36.

Bakhtin, Mikhail. 1963. *Problemy poetiki Dostoevskogo*. Moscow: Sovetskii pisatel'.

———. 1975. "Slovo v romane" (1934–35). In *Voprosy literatury i estetiki. Issledovaniia raznyk let*, 72–233. Moscow: Khudozhestvennaia literatura.

———. 1981. "Discourse in the Novel." In Bakhtin, *The Dialogic Imagination*, translated by Caryl Emerson and Michael Holquist, edited by Holquist, 259–422. Austin: University of Texas Press.

———. 1984. *Problems of Dostoevsky's Poetics*. Translated and edited by Caryl Emerson. Theory and History of Literature 8. Minneapolis: University of Minnesota Press. (Translation of Bakhtin 1963.)

Banfield, Ann. 1982. *Unspeakable Sentences*. Boston: Routledge & Kegan Paul.

Baring, Maurice. 1909. "Tolstoy and Turgeniev." *Quarterly Review* 211.420 (July): 180–202.

———. 1910. *Landmarks in Russian Literature*. New York: Macmillan.

Bassnett, Susan and André Lefevere, eds. 1990. *Translation, History and Culture*. London: Pinter Publishers.

Belaia, Galina. 1983. *Khudozhestvennyi mir sovremennoi prozy*. Moscow: Nauka.

Bely, Andrei. 1978. *Petersburg*. Translated by Robert A. Maguire and John Malmstad. Bloomington: Indiana University Press.

Benjamin, Walter. 1968*a*. "The Storyteller." In his *Illuminations*, translated by Harry Zohn, edited by Hannah Arendt, 83–109. New York: Harcourt.

———. 1968*b*. "The Task of the Translator." In his *Illuminations*, translated by Harry Zohn, edited by Hannah Arendt, 69–82. New York: Harcourt.

Bird, George, trans. See *Dostoevsky* 1973*b*.

Blum-Kulka, Shoshana. 1986. "Shifts of Cohesion and Coherence in Translation." In *Interlingual and Intercultural Communication*, edited by Juliane House and Blum-Kulka, 17–36. Tübingen: Gunter Narr Verlag.

Bouis, Antonina, trans. *See* Rasputin 1978*a*, 1978*b*; Tolstaya 1987*a*, 1987*b*.

Bristow, Eugene K. 1977. "Introduction: On Translating Chekhov." *Anton Chekhov's Plays*, translated and edited by Bristow, xv–xxxii. Norton Critical Edition. New York: Norton.

Brooks, Peter. 1986. "Psychoanalytic Constructions and Narrative Meanings." *Paragraph* 7 (March): 53–76.

Bryner, Cyril. 1958. "Turgenev in the English-Speaking World." In *Three Papers in Slavonic Studies*, by Bryner et al., 5–19. Vancouver: University of British Columbia.

Bulgakov, Mikhail. 1973. *Master i Margarita*. In his *Romany*, 423–812. Leningrad: Khudozhestvennaia literatura.

    The Master and Margarita. Translated by Mirra Ginsburg. New York: Grove Press, 1967.

    The Master and Margarita. Translated by Michael Glenny. New York: Harper & Row, 1967.

Burlingame, Helen, trans. *See* Trifonov 1986*a*.

Catford, J. C. 1965. *A Linguistic Theory of Translation*. London: Oxford University Press.

Chekhov, A. P. 1977. "Step'." 1888. In vol. 7 of *Polnoe sobranie sochinenii i pisem v tridtsati tomakh*, 13–104. Moscow: Nauka.

⸻. "The Steppe." In *The Bishop and Other Stories*, translated by Constance Garnett, 161–302. New York: Macmillan, 1919.

Chesterton, G. K. 1912. "Simplicity and Tolstoy." In his *Simplicity and Tolstoy*, 1–28. London: Arthur Humphreys.

Chukovsky, Kornei. 1988. *Vysokoe iskusstvo*. 1941. Moscow: Sovetskii pisatel'.

⸻. 1984. *The Art of Translation: Kornei Chukovsky's "A High Art"*. Translated and edited by Lauren Leighton. Knoxville: University of Tennessee Press.

Clark, Richard C. 1972. "Approaches to the History of Russian Literature." Review article. *Review of National Literatures* 3 (Spring): 242–61.

Cohn, Dorrit. 1966. "Narrated Monologue: Definition of a Fictional Style." *Comparative Literature* 18 (Spring): 97–112.

Conrad, Joseph. 1928. *Letters from Joseph Conrad, 1895–1924*. Edited by Edward Garnett. Indianapolis: Bobbs-Merrill.

⸻. 1956. *Under Western Eyes*. 1910. (Introduction 1926.) London: Thomas Nelson & Sons.

Coulson, Jessie, trans. *See* Dostoevsky, 1972*b*, 1973*a*.

Crankshaw, Edward. 1947. "Work of Constance Garnett." *The Listener*, 30 January, 195–96.

Cross, A. G. 1969. "The Reverend William Tooke's Contribution to English Knowledge of Russia at the End of the Eighteenth Century." *Canadian Slavic Studies* 3 (Spring): 106–15.

Davie, Donald. 1965. "Introduction." In *Russian Literature and Modern English Fiction*, edited by Davie, 1–13. Chicago: University of Chicago Press.

⸻. 1990. "Mr. Tolstoy, I Presume? The Russian Novel through Victorian Spectacles." In his *Slavic Excursions*, 271–80. Chicago: University of Chicago Press.

Decker, Clarence. 1937. "Victorian Comment on Russian Realism." *PMLA* 52 (June): 542-49.

Dillon, George L. 1978. *Language Processing and the Reading of Literature*. Bloomington: Indiana University Press.

Dostoevsky, F. M. 1972*a*. *Brat'ia Karamazovy*. 1880. Vols. 14–15 of *Polnoe sobranie sochinenii v tridtsati tomakh*. Leningrad: Nauka.

⸻. *The Brothers Karamazov*. Translated by Constance Garnett. 1912. Revised and edited by Ralph E. Matlaw. Norton Critical Edition. New York: Norton, 1976.

⸻. *The Brothers Karamazov*. Translated by Andrew H. MacAndrew. 1970. Toronto: Bantam, 1981.

⸻. *The Brothers Karamazov*. Translated by David Magarshack. 1958. New York: Viking Penguin, 1988.

The Brothers Karamazov. Translated by Richard Pevear and Larissa Volokhonsky. San Francisco: North Point Press, 1990.

The Brothers Karamazov. Translated by David McDuff. London: Penguin, 1993.

Les Frères Karamazov. Translated by Henri Mongault. Paris: Gallimard, 1952.

―――. 1972*b*. *Dvoinik*. 1846. In vol. 1 of *Polnoe sobranie sochinenii v tridtsati tomakh*, 109–229. Leningrad: Nauka.

"The Double." In *The Short Novels of Dostoevsky*, translated by Constance Garnett, introduction by Thomas Mann, 475–615. New York: Dial Press, 1945.

"The Double." In *Notes from Underground and The Double*, translated by Jessie Coulson, 127–287. Harmondsworth: Penguin, 1972.

The Double: Two Versions. Translated by Evelyn Harden. Ann Arbor: Ardis, 1985.

The Double. Translated by George Bird. Bloomington: Indiana University Press, 1958.

―――. 1973*a*. *Prestuplenie i nakazanie*. 1866. Vol. 6 of *Polnoe sobranie sochinenii v tridtsati tomakh*. Leningrad: Nauka.

Crime and Punishment. Translated by Constance Garnett. 1914. New York: Macmillan, 1922.

Crime and Punishment. Translated by David Magarshack. London: Penguin, 1951.

Crime and Punishment. Translated by Jessie Coulson. 1953. Oxford: Oxford University Press, 1980.

Crime and Punishment. Translated by Sidney Monas. New York: Signet, 1968.

Crime and Punishment. Translated by David McDuff. London: Penguin, 1991.

Crime and Punishment. Translated by Richard Pevear and Larissa Volokh-onsky. New York: Knopf, 1992.

―――. 1973*b*. *Zapiski iz podpol'ia*. 1864. In vol. 5 of *Polnoe sobranie sochinenii v tridtsati tomakh*, 99–179. Leningrad: Nauka.

Notes from Underground. In *The Short Novels of Dostoevsky*, translated by Constance Garnett, introduction by Thomas Mann, 127–222. New York: Dial Press, 1945.

Notes from Underground. In *Notes from Underground and the Grand Inquisitor*, translated by Ralph E. Matlaw, 3–115. New York: Dutton, 1960.

Notes from Underground. Translated by Michael R. Katz. New York: Norton, Norton Critical Edition. 1989.

Notes from Underground. In *Notes from Underground and the Gambler*, translated by Jane Kentish, 1–123. Oxford: Oxford University Press, 1991.

Notes from Underground. Translated by Richard Pevear and Larissa
   Volokhonsky. New York: Knopf, 1993.

———. 1974. *Idiot.* 1868. Vol. 8 of *Polnoe sobranie sochinenii v tridtsati
   tomakh.* Leningrad: Nauka.

The Idiot. Translated by Frederick Whishaw. Vizetelly's Russian Novels. London: Vizetelly, 1887.

The Idiot. Translated by Constance Garnett. New York: Macmillan, 1916.

The Idiot. Translated by David Magarshack. Harmondsworth: Penguin,
   1955.

Edwards, Jacqueline, and Mitchell Schneider, trans. *See* Abramov 1982a.

Eikhenbaum, Boris M. 1919. "Kak sdelana 'Shinel'" Gogolia." In vol. 3 of his
   Poetika: Sborniki po teorii poeticheskogo iazyka, 151–65. Petrograd:
   Gos. tipografiia Leshtukov per.

———. 1924. "Illiuziia skaza." In his *Skvoz' literaturu,* 152–56. Leningrad:
   Akademiia.

Emerson, Caryl. 1983. "Translating Bakhtin: Does His Theory of Discourse
   Contain a Theory of Translation?" *University of Ottawa Quarterly*
   53.1:23–33.

———. 1991. "The Brothers, Complete." *Hudson Review* 44:309–16.

———, trans. *See* Bakhtin 1981, 1984.

Enkvist, Nils Erik. 1971. "On the Place of Style in Some Linguistic Theories."
   In *Literary Style: A Symposium,* edited by Seymour Chatman, 47–61.
   London: Oxford University Press.

———. 1978. "Stylistics and Text Linguistics." In *Current Trends in Textlin-
   guistics,* edited by Wolfgang Dressler, 174–190. Berlin: Walter de Gruyter.

———. 1985. "Text and Discourse Linguistics, Rhetoric and Stylistics." In
   Discourse and Literature, edited by Teun A. van Dijk, 11–38. Amster-
   dam: John Benjamins.

Erofeev, Viktor. 1990. "The Parakeet." Translated by Leonard J. Stanton. In
   Glasnost: An Anthology of Russian Literature under Gorbachev, edited by Helena Goscilo and Byron Lindsey, 367–78. Ann Arbor: Ardis.

Falla, Paul, trans. *See* Tendriakov.

Faulkner, William. 1959. *The Mansion.* New York: Random House.

   "Osobniak." Translated by Rita Rait-Kovaleva. In vol. 5 of *Sobranie
   sochinenii v shesti tomakh,* 5–390. Moscow: Khudozhestvennaia literatura, 1987.

Fyodorov, A. V. 1986. *Osnovy obshchei teorii perevoda.* Moscow: Vysshaia
   shkola.

Fiene, Donald M. 1981. "A Comparison of the Soviet and Possev Editions of
   The Master and Margarita, with a Note on Interpretation of the
   Novel." *Canadian-American Slavic Studies* 15 (Summer–Fall): 330–54.

Fish, Stanley. 1980. "Literature in the Reader: Affective Stylistics." In *Reader Response Criticism: From Formalism to Post-Structuralism,* edited
   by Jane P. Tompkins, 70–100. Baltimore: Johns Hopkins University Press.

Floyd, David, trans. *See* Abramov 1991.

Frierson, William C. 1965. *The English Novel in Transition*. New York: Cooper Square.

Galagan, G. Ia. 1966. "'Dvorianskoe gnezdo.' *Spectator* o perevode Rol'stona." In vol. 2 of *Turgenevskii sbornik: Materialy k polnomu sobraniiu sochinenii i pisem I. S. Turgeneva*, 143–46. Moscow: Nauka.

Galsworthy, John. 1934. *Letters from John Galsworthy, 1900–1932*. Edited by Edward Garnett. New York: Scribner's.

Galton, D. 1970. "The Anglo-Russian Literary Society." *Slavonic and East European Review* 48:272–82.

Garnett, Constance. 1947. "Russian Literature in English." *The Listener*, 30 January, 195.

———, trans. *See* Chekhov; Dostoevsky; Gogol; Turgenev.

Garnett, Richard. 1991. *Constance Garnett: A Heroic Life*. London: Sinclair-Stevenson.

Gettmann, Royal A. 1941. *Turgenev in England and America*. Illinois University Studies in Language and Literature, vol. 27. Urbana: University of Illinois Press.

Gibian, George. 1957. "Bridling the Runaway Soviet Literary Revolt." *New Republic*, 22 April, 16–18.

———. 1958. Review of *The Idiot*, by F. Dostoevsky, translated by David Magarshack. *SEEJ* 16 (Summer): 152–54.

Ginsburg, Mirra, trans. *See* Bulgakov.

Gleason, John Howes. 1950. *The Genesis of Russophobia in Great Britain*. Harvard Historical Studies 57. Cambridge: Harvard University Press.

Glenny, Michael, trans. *See* Bulgakov; Trifonov 1986*b*, 1986*c*.

Gogol, N. V. 1951. *Mertvye dushi*. 1842. Vol. 6 of *Polnoe sobranie sochinenii*. Leningrad: Nauka.

Home Life in Russia. "By a Russian Noble. Revised by the editors." 2 vols. London: Hurst & Blackett, 1854.

Dead Souls. Translated by Stephen Graham. 1893. 3d ed. New York: Frederick A. Stokes, 1915.

Dead Souls. Translated by D. J. Hogarth. Everyman's Library. London: J. M. Dent, 1915.

Dead Souls. Translated by Constance Garnett. 1923. New York: Modern Library, 1936.

Dead Souls. Translated by David Magarshack. Harmondsworth: Penguin, 1961.

Dead Souls. Translated by George Reavey. Edited by George Gibian. New York: W. W. Norton, 1985.

———. 1938. "Shinel'." In vol. 3 of *Polnoe sobranie sochinenii*. Leningrad: Nauka.

"The Overcoat." Translated by Constance Garnett. In *Six Russian*

Short Novels. Edited by Randall Jarrell, 1–36. Garden City, N.Y.: Anchor-Doubleday, 1963.

"The Overcoat." In The Collected Tales and Plays of Nikolai Gogol, translated by Constance Garnett, revised and edited by Leonard J. Kent, 562–92. New York: Pantheon, Random House, 1964.

"The Overcoat." In Tales of Good and Evil, translated by David Magarshack, 233–71. Garden City, N.Y.: Doubleday, 1957.

"The Overcoat." Diary of a Madman and Other Stories, translated by Ronald Wilks, 71–108. Harmondsworth: Penguin, 1972.

Gordon, Maria, trans. See Zoshchenko.

Gorky, Maksim. 1953. "O proze." 1933. Vol. 26 of Sobranie sochinenii v tridtsati tomakh, 387–408. Moscow: Khudozhestvennaia literatura, 1953.

Goscilo, Helena. 1990. "Introduction: A Nation in Search of Its Authors." In Glasnost: An Anthology of Russian Literature under Gorbachev, edited by Goscilo and Byron Lindsey, xv–xlv. Ann Arbor: Ardis.

Graham, Joseph, ed. 1985. Difference in Translation. Ithaca: Cornell University Press.

Grice, H. Paul. 1975. "Implicature." In Syntax and Semantics, Vol. 3: Speech Acts, edited by P. Cole and J. L. Morgan, 43–58. New York: Academic Press, Harcourt Brace Jovanovich.

Hapgood, Isabel, trans. See Turgenev.

Harari, Manya. 1959. "On Translating 'Zhivago.'" Encounter 7 (May): 51–53.

———, trans. See Kazakov; Pasternak.

Harden, Evelyn, trans. See Dostoevsky 1972b.

Hayward, Max, trans. See Pasternak; Solzhenitsyn.

Heilbrun, Carolyn G. 1961. The Garnett Family. London: George Allen & Unwin.

Hemmings, F. W. J. 1950. The Russian Novel in France, 1884–1914. Oxford: Oxford University Press.

Herbst, Josephine. 1931. "Literature in the U.S.S.R." New Republic 29 April, 305–6.

Hermans, Theo, ed. 1985. The Manipulation of Literature. London: Croom Helm.

Hersey, John. 1944. "Engineers of the Soul." Time, 9 October, 99–102.

Hingley, Ronald, trans. See Solzhenitsyn.

Hinrichs, Uwe. 1983. Die sogenannten "Vvodnye slova" (Schalworter/ Modalworter) im Russischen. Berlin: Otto Harrassowitz.

Hosking, Geoffrey. 1980. Beyond Socialist Realism. London: Granada.

Hughes, Anne C. 1977. "From a Didactic to an Exploratory Conception of Literature: Trends in Recent Soviet Prose Fiction." Ph.D. diss., Lancaster University.

Hugo, Victor. 1976. Nôtre Dame de Paris, 1482. 1831. Paris: Garnier.

———. Notre-Dame de Paris. 1910. Translator unnamed. Everyone's

Library. London: J. M. Dent, 1964.

———. *The Hunchback of Notre Dame*. Translator unnamed. New York: Modern Library, n.d.

"In Praise of *War and Peace*." 1942. In L. N. Tolstoy, *War and Peace*. Inner Sanctum Edition. Translated by Louise and Aylmer Maude. New York. Simon & Schuster.

"Is the Art of Chekhov a Distilled Poison?" 1942. *Current Opinion* 71 (October): 505–7.

Iser, Wolfgang. 1980*a*. "Interaction between Text and Reader." In *The Reader in the Text*, edited by Susan R. Suleiman and Inge Crosman, 106–19. Princeton: Princeton University Press.

———. 1980*b*. "The Reading Process: A Phenomenological Approach." In *Reader Response Criticism: From Formalism to Post-Structuralism*, edited by Jane P. Tompkins, 50–69. Baltimore: Johns Hopkins University Press.

Jakobson, Roman. 1987. "On Linguistic Aspects of Translation." In his *Language in Literature*, 428–35. Cambridge: Harvard University Press.

James, Henry. 1984. *Literary Criticism*, Vol. 2: *French Writers; Other European Writers*. New York: Literary Classics of the United States.

Johnson, Vida Taranovski. 1981. "The Thematic Function of the Narrator in *The Master and Margarita*." *Canadian-American Slavic Studies* 15. (Summer–Fall): 271–86.

Joseph, Larry, and Rachel May, trans. *See* Tertz 1992*b*.

Katz, Michael, trans. *See* Dostoevsky 1973*b*.

Kazakov, Yurii. "Aktur—gonchii pes." In his *Izbrannoe*, 117–34. Moscow: Khudozhestvennaia literatura.

———. 1977. "Acturus the Hunting Dog." Translated by Manya Harari and Andrew Thompson. In *Russian Writing Today*, edited by Robin Milner-Gulland and Martin Dewhirst, 270–91. Harmondsworth: Penguin.

Kent, Leonard J. 1964. "About the Translation." In *The Collected Tales and Plays of Nikolai Gogol*, translated by Constance Garnett, revised and edited by Leonard J. Kent, xi. New York: Pantheon, Random House.

Kentish, Jane, trans. *See* Dostoevsky 1973*b*.

Kim, Anatolii. 1985. "Prikliucheniia m. n. s." *Oktiabr'* 8:76–85.

———. 1989. *Otets-les*. Moscow: Sovetskii pisatel'.

Klimoff, Alexis. 1973. "Solzhenitsyn in English: An Evaluation." In *Aleksandr Solzhenitsyn: Critical Essays and Documentary Materials*, edited by John Dunlop, Richard Hough, and Klimoff, 533–57. Belmont, Mass.: Nordland Publishing Co.

Koen, Frank, Alton Becker, and Richard Young. 1969. "The Psychological Reality of the Paragraph." *Journal of Verbal Learning and Verbal Behavior* 8:49–53.

Komissarov, V. N. 1980. *Lingvistika perevoda*. Moscow: Mezhdunarodnoe otnoshenie.

Knowlton, Edgar C. 1916. "A Russian Influence on Stevenson." *Modern Philology* 14 (December): 449–54.

Langleben, Maria M. 1979. "On the Triple Opposition of a Text to a Sentence." In vol. 1 of *Text vs. Sentence: Basic Questions of Text Linguistics*, edited by János S. Petöfi, 246–57. Hamburg: Helmut Buske Verlag.

Leggett, Glenn, et al., eds. 1988. *Prentice Hall Handbook for Writers*. 10th ed. Englewood Cliffs, N.J.: Prentice Hall.

Leighton, Lauren G. 1978. "On Translation: 'One Day in the Life of Ivan Denisovič. '" *Russian Language Journal* 32 (Winter): 117–30.

———. 1984. "Translator's Introduction." In *The Art of Translation: Kornei Chukovsky's "A High Art"*, translated and edited by Leighton, ix–xxxii. Knoxville: University of Tennessee Press.

———. 1991. *Two Worlds, One Art*. DeKalb: Northern Illinois University Press.

[Lermontov, M. Iu]. 1853. *Sketches of Russian Life in the Caucusus*. "By a Russe, many years resident amongst the various tribes." London: Ingram, Cooke & Co.

Levenston, E. A., and G. Sonnenschein. 1986. "The Translation of Point-of-View in Fictional Narrative." In *Interlingual and Intercultural Communication*, edited by Juliane House and Shoshana Blum-Kulka, 49–59. Tübingen: Gunter Narr Verlag.

Levine, Suzanne Jill. 1991. *The Subversive Scribe: Translating Latin American Fiction*. St. Paul: Greywolf Press.

———. 1992. "Translation as (Sub)version: On Translating *Infante's Inferno*." In *Rethinking Translation*, edited by Lawrence Venuti, 75–85. New York: Routledge.

Levinson, Stephen C. 1983. *Pragmatics*. Cambridge: Cambridge University Press.

Lewis, Philip. 1985. "The Measure of Translation Effects." In *Difference in Translation*, edited by Joseph Graham, 31–62. Ithaca: Cornell University Press.

Lovett, Robert Morss. 1925. Review of *The Life and Letters of Anton Tchekhov*, edited by S. S. Kotelianksy and P. Tomlinson. *New Republic* 4 November, 286–87.

Luplow, Richard. 1971. "Narrative Style and Structure in 'One Day in the Life of Ivan Denisovich.'" *Russian Literature Triquarterly* 1:399–412.

MacAndrew, Andrew T., trans. See Dostoevsky 1972*a*.

Magarshack, David, trans. See Dostoevsky 1972*a*, 1973*a*, 1974; Gogol.

Maguire, Robert A., and John Malmstad. 1978. "Translators' Introduction." In *Petersburg*, by Andrei Bely, translated by Maguire and Malmstad, vii–xxvii. Bloomington: Indiana University Press.

Markov, Vladimir. 1959. "Notes on Pasternak's 'Doctor Zhivago.'" *Russian Review* 18 (January): 14–22.

Martínez-Bonati, Félix. 1981. *Fictive Discourse and the Structures of Literature*. Ithaca: Cornell University Press.

Matlaw, Ralph, ed. 1979. *Anton Chekhov's Short Stories*, translated by Constance Garnett, Ivy Litvinov, Marian Fell, and Ralph Matlaw. Norton Critical Edition. New York: Norton.

———, ed. and rev. 1966. *Fathers and Sons*. By Ivan Turgenev. Translated by Constance Garnett. Norton Critical Edition. New York: Norton.

———, ed. and rev. 1976. *The Brothers Karamazov*. By Fyodor Dostoyevsky, translated by Constance Garnett. Norton Critical Edition. New York: Norton.

———, trans. *See* Dostoevsky 1973*b*.

Matthews, P. H. 1981. *Syntax*. Cambridge: Cambridge University Press.

McDuff, David, trans. *See* Dostoevsky 1972*a*, 1973*a*.

McLean, Hugh. 1964. "Abram Tertz and his Translators." *SEEJ* 8.4:434–40.

———, trans. *See* Zoshchenko.

Meyer, Priscilla. 1971. "Hoist by the Socialist-Realist Petard: American Intepretations of Soviet Literature." *RLT* 1:420–23.

Miller, Robin. 1981. *Dostoevsky and "The Idiot."* Cambridge: Harvard University Press.

Mirsky, D. S. 1931. "Books and Films in Russia." *Yale Review* 20 (March): 472–87.

———. "Chekhov." 1979. In *Anton Chekhov's Short Stories*, edited by Ralph Matlaw, 291–301. Norton Critical Edition. New York: Norton.

Monas, Sidney, trans. *See* Dostoevsky 1973*a*.

Mongault, Henri, trans. *See* Dostoevsky 1972*a*.

Moser, Charles A. 1988. "The Achievement of Constance Garnett." *American Scholar*, Summer: 431–38.

Muchnic, Helen. 1938–39. "Dostoevsky's English Reputation (1881–1936)." *Smith College Studies in Modern Languages* 20.3–4.

Nabokov, V. V. 1981. "The Art of Translation." In his *Lectures on Russian Literature*, 315–21. New York: Harcourt.

———. 1944. *Nikolai Gogol*. New York: New Directions.

Neuschäffer, Walter. 1935. *Dostojewskijs Einfluß auf den englischen Roman*. Anglistische Forschungen, Heft 81. Heidelberg: Carl Withers Universitätsbuchhandlung.

Nichols, John. 1974. *The Milagro Beanfield War*. New York: Random House.

Niranjana, Tejaswini. 1992. *Siting Translation*. Berkeley and Los Angeles: University of California Press.

Nunberg, Geoffrey. 1990. *The Linguistics of Punctuation*. CSLI Lecture Notes, no. 18. Stanford: Center for the Study of Language and Information.

Oomen, Ursula. 1979. "Texts and Sentences." In vol. 1 of *Text vs Sentence: Basic Questions of Text Linguistics*, edited by János S. Petöfi, 272–80. Hamburg: Helmut Buske Verlag.

Orel, Harold. 1954. "English Critics and the Russian Novel: 1850–1917." *Slavonic and East European Review* 33 (December): 457–69.

———. 1977. "The Victorian View of Russian Literature." *Victorian Newsletter* 51:1–5.

Parker, Ralph, trans. *See* Solzhenitsyn.

Parthé, Kathleen. 1986. Review of *Two Winters and Three Summers*, by Fyodor Abramov, translated by D. B. Powers and Doris C. Powers. *Slavic and East European Journal* 30 (Winter): 585–86.

———. 1992. *Russian Village Prose: The Radiant Past*. Princeton: Princeton University Press.

Pascal, Roy. 1977. *The Dual Voice*. Manchester: Manchester University Press.

Pasternak, Boris. 1958. *Doktor Zhivago*. Ann Arbor: University of Michigan Press.

Doctor Zhivago. Translated by Max Hayward and Manya Harari. New York: Pantheon, 1958.

Pause, Eberhard. 1983. "Context and Translation." In *Meaning, Use, and Interpretation of Language*, edited by Rainer Bauerle et al., 384–99. Berlin: Walter de Gruyter.

Pearson, T. R. 1985. *A Short History of a Small Place*. New York: Simon & Schuster.

Peterson, Dale E. 1992. "Justifying the Margin: The Construction of 'Soul' in Russian and African-American Texts." *Slavic Review* 51 (Winter): 749–57.

Petrushevskaya, Lyudmila. 1990. "Our Crowd." Translated by Helena Goscilo. In *Glasnost: An Anthology of Russian Literature under Gorbachev*, edited by Goscilo and Byron Lindsey, 3–24. Ann Arbor: Ardis.

Pevear, Richard and Larissa Volokhonsky, trans. *See* Dostoevsky 1972*a*, 1973*a*, 1973*b*.

Phelps, Gilbert. 1956. *The Russian Novel in English Fiction*. London: Hutchinson University Library.

———. 1958. "The Early Phases of British Interest in Russian Literature." *Slavonic and East European Review* 36 (June): 418–33.

———. 1960. "The Early Phases of British Interest in Russian Literature" Part 2. *Slavonic and East European Review* 38.91 (June): 415–30.

Phelps, W. L. 1917. *Essays on Russian Novelists*. 1910. New York: Macmillan.

Polubichenko, Lydia V. 1984. "Philological Topology and the Translation of Fiction." *Quinquereme* 7.2:199–210.

Powers, D. B., and Doris C. Powers, trans. *See* Abramov 1982.

Pritchett, V. S. 1988. *Chekhov: A Spirit Set Free*. New York: Random House.

Proffer, Carl. 1964. "*Dead Souls* in Translation." *Slavic and East European Journal* 8.4:420–33.

———. 1984. "Russian Prose 1961–84: Its Relationship to Union Officers, Border Guards, an Executioner, Tests of Character, the Dangers of Form, Emigration, and the Future." In *The Barsukov Triangle, The*

Two-Toned Blond, and Other Stories, edited by Proffer and Proffer, vii–xxx. Ann Arbor: Ardis.

Proffer, Carl, and Ellendea Proffer. 1982. "Introduction: Russian Fiction into the Eighties." In *Contemporary Russian Prose*, edited by Proffer and Proffer, vii–xxix. Ann Arbor: Ardis.

Quirk, Randolph et al., eds. 1972. *A Grammar of Contemporary English*. Harlow, Essex: Longman.

Rabinowitz, Peter J. 1987. *Before Reading: Narrative Conventions and the Politics of Interpretation*. Ithaca: Cornell University Press.

Rait-Kovaleva, Rita, trans. *See* Faulkner.

Ralston, W. R. S., trans. *See* Turgenev 1969.

Rapoport, Semion. 1928. "Translations and Translators." *Contemporary Review* 133:500–508.

Rasputin, Valentin. 1978*a*. *Proshchanie s Materoi*. 1976. In his *Povesti*, 201–383. Moscow: Sovetskaia Rossiia.
> *Farewell to Matyora*. Translated by Antonina Bouis. New York: Macmillan, 1980.

———. 1978*b*. *Zhivi i pomni*. 1974. In his *Povesti*, 7–200. Moscow: Sovetskaia Rossiia.
> *Live and Remember*. Translated by Antonina Bouis. New York: Macmillan, 1978.

———. 1984*a*. "Poslednii srok." 1970. In his *Izbrannye proizvedeniia v dvukh tomakh*, 127–289. Moscow: Molodaia gvardiia.

———. 1984*b*. "Rudol'fio." 1965. In his *Izbrannye proizvedeniia v dvukh tomakh*, 318–31. Moscow: Molodaia gvardiia.
> "Rudolphio." Translated by Meredith Heinemeier and Liza Valova. In *The Barsukov Triangle, The Two-Toned Blond, and Other Stories*, edited by Carl Proffer and Ellendea Proffer, 113–28. Ann Arbor: Ardis, 1984.

Reavey, George, trans. *See* Gogol 1951.

Reid, Robert. 1986. "The Critical Uses of Translation (Lermontov's *A Hero of Our Time*)." *Essays in Poetics* 11.2:55–90.

"The Renaissance of Interest in Russian Literature." 1915. *Current Opinion* 58 (March): 197–98.

Robin, Régine. 1992. *Socialist Realism: An Impossible Aesthetic*. Stanford: Stanford University Press.

Robinson, Douglas. 1991. *The Translator's Turn*. Baltimore: Johns Hopkins University.

Rozental', D. E. 1977. *Prakticheskaia stilistika russkogo iazyka*. 4th ed. Moscow: Vysshaia shkola.

Rubenstein, Roberta. 1972. "Virginia Woolf and the Russian Point of View." *Comparative Literature Studies* 9:196–206.

———. 1974. "Genius of Translation." *Colorado Quarterly* 22.3:359–68.

Rutherford, William E. 1970. "Some Observations Concerning Subordinate Clauses in English." *Language* 46.1:97–115.

Sakharov, V. I. 1987. "M. V. Lomonosov i polemika o 'Starom i novom sloge' (konets XVIII–nachalo XIX v.)." In *Lomonosov i russkaia literatura*, edited by A. S. Kurilov, 280–95. Moscow: Nauka.

Schaarschmidt, G. 1966. "Interior Monologue and Soviet Literary Criticism." *Canadian Slavonic Papers* 8:143–52.

Schlesinger, I. M. 1968. *Sentence Structure and the Reading Process*. Janua Linguarum series minor 69. The Hague: Mouton.

Scholes, Robert and Robert Kellogg. 1966. *The Nature of Narrative*. New York: Oxford University Press.

Schulte, Rainer. 1988. "A Word for Translation Criticism." *Translation Review* 27:1–2.

Sendich, Munir. 1978. Review of *Doctor Zhivago*, by Boris Pasternak, translated by Max Hayward and Manya Harari. *Russian Language Journal* 32.113:241–49.

Sherman, Stuart P. 1912. Review of *Essays on Russian Novelists*, by W. L. Phelps. *Yale Review* 1:321–25.

Shklovskii, V. 1925. "Iskusstvo kak priem." In his *O teorii prozy*, 7–20. Moscow: Krug.

Sholokhov, Mikhail. 1955–57. *Tikhii Don*. 1928–40. Vols 2–5 of *Sobranie sochinenii v semi tomakh*. Moscow: Molodaia gvardiia.
   And Quiet Flows the Don. Translated by Stephen Garry. 1934. Harmondsworth: Penguin, 1967.

Shukshin, V. 1979. "Neprotivlenets Makar Zherebtsov." 1969. In his *Rasskazy*. Moscow: Russkii iazyk.

———. 1984. "Makar Zherebtsov." Translated by Margaret Mabson. In *The Barsukov Triangle, The Two-Toned Blond, and Other Stories*, edited by Carl Proffer and Ellendea Proffer, 149–58. Ann Arbor: Ardis.

———. 1985. "Vybiraiu derevniu na zhitel'stvo." 1973. In vol. 3 of *Sobranie sochinenii v trekh tomakh*, 146–53. Moscow: Molodaia gvardiia.
   "Moving to the Country." Translated by Natasha Ward and David Iliffe. In *Roubles in Words, Kopeks in Figures*. London: Marion Boyars, 1985.

Silliman, Ron. 1989. *The New Sentence*. New York: Roof Press.

Simmons, Ernest J. 1944. "Russian Studies at Cornell." *New Republic*, 15 May, 674–75.

———. 1952. "Soviet Writing Today." *Nation*, 23 February, 175–77.

Simon, Paul. 1980. *The Tongue-tied American*. New York: Continuum.

Simon, Sherry. 1992. "The Language of Cultural Difference: Figures of Alterity in Canadian Translation." In *Rethinking Translation*, edited by Lawrence Venuti, 157–76. New York: Routledge.

Smith, Winifred. 1916. "New Translations of Slavic Fiction." *Dial* 15 August, 103–4.

Sokolova, L. 1968. *Nesobstvenno-avtorskaia (nesobstvenno-priamaia) rech' kak stilisticheskaia kategoriia*. Tomsk: Izdatel'stvo Tomskogo universiteta.

Solzhenitsyn, Aleksandr. 1962. *Odin den' Ivana Denisovicha*. *Novyi mir* 11:8–74.

  One Day in the Life of Ivan Denisovich. Translated by Max Hayward and Ronald Hingley. New York: Praeger, 1963.

  One Day in the Life of Ivan Denisovich. Translated by Ralph Parker. New York: Dutton, 1963.

  One Day in the Life of Ivan Denisovich. Translated by Thomas P. Whitney. New York: Fawcett, 1963.

  One Day in the Life of Ivan Denisovich. Translated by G. Aitken. London: Sphere Books, 1970.

  One Day in the Life of Ivan Denisovich. Translated by H. T. Willetts. New York: Farrar, Straus and Giroux, 1991.

Stein, Gertrude. 1973. "Sentences." In her *How to Write*. Paris: Plain Editions, 1931. Reprint, Barton, Vt.: Something Else Press.

Stoliarov, M. 1939. "Iskusstvo perevoda khudozhestvennoi prozy." *Literaturnyi kritik* 5–6:242–54.

Streeter, Victor. 1973. "A Look at Sentence-type Cohesion." *Language and Style* 6.2:109–16.

Struve, Gleb. 1964. "Western Writing on Soviet Literature." *Survey* 50 (January): 137–45.

Stubbs, Michael. 1983. *Discourse Analysis*. Chicago: University of Chicago Press.

Suleiman, Susan R., and Inge Crosman, eds. 1980. *The Reader in the Text*. Princeton: Princeton University Press.

Tendriakov, Vladimir. 1965. "Podenka—vek korotkii." In his *Perevertyshi*, 355–430. Moscow: Sovremennik.

  "Creature of a Day." In *Three, Seven, Ace*, translated by Paul Falla. New York: Harper & Row, 1973.

Tertz, Abram (Andrei Sinyavsky). 1992a. "Grafomani." 1960. In vol. 1 of *Sobranie sochinenii v dvukh tomakh*, 154–79. Moscow: SP "Start."

  "Graphomaniacs." In *Fantastic Stories*, translated by Ronald Hingley. New York: Random House, 1963.

———. 1992b. *Kroshka tsores*. 1980. In vol. 2 of *Sobranie sochinenii v dvukh tomakh*, 611–54. Moscow: SP "Start."

  Little Jinx. Translated by Larry Joseph and Rachel May. Evanston, Ill.: Northwestern University Press, 1992.

———. 1992c. *Spokoinoi nochi*. In vol. 2 of *Sobranie sochinenii v dvukh tomakh*, 337–609. Moscow: SP "Start."

  Goodnight! Translated by Richard Lourie. New York: Viking Penguin, 1989.

Titunik, I. R. 1971. "Mikhail Zoscenko and the problem of *skaz*." *California Slavic Studies* 6:83–96.

Tobenkin, Elias. 1928. "Russia's New Literature." *Bookman* 66 (January): 537–41.

Tolstaya, Tatyana. 1987*a*. "Na zolotom kryl'tse sideli..." In her *Na zolotom kryl'tse sideli...*, 40–48. Moscow: Molodaia gvardiia.

"On the Golden Porch." In *On the Golden Porch*, translated by Antonina Bouis, 41–50. New York: Vintage/Random House, 1990.

———. 1987*b*. "Svidanie s ptitsei." In Tolstaya, *Na zolotom kryl'tse sideli...*, 110–24. Moscow: Molodaia gvardiia. 110–24.

"Date with a Bird." In *On the Golden Porch*, translated by Antonina Bouis, 116–30. New York: Vintage/Random House, 1990.

Tove, Augusta L. 1958. "Konstantsiia Garnet—perevodchik i propagandist russkoi literatury." *Russkaia literatura* 4:193–98.

———. 1963. "Perevody Chekhova v Anglii i SShA." *Nauchnye doklady vysshei shkoly: Filologicheskie nauki* 1:144–51.

———. 1966. "'Dvorianskoe gnezdo.' Pervyi angliiski perevod." In vol. 2 of *Turgenevskii sbornik*, 133–43. Moscow: Nauka.

Trifonov, Yurii. 1986*a*. *Dolgoe proshchanie*. 1976. In vol. 2 of *Sobranie sochinenii v chetyrekh tomakh*, 131–216. Moscow: Khodozhestvennaia literatura.

"The Long Goodbye." In *The Long Goodbye*, translated by Helen Burlingame, 201–353. New York: Harper & Row, 1978.

———. 1986*b*. *Dom na naberezhnoi*. 1976. In vol. 2 of *Sobranie sochinenii v chetyrekh tomakh*, 363–494. Moscow: Khodozhestvennaia literatura.

"The House on the Embankment." In *Another Life and the House on the Embankment*, translated by Michael Glenny, 187–350. New York: Simon & Schuster, 1986.

———. 1986*c*. *Drugaia zhizn'*. 1975. In vol. 2 of *Sobranie sochinenii v chetyrekh tomakh*, 219–360. Moscow: Khodozhestvennaia literatura.

"Another Life." In *Another Life and the House on the Embankment*, translated by Michael Glenny, 9–186. New York: Simon & Schuster, 1986.

Turgenev, I. S. 1964. *Dvorianskoe gnezdo*. In vol. 7 of *Polnoe sobranie sochinenii i pisem*, 123–292. Moscow: Nauka.

A House of Gentlefolk. Translated by Constance Garnett. 1894. London: W. Heinemann, 1906.

Liza. Translated by W. R. S. Ralston. London: Chapman and Hall, 1869.

A Nobleman's Nest. Translated by I. Hapgood. 1903–4. Vol. 4 of *The Novels and Stories of Ivan Turgenev*. New York: Scribner's, 1922.

Russian Life in the Interior (Or: The Experiences of a Sportsman). Translator (from French) unnamed. Edited by James D. Meiklejohn. Edinburgh: Adam and Charles Black, 1885.

Tymoszko, Maria. 1990. "Translation in Oral Tradition as a Touchstone for

Translation Theory and Practice." In *Translation, History and Culture,* edited by Susan Bassnett and André Lefevere, 46–55. London: Pinter Publishers.

Tynianov, Iu. N. 1977. "Literaturnoe segodnia." *Poetika; Istoriia literatury; Kino.* Moscow: Nauka.

Uspenskii., B. A. 1970. *Poetika kompozitsii.* Moscow: Iskusstvo.

Vasil'eva, A. N. 1976. *Kurs lektsii po stilistike russkogo iazyka.* Moscow: Russkii iazyk.

Venuti, Lawrence. 1986. "The Translator's Invisibility." *Criticism* 38.2: 179–212.

———, ed. 1992. *Rethinking Translation.* New York: Routledge.

Vinogradov, V. V. 1966. "Problema skaza v stilistike." In *Poetika: Sbornik statei,* by B. Kazanskii et al., 24–40. 1926. The Hague: Mouton.

———. 1976. "K morfologii natural'nogo stilia." 1921–22. In *Poetika russkoi literatury,* 101–40. Moscow: Nauka.

———. 1979. "On the Tasks of Stylistics: Observations Regarding the Style of 'The Life of the Archpriest Avvakum.'" In *The Life Written by Himself,* by Archpriest Avvakum, translated by Kenneth N. Brostrom, 117–46. Michigan Slavic Translations, no. 4. Ann Arbor: Michigan Slavic Publications.

———. 1986. *Russkii iazyk.* 3d ed. Moscow: Vysshaia shkola.

Vinogradova, V. N. 1979. "O stilizatsii razgovornoi rechi v sovremennoi khudozhestvennoi proze." In *Ocherki po stilistike khudozhestvennoi rechi,* edited by A. N. Kozhin, 66–76. Moscow: Nauka.

Vinokur, T. G. 1965. "O iazyke i stile povesti A. I. Solzhenitsyna 'Odin den' Ivana Denisovicha.'" *Voprosy kul'tury rechi* 6:16–31.

de Vogüé, E. M. 1887. *The Russian Novelists.* Translated by Jane Loring Edmands. Boston: D. Lothrop Co.

Voloshinov, V. N. 1929. *Marksizm i filosofiia iazyka. Osnovnye problemy sotsiologicheskogo metoda v nauke o iazyke.* Leningrad.

Ward, Natasha, and David Iliffe, trans. See Shukshin 1985.

Wells, H. B. 1932. "The Russian Language in the United States." *American Mercury* 25 (April): 448–51.

West, Rebecca. 1976. "The Strange Necessity." In *The Strange Necessity: Essays and Reviews,* 1–213. London: J. Cape, 1928. Reprint, Saint Clair Shores, Mich.: Scholarly Press.

Whishaw, Fredrick, trans. See Dostoevsky 1973b.

Wilks, Ronald, trans. See Gogol 1938.

Wilson, Edmund. 1936. "Letters in the Soviet Union." *New Republic,* 1 April, 212–14.

———. 1958. "Doctor Life and His Guardian Angel." Review of *Doctor Zhivago,* by Boris Pasternak, translated by Max Hayward and Manya Harari. *New Yorker,* 15 November, 213–38.

Woolf, Virginia. 1925a. "Modern Fiction." In *The Common Reader,* First Series, 207–18. New York: Harcourt, Brace.

————. 1925*b*. "The Russian Point of View." In *The Common Reader*, First Series, 243–56. New York: Harcourt, Brace.

————. 1935. "The Novels of George Meredith." In *The Common Reader*, Second Series, 226–36. 1932. London: Hogarth Press.

Wright, C. T. Hagberg. 1921. "The Meaning of Russian Literature." *Quarterly Review* 446:102–20.

Zoshchenko, Mikhail. 1977. "Zabavnoe prikliuchenie." 1935. In his *Rasskazy; Sentimental'nye povesti; Komedii; Fel'etony*, 139–46. Moscow: Sovetskaia Rossiia.

"An Amusing Adventure." In *Nervous People and Other Satires*, translated by Maria Gordon and Hugh McLean, 218–27. New York: Random House, 1963.

Zytaruk, George J. 1971. *D. H. Lawrence's Response to Russian Literature*. The Hague and Paris: Mouton.

Index

Numbers in italics refer to the translation examples.

Abramov, Fedor: and colloquial narration, 65, 175n. 15; critique of Stalinist narration by, 61–62, 64; use of deictics by, *67, 98. See also* village prose
abusive translation: as assertion of translator's rights, 86; defined, 8–9; in recent translations, 50–52, *51*
Aitmatov, Chingiz: *The Day Lasts More than a Hundred Years,* 75
Alice in Wonderland. See Carroll, Lewis
ambiguity. *See* literary translation: of ambiguity
American attitudes toward Russian literature. *See* reception of translations, America
American regional fiction, as a model for translation, 108
Anglo-Russian Literary Society, 170n. 32
author. *See* implied author; translator: and author
authority: and ownership of text, 1, 4, 9. *See also* translator: and author

Bakhtin, Mikhail: "Discourse and the Novel," 2–6; and heteroglossia, 53–55, 83, 90, 114–15; *Problems of Dostoevsky's Poetics,* 28, 109–10; and sentence, 137; and terminology, 177n. 1
Banfield, Ann, 106, 142, 178n. 4; strict interpretation of English grammar by, 108, 179n. 11
Baring, Maurice, 24, 28
Bassnett, Susan, 38
Benjamin, Walter, 7–8, 86–87

Bird, George: translation of Dostoevsky's "Double," 161–66, 185n. 9
Bouis, Antonina, *51. See also* Rasputin, Valentin
boundaries, 2–6, 144; between languages, cultures, 3, 8, 24; between text and context, 2–6; between voices in text, 3–4, 90–91, 94, 100; between written texts and oral speech, 55, 91, 178n. 5; of sentence, 120–21, 123, 127–29, *128,* 133, 135–39
Bowring, Sir John, 13
Brooks, Peter, 85–86, 143, 180n. 21
Brothers Karamazov, The. See Dostoevsky, F. M.
Bulgakov, Mikhail: *The Master and Margarita,* 46, 145–53, 183–84

canonization of translations, 12, 38–42
Carroll, Lewis: *Alice in Wonderland,* in Russian, 7, 123
"centripetal" and "centrifugal" forces on translation, 2, 3, 5, 6, 9, 52, 59, 143
Chekhov, Anton, 35–36, 39, 40, 41, 42, 100, 132, 172n. 51
Chukovsky, Kornei, 38, 40
Cohn, Dorrit, 89–90, 177n. 1, 177n. 3
colloquial language, 47, 49, 68, 75, 77–83, *79, 80;* in America, 174n. 4; contrast to English, 82–83, 176n. 18, 176n. 19; in Russia, 59–66, 81–82, 175n. 15, 176n. 17. *See also* interjections; modal particles; oral speech; parentheticals; pragmatic connectors; tense shifts
Conrad, Joseph, 25, 34, 37, 38, 170n. 30, 172n. 53
Crime and Punishment. See Dostoevsky, F. M.

205

dash, 132–33, 134. *See also* punctuation
Dead Souls. *See* Gogol, Nikolai
deictics, 65–68, *67, 69,* 83, 84, 89, 115, 174n. 11
Descriptive Translation Studies, 6–7, 9
de Vogüé, Viscount E. M. *See* Vogüé, Viscount E. M. de
diglossia, 55, 60–61. *See also* Bakhtin, Mikhail
Doctor Zhivago. *See* Pasternak, Boris
Dorosh, Efim, 61, 64
Dostoevsky, F. M.: humor in, 69; and narrated monologue, 105–6; new translations of, 53–55, *54,* 86; and "penetrated word," 109–15; and "Russian craze," 32–35, *33,* 38–41; translations from French or German, 19; Victorian antipathy to, 22–25, 27–29, 31. Works: *The Brothers Karamazov,* 30–34, *33,* 41, 53–54, *54,* 70–71, *70,* 110–12, 129; *Crime and Punishment,* 27, 28, 32, 112–14, *113,* 170n. 31, 171n. 37 ; "The Double," 109–10, *111; The Idiot, 44,* 110; *Notes from Underground,* 50, 53, 116–17, *117,* 135. *See also* Bakhtin, Mikhail; Garnett, Constance
"Double, The." *See* Dostoevsky, F. M.

Eikhenbaum, Boris, 81, 155–61
ellipsis, 116–17, *117,* 130–31, *131,* 175n. 16, 181n. 8
Emerson, Caryl: on translating Dostoevsky, 135, 137, 180n. 18
emotive speech: translation of, 92–93
emphatic expressions: translation of, 66, 68, 73, 84, 92–93
erlebte Rede, 177n. 1. *See also* narrated monologue
explanatory apparatus with translation, 4, 86
explanatory translation, 84–86, 93, 114–15, 129, 133–34, *134,* 136

Falla, Paul. *See* Tendriakov, Vladimir, "The Mayfly"
Faulkner, William, 57, 62, 133–34, *135,* 136, 139
Fiene, Donald, 152, 183n. 1, 183n. 2, 184n. 3
Fish, Stanley, 135–36
Flaubert, Gustave, 105, 123, 129, 132
fluency in translation, 5, 27, 180n. 17
formalism, 61, 142, 155–66, 174n. 2

France: reception of Russian literature in, 14, 19, 21, 30, 43, 170n. 31; translations in, 14, 18–20, 27, 32, *70,* 169n. 16, 170n. 34

Garnett, Constance, 24–42, 43–45, 128–29; canonization of translations of, 37–42, 143; Russian contacts, 20; stylistic smoothing in translations by, 44, 53–54, *54, 58;* as translator of Chekhov, 35–36; as translator of Dostoevsky, 31–34, *33,* 38–41, *44, 70,* 70–71, 110–13, *111,* 116, *117,* 129, 143, 179n. 15, 185n. 7; as translator of Gogol, *58,* 58–59, 129; as translator of Turgenev, 24–27
Garnett, Edward, 30, 172n. 53
gender in translation, 4
Germany: reception of Russian literature in, 14, 18–19, 43; translations in, 18, 34
Ginsburg, Mirra: as translator of *Master and Margarita,* 145–53, 183n. 2
glasnost' and translation, 49–52
Glenny, Michael: as translator of Bulgakov, 145–53; as translator of Trifonov, 75, 92, 136
Gogol, Nikolai: 35, 38, 40–41, 45; *Dead Souls,* 15–17, 27, 30, 34, 40, 84, 128–29, 169n. 16, 176n. 21; European reception of, 13–14, 15–17, 19, 21–22, 23–27, 29, 30; "The Overcoat," 57–59, *58,* 155–60
Gorky, Maxim, 30, 35, 61, 62, 64, 86, 175n. 15
Goscilo, Helena, 50, 52
Grice, H. Paul. *See* implicature
grotesque: translation of, 49, 155–66

Hapgood, Isabel, 25, 27
Hayward, Max: as translator of Pasternak (with M. Harari), 45, 46–47; as translator of Solzhenitsyn (with R. Hingley), *48, 74, 80,* 81, *92,* 94, *95,* 107, *124,* 125–27, *126,* 129, 133, *134*
Hemingway, Ernest, 136
Hermans, Theo, 6–7, 167n. 3
Herzen, Alexander, 14, 19
Hingley, Ronald: as translator of Chekhov, 132; as translator of Solzhenitsyn, *48, 74, 80,* 81, *92,* 94, *95,* 107, *124,* 125–27, *126,* 129, 133, *134*
Hugo, Victor, 114–15
humor in translation, 21, 23, 36, 69, 72, 153, 155, 159, 184n. 6

Index

Idiot, The. See Dostoevsky, F. M.

impersonal constructions, 96, 102–4, 107; in Russian vs. in English, 4, 96, 99–102, *101*

implicature, rules of, 151–52

implied author, 1, 4, 115, 167n. 2

indirect speech, 110; compared to narrated monologue, 65, 89–91; vs. direct speech, 89–90, 94, 98, 106; grammar of, Russian vs. English, 4, 96, 179n. 12

"informational" translation, 8, 13–18, 29, 34, 45, 46, 49, 86

interior monologue. *See* narrated monologue

interjections into narrative voice: disappearance of, in translation, 83, 148, 173n. 61; Russian grammar and, 81, 84; as sign of intrusive narrator, 62, 65, 68–71, *69, 70;* as sign of narrated monologue, 91–96, *92, 95*

internal citation, 5, 110–14, *111, 113,* 164–65, 179n. 15

intonation in literary text, 79–81, 87, 119, 155, 159–60

intrusive narrator: and direct address to reader, 76, 82–83, 84, 148; and opacity of language, 83, 113. *See also* colloquial language; interjections

irony: translation of, 71, 94, 114–15, 116–17, 162, 179n. 14

Iser, Wolfgang, 135–36, 138, 167n. 2, 182n. 12

Jakobson, Roman, 86, 176n. 23

James, Henry, 23–24, 28

Joyce, James, 62, 136

Katz, Michael. *See* Dostoevsky, F. M., *Notes from Underground*

Kent, Leonard J., 40–41

Kentish, Jane. *See* Dostoevsky, F. M., *Notes from Underground*

Kim, Anatolii, 127–29, *128,* 133, 138–39

Lawrence, D. H., 32, 34

Lefevere, André, 7, 38

Leighton, Lauren, 47, 79–80, 174n. 2

Lermontov, Mikhail: translations into English, 7, 14–15, 172n. 48

Lewis, Philip, 7–8, 86

literary language: and language of literature (boundaries of acceptability in English), 106–9, 112; vs. colloquial, 61–65, 77,
80–82, 179n. 14

literary theory and translation, 4–9, 52–55, 86–87, 115–17, 155–66

literary translation: vs. adaptation, 14; of ambiguity, 4–5, 67–68, 96, 100–108, *101, 103;* apparatus of, 4, 6; changing requirements on, 41; and creation of "corporate text," 7; definition of, 6; history of, 5, 11–55, 169n. 17; vs. "informational," 12, 15–17, 47, 49; of "materiality" or "opacity" of language, 5, 52, 58–59, 61, 86, 130, 143; as profession, 21, 24, 37–38, 47; reviews and criticism of, 6, 7, 24–25, 27, 28, 29, 37–38, *39. See also* canonization of translations

MacAndrew, Andrew, 45, 70

Magarshack, David, 41, 43–45, *44;* as translator of Dostoevsky, *70,* 106, 111–13, *111, 113,* 173n; as translator of Gogol, 58, *58,* 128, 180n. 16

Maguire, Robert, 45–46, 47, 52

Malmstad, John, 45–46, 47, 52

Master and Margarita, The. See Bulgakov, Mikhail

Matlaw, Ralph: as editor of Garnett translations, 41; as translator of Dostoevsky, 116

modal particles, 57–59, 69, *70,* 71, 121, 147, 175n. 16. *See also* parentheticals

Nabokov, Vladimir, 6, 38, 105, 167–68

narrated monologue, 89–117; defined, 3, 4, 89–90, 177n. 1, 177n. 3, 178n. 4; in Dostoevsky, 110–15, *111, 113;* and English language, 106–9, 177n. 3, 179n. 11; and Russian language, 103–4, 105–6, 178n. 6; and Russian literary traditions, 91, 105–6; and Soviet literary policy, 62–65, *64,* 178n. 5; in village prose, 65. *See also* impersonal constructions; interjections; intrusive narrator; repetition; tense shifts

narrator and reader, 62, 73, 76, 77–78, 84–86, *85,* 106, 147–49, 184n. 5

Nichols, John: *The Milagro Beanfield War,* 77–78, 82

Nunberg, Geoffrey, 120–22, 133

objectivity: and deictics, 66–68, 178n. 4; as literary virtue, 28, 64; translators' inclination toward, 83–86. *See also* subjectivity

oral culture and translation, 119

oral speech: illusion of, as literary device, 4,

ـdex

, 80–81, 91, 132; vs. written
9, 122, 133, 175n. 16, 179n. 14

breaks: and stylistic rhythm,
, 123, 128, 132–33, 136–37, 181n.
n. 5; treatment of, in translation,
126–27, 129
theticals, 68–72, 70, 71
r, Ralph. *See* Solzhenitsyn, Aleksandr,
ne Day in the Life of Ivan Denisovich
thé, Kathleen, 99
rticles. *See* modal particles
scal, Roy, 90, 106
asternak, Boris: *Doctor Zhivago*, 46–47
Pavlova, Karolina, 18, 169n. 15
Peterson, Dale, 55, 108
Pevear, Richard, and Larissa Volokhonsky,
53–54, 54, 117, 143, 180n. 22
pirate translations, 14–17, 168n. 8
political implications of literary style, 42–43,
52, 59–65, 63, 77
political influences on translation, 12,
14–17, 31, 46–47, 49, 141, 144, 173n. 59
Polubichenko, Lydia, 7, 123, 129
pragmatic connectors, 72–76, 72, 74, 159,
175n. 13
Proffer, Carl and Ellendea, 48–49
pronouns, 93–95, 95, 96, 100, 102–4, 103,
107, 108, 115
prostorechie, 50, 77, 82, 176n. 17, 176n. 18.
See also colloquial language
puns, translation of, 146, 155–57
punctuation, 119–39; circularity of definition, 119–21; conventional nature of,
120–22, 132, 175n. 13, 181n. 2; flouting
of rules of, 121, 127; foregrounded in literature, 130–31, 131; as indicator of
rhythms of speech, 73, 81–82; and "intonation," 79–81, 93; translation of, 6, 73;
translator's license respecting, 6, 73,
121–22, 129, 132–34, 137–39. *See also*
dash; ellipsis; paragraph breaks; pragmatic connectors; sentence breaks; topic and
focus

quasi-direct discourse. *See* narrated monologue
Quiet Don. See Sholokhov, Mikhail
quotation. *See* internal citation
quotation marks, to create boundaries
between voices, 110

Rabinowitz, Peter, 99, 105, 108, 175n. 13
Ralston, W. R. S., 17, 24–25, 26, 29, 123,
169n. 25
Rasputin, Valentin, 47, 65. Works: *Farewell
to Matera*, 75–76, 76, 77, 78, 79, 100–12,
101, 108; *Live and Remember*, 51, 67,
79, 97, 98; "Rudolfio," 67
reader. *See* narrator and reader; punctuation, conventional nature of; reception of
translations; sentence breaks; translator
and reader
reception of translations: in America, 17–18,
22–24, 27, 29, 34, 42, 43, 142, 168n. 11,
169n. 13, 173n. 59; in England, 12–13,
20–25, 28–29, 32, 34. *See also* France;
Germany
register, shifts in, 147, 159–60, 184n. 4. *See
also* colloquial language
Reid, Robert, 7, 15
repetition: translation of, 41, 58–59, 73–75,
74, 110–14, 111, 113, 148–50, 155–59,
160–66, 179n. 15, 182n. 13, 184n. 5,
185n. 9
Robinson, Douglas, 9, 86, 116
"Russian craze," 30–36
Russian language: contrast to English, 81,
103–6
russophobia, 13–17, 168n. 6

sentence: as fundamental unit of writing or
reading, 120, 133, 181n. 1, 182n. 9; compound vs. simple, 122, 175n. 16. *See also*
tense shifts
sentence breaks: meaning of, 122–29; and
ownership of text, 136–38; and reading
process, 133–39, 135; and style, 133,
136–37, 175n. 16. *See also* pragmatic
connectors
shifters. *See* pronouns
Sholokhov, Mikhail, 64–65; *The Quiet Don*,
42–43, 62, 63
Shukshin, Vasilii, 47, 85
Silliman, Ron, 120, 122, 133, 136, 137
Sinyavsky, Andrei. *See* Tertz, Abram
skaz, 47, 62, 64, 72, 83, 109, 114, 175n. 15,
176n. 20. *See also* intrusive narrator; narrator and reader
Solzhenitsyn, Aleksandr, *One Day in the
Life of Ivan Denisovich*: colloquial language in, 47, 65, 77; impersonal constructions in, 107; intonation in, 79–81,
80; new translation of, 48, 83; paragraph-

Index

ing in, 129; pragmatic connectors in,
73–75, *74;* punctuation in, 132–33, *134;*
rush to publish translation of, 46; shifts in
perspective in, *92,* 93, 94, *95;* topic and
focus in, 123–27, *124, 126. See also* Willetts, H. T.
somatic response to language, 9, 25, 114,
116
Soviet "school" of translation, 174n. 2
Stalin era: and American attitudes toward
Russian literature, 42–44; official attitudes toward literary style during, 61–62,
64; reaction to literary dogmas after,
62–65, 86, 91
Stein, Gertrude, 137
Stevenson, Robert Louis, 28
Struve, Gleb, 42
subjectivity: in Dostoevsky's works, 28; vs.
"objective" or expository style, 48, 59,
178n. 4. *See also* deixis; modal particles;
narrated monologue; parentheticals;
tense shifts

teaching literature in translation, 2, 11, 43,
141–44, 166, 183n. 2
Tendriakov, Vladimir, 65; "The Mayfly," *92,*
93–94, *95,* 97, 102–5, *103*
tense shifts, 76–77, *77,* 91, 96–99, *97,*
106–7, 179n. 12; differences between
Russian and English systems of, 97–98;
history of Russian system of, 96–97
tenseless expressions, 97–98, *98*
Tertz, Abram: *Goodnight,* 131; "Graphomaniacs," 130, 137–38; *Little Jinx,* 49,
130–31, *131*
Tolstaya, Tatyana: *On the Golden Porch,* 51
Tolstoy, Lev Nikolaevich: "Childhood and
Youth," 17; reception of, in America, 23,
29, 171n. 39; reception of, in England,
17, 19–20, 26, 29–30, 31, 34, 35, 171n.
40, 171n. 42, 172n. 45; style of, 123
Tooke, Rev. William, 13
topic and focus, 122–29, *124, 126, 128,* 135,
181n. 3
translated text, as signifier or signified, 86,
142–43
translation. *See* literary translation
translation studies, history of, 2
translator: and author, 4–6, 34, 40, 52,
83–86, 87, 121, 136–39, 142–43, 167n. 3,
168n. 1; and narrator, 9, *33,* 40, 52,
65–87, 104, 109–17; and publisher, 1, 5;

and reader, 11–12, 37–38, 93, 114–17,
121, 138–39, 142–43, 183n. 3; tendency
to impose logic in texts, 150–53; tendency toward psychological normalization of
text, 166, 180n. 21, 185n. 9
Trifonov, Yurii, 47, 65, 68–69, *69,* 75, 91,
92, 136
Turgenev, Ivan: as translator, 132; *A Noblemen's Nest (Liza),* 24–25, *26,* 169n. 25;
reception of, in America, 17–18, 168n.
11, 169n. 13; reception of, in England,
17–18, 19, 20, 22–27, 30–31, 34; *A
Sportsman's Sketches,* 14–15, 19; style of,
40, 109; translations of, into English, 38,
40–41, 123; translations of, into French,
14; translations of, into German, 14; vs.
Dostoevsky, 171n. 35

Venuti, Lawrence, 5, 8, 12, 61, 83–84, 86
Victorian culture, 20, 22–27, 37–40, 174n. 4
village prose, 49, 64, 65, 78, 84, 86, 99–100.
See also Rasputin, Valentin; Abramov,
Fedor
Vinogradov, V. V.: on "The Double,"
109–10, 155, 160–66, 178n. 8, 179n. 15;
on intonation, 81; on parentheticals, 69;
on Russian tense system, 96
Vizetelly, Henry, 20, 29
Vogüé, Viscount E. M. de, 19, 21–22, 23,
27, 170n. 33, 170–71n. 34
Volokhonsky, Larissa, and Richard Pevear,
53–54, *54,* 117, 143, 180n. 22
Voloshinov, Maximilian, 90–91, 105, 107,
137
vvodnye slova. See parentheticals

Wilks, Ronald. *See* Gogol, Nikolai, "The
Overcoat"
Willetts, H. T., *48,* 83, 86, 99, 107. *See also*
Solzhenitsyn, Aleksandr, *One Day in the
Life of Ivan Denisovich*
Woolf, Virginia, 36, 42, 173n. 56
word order in translation, 178n. 6
written text. *See* oral speech vs. written text

Yarmolinsky, Avrahm: revision of Garnett
translations by, 165–66, 185n. 8

Zamiatin, Evgenii, 42, 62, 173n. 57
Zola, Émile, 29, 129
Zoshchenko, Mikhail, 46, 47, 72, 72

209